A BOOK OF LONDON

A BOOK OF LONDON

edited by

IVOR BROWN

With 54 photographs from

THE TIMES

COLLINS
LONDON AND GLASGOW

GENERAL EDITOR: J. B. FOREMAN, M.A.

First published, 1961
Latest reprint, 1964

ACKNOWLEDGMENTS

The publishers gratefully acknowledge the co-operation of the following authors, owners of copyright, publishers and literary agents who have given permission for poems and prose passages to appear in these pages.

JONATHAN CAPE LTD. and the late MR. JAMES BONE for the extract from *London Perambulator* by James Bone.

JONATHAN CAPE LTD. for the extract from *Travels in England* by Thomas Platter, translated and edited by Clare Williams.

CHATTO AND WINDUS LTD. for the extract from *The Right Place* by C. E. Montague.

CHATTO AND WINDUS LTD. and HARCOURT, BRACE AND COMPANY INC. for the extract from *Queen Victoria* by Lytton Strachey.

CHATTO AND WINDUS LTD. and THE VIKING PRESS INC. for the extract from *Under the Net* by Iris Murdoch. Copyright, 1954, by Iris Murdoch.

CHATTO AND WINDUS LTD. and HARPER & BROTHERS for the extract from the poem *Theatre of Varieties* from *The Cicadas and Other Poems* by Aldous Huxley. Copyright, 1929, 1931, by Aldous Huxley.

THE CLARENDON PRESS, OXFORD for the poem *London Snow* from *The Shorter Poems of Robert Bridges*.

MR. NEVILL COGHILL and PENGUIN BOOKS LTD. for the extract from Nevill Coghill's translation of Chaucer's *The Cook's Tale*.

MISS D. E. COLLINS and METHUEN & CO. LTD. for the extract *Cockneys and their Jokes* from the *Selected Essays* of G. K. Chesterton.

CONSTABLE AND CO. LTD. and HARCOURT, BRACE AND COMPANY INC. for the extract from *More Trivia* by Logan Pearsall Smith.

J. M. DENT & SONS LTD. and E. P. DUTTON & CO. INC. for the extracts from *Diary of a Nobody* by George and Weedon Grossmith.

SIR GEORGE ROSTREVOR HAMILTON and WILLIAM HEINEMANN LTD. for the poem *Seeing Miss Hilary* from *Collected Poems and Epigrams* by Sir George Rostrevor Hamilton.

WILLIAM HEINEMANN LTD. and CHARLES SCRIBNER'S SONS for the extract from *The Man of Property* by John Galsworthy.

SIR COMPTON MACKENZIE and MACDONALD & CO. (PUBLISHERS) LTD. for the extract from *Carnival* by Compton Mackenzie.

JOHN MURRAY LTD. and HOUGHTON MIFFLIN INC. for the poems *Essex* and *Parliament Hill Fields* from the *Collected Poems* of John Betjeman.

MAX PARRISH & CO. LTD. for the extract from *The Last Bassoon—A Diary* by Fred Bason.

A. D. PETERS for two extracts from *Angel Pavement* by J. B. Priestley, an extract from *Bond Street Story* by Norman Collins, and an extract from *Winter in London* by Ivor Brown.

PHOENIX HOUSE LTD. for the extract from *A Book of London Yesterdays* by Frederick Willis.

THE SOCIETY OF AUTHORS, DR. JOHN MASEFIELD, O.M., and THE MACMILLAN COMPANY, NEW YORK for the poems *Biography* and *London Town* from the *Collected Poems* of John Masefield.

MR. RAGLAN SQUIRE, MACMILLAN & CO. LTD., ST. MARTIN'S PRESS INC., NEW YORK and THE MACMILLAN COMPANY OF CANADA LTD. for the poem *After the Jubilee, 1935* from the *Collected Poems* of Sir John Squire.

THE TRUSTEES OF THE HARDY ESTATE, THE MACMILLAN COMPANY OF CANADA LTD. and THE MACMILLAN COMPANY, NEW YORK for the extract from the poem *Reminiscences of a Dancing Man* from the *Collected Poems* of Thomas Hardy.

CONTENTS

For and Against

8   CONTENTS

History

Characters

Green Islands

Shops

Riverside

Streets

At Plays and Play

Inns and Lodgings

ILLUSTRATIONS

13

INTRODUCTION

This anthology of London is a successor to similar volumes whose themes were England, Scotland, Wales, and Ireland. The support given to those has encouraged the publishers to issue this further book whose theme is a single city.

A city? So it was, and so in name it is. But the city has become a region and a monster which sprawls across the south-east corner of England. The so-called Home Counties are becoming all homes and no county. "Green belts" are ordained to check this devouring of the countryside, but a tightened belt does not efficiently disguise or contain the belly of a fat man which sags out around the girdle. Cobbett's "wen" has become a series of protuberances now called by town-planners a conurbation. This is deemed by some to be a vile word, but it does describe the linked chain of "development" which is more and more confining Londoners within their ever-greater London. Escape by road at week-ends and holiday periods is increasingly difficult and even hazardous. To be incarcerated in a five-mile traffic jam is scarcely to be deemed a vacational pleasure, while getting to and from work involves appalling discomforts and delays. Yet the number of people who are ready and eager to settle in London is greater than the number of those wanting to get out. London has not lost its fascination; the monster remains magnetic.

This unfailing charm of even the noisy and the swollen conurbation is something to which the writer or selector of writings about London must be fair, balancing the appreciations of those who have found and acknowledged ample London happiness with the denunciations of those who have seen London only as a swarming-ground of avarice, folly, and vulgarity, and have found their pleasure in laying on the lash. Being rude about London, as some of the ancient Romans were very rude about their Rome, is a very old habit; but we must remember the city's long tradition of hospitality to strangers as well as of craftsmanship and honourable commerce. A capital reflects the moods and morals of passing centuries and when England was most cruel, Tyburn and the Tower were inevitably the headquarters of legal and sometimes of illegal savagery. But even at the worst of times there have been those who discovered in London a kindlier guest-house than other great cities were providing. And the blackest periods of the city's moral life have been lit not only with the fires of persecution but with the lamps of poetry and architecture at their finest.

The anthologist's life is a vexing one because there is so much that he has to leave out. But it has its compensations. Faced with the huge assemblage of writing about London, I find myself in the position of Dickens's Mrs. Todgers while she was preparing savoury dishes for the party of commercial gentlemen eager to welcome Mr. Pecksniff and especially his daughters. As described by Master Bailey, Mrs. Todgers, when cooking, stood over the fire, " dodging among the tender pieces with a fork and eating of 'em." The anthologist, fork in hand, selects from richness and can eat as he works until he at last announces, again in Master Bailey's words, " The wittles is up."

In the banquet of London life there must, of course, be " wittles " that are tough and sour as well as soft and succulent in the meal that results. There have been such notable miseries and muddles, brutalities and squalors in the history of London that the early tribute from Scotland, William Dunbar's praise of this " gem of all joys " and " flower of cities all," can be made to look sufficiently ridiculous. Against London one must select from the snarling Tudor and Jacobean pamphlet-eers, from Ned Ward's gloating espionage on the metropolitan misdemeanours of a century later, from the rhymes of Swift and Gay on the street-spectacle, and from the many terrifying pictures of nineteenth century dirt and destitution, which were so magnif-icently painted by Charles Dickens. I have seen Dickens described as one who sentimentalised London poverty, presumably because he knew that the poor who lacked so much had none the less retained the gift of laughter. Dickens was as little sentimental in his views of society as any angry young Radical has ever been. Either in youth, when writing the " Boz " papers, or later on when surveying the crumbling specimens of old mortality in the Marshalsea Prison and hurling the harpoon that was his pen into the swarms of " city sharks " and the complacent monopolists of office in Westminster and Whitehall, he drove as surely into the cruelty as he did into the kindness of London's various characters and classes.

When one selects from London writings there is the further difficulty that one may be presenting the seamy side to such an extent as to give a distorted view of a vast human amalgam and overlook the happiness which has been none the less real because it has been much less conspicuous. For the satirist the sins of a city are the obvious target. For the genial humorist, whose intention is less sharp, it is natural to choose the follies, absurdities, and failures of urban administration and social practice as his raw material in the construction of the London comedy. The critics of the arts as well as of behaviour know that it is much easier to seem smartly clever if one derides than if one approves. Fleet Street works on the principle that virtue is not news and the satirist knows that well-being and contentment are of little use to him. Consequently much of the most easily readable and most widely relished descriptions of London

life have given a poor view of a city whose endurances
have certainly been gallant and whose enjoyments have
also been genuine. I have done my best to present a
balanced view of the London scene down the centuries
and to extract from the city's literature a fair measure
of appreciation along with the inevitable sneers and
scoldings of the man who wants to score his sardonic
points and to be applauded for his indignation.

One of the surprising facts that emerges is the age-long
repetition of the same grievances and accusations. For
example, the hustling speed, the crowding and the perils
of London traffic were as much denounced by the Tudor
publicists in their time as they are to-day by a leader-
writer who is commenting on the latest list of street-
casualties. Dickens alluded to the dreadful hazards of
the road to Brighton a hundred and thirty years ago when
the coaches in racing competition were frequently over-
turned with disaster to the passengers. The inhabitants
of the city objected in Jacobean times to a new theatre in
the Blackfriars district because of the traffic chaos which
it caused. Nor are industrial pressure and Trade Union
activities recent phenomena; in Shakespeare's time
the organised watermen bitterly complained that, by
setting up play-houses north of the river, the damnable
play-actors were ruining the ferrying-trade which
carried their audiences to Southwark. Nobody has even
been more angrily outspoken about the nuisance of
urban smoke than the seventeenth-century diarist,
Evelyn. So readers of this anthology will be constantly
reminded that many of our present discontents are as old
as the timbers of Westminster Hall. Is contemporary
life producing unbearable hustle and strain? Read
Thackeray on what he considered the exhausting labours
and stresses in the daily round of a prosperous Victorian
London lady.

An anthology, drawing mainly on the writers whose
work has survived by its excellence, must tell more of

London past than of London present. No harm in that. London present is changing its structural face so rapidly and its habits so steadily that any picture of it in the early nineteen-sixties will cease to be typical as soon as it is written. In the face of this hurry-scurry of social change it may be well to see the years in the light of the centuries and to look for the abiding unities of London life amid the superficial variations in its fabric. To that end historians conduct their profession and an anthology of this kind must seek to be history condensed, a record of popular fun and of rebellious furies, of elegant manners and of proletarian humours, which will present a just pattern of the civic qualities, some transient, some surviving.

In attempting to do this I have been greatly assisted by my colleagues in the House of Collins, especially Mr. J. B. Foreman, and by the pictorial collaboration of *The Times* newspaper. To them, as to all the owners of copyright work on which I have drawn, I am extremely grateful.

IVOR BROWN

LONDON: OBSERVATIONS

Good for Poetry

> Mine is an urban Muse and bound
> By some strange law to paven ground;
> Abroad she pouts: she is not shy
> On London stones.

AUSTIN DOBSON

Good for Growing Up

London is the only place in which the child grows completely up into the man.

WILLIAM HAZLITT

Good as a Ghost

> Go where we may, rest where we will
> Eternal London haunts us still.

THOMAS MOORE

Good for Dark Nights

> The night was dark and stormy
> But blithe of heart were they,
> For shining in the distance
> The lights of London lay.

GEORGE R. SIMS

Good for all Seasons

> Oh mine in snows and summer heats
> Those good old Tory brick-built streets!
> WILFRED WHITTEN

Bad for Taste

> London has a great belly, but no palate.
> THOMAS HOBBES

Bad for Security

> Ye Towers of Julius, London's lasting shame,
> With many a foul and midnight murder fed.
> THOMAS GRAY

Bad for Men of Property and Faith

> Here falling houses thunder on your head
> And here a female atheist talks you dead.
> DR. SAMUEL JOHNSON

Bad for Lovers of a Cold Climate

> Hell is a city much like London.
> P. B. SHELLEY

Bad for Moral Sanitation

London, that great cesspool into which all the loungers of the Empire are irresistibly drained.

SIR ARTHUR CONAN DOYLE
Opinion of Dr. Watson expressed in
A Study in Scarlet

For and Against

REBUKE TO COURT AND CITY

Go, soul, the body's guest,
   Upon a thankless arrant.
Fear not to touch the best;
   The truth shall be thy warrant.
   Go, since I needs must die,
   And give the world the lie.

Say to the court, it glows
   And shines like rotten wood;
Say to the church, it shows
   What's good, and doth no good.
   If church and court reply,
   Then give them both the lie.

Tell potentates, they live
   Acting by others' action,
Not loved unless they give,
   Not strong but by affection.
   If potentates reply,
   Give potentates the lie.

Tell men of high condition
   That manage the estate,
Their purpose is ambition,
   Their practice only hate;
   And if they once reply,
   Then give them all the lie.

Tell them that brave it most,
    They beg for more by spending,
Who, in their greatest cost,
    Like nothing but commending:
    And if they make reply,
    Then give them all the lie.

Tell zeal it wants devotion;
    Tell love it is but lust;
Tell time it meets but motion;
    Tell flesh it is but dust;
    And wish them not reply,
    For thou must give the lie.

Tell age it daily wasteth;
    Tell honor how it alters;
Tell beauty how she blasteth;
    Tell favor how it falters;
    And as they shall reply,
    Give every one the lie.

Tell wit how much it wrangles
    In tickle-points of niceness;
Tell wisdom she entangles
    Herself in over-wiseness;
    And when they do reply,
    Straight give them both the lie.

Tell physic of her boldness;
    Tell skill it is prevention;
Tell charity of coldness;
    Tell law it is contention;
    And as they do reply,
    So give them still the lie.

Tell fortune of her blindness;
　　Tell nature of decay;
Tell friendship of unkindness;
　　Tell justice of delay;
　　And if they will reply,
　　Then give them all the lie.

Tell arts they have no soundness,
　　But vary by esteeming;
Tell schools they want profoundness,
　　And stand too much on seeming;
　　If arts and schools reply,
　　Give arts and schools the lie.

Tell faith it's fled the city;
　　Tell how the country erreth;
Tell manhood shakes off pity,
　　Tell virtue least preferred;
　　And if they do reply,
　　Spare not to give the lie.

So when thou hast, as I
　　Commanded thee, done babbling;
Because to give the lie
　　Deserves no less than stabbing.
　　Stab at thee he that will—
　　No stab thy soul can kill.

SIR WALTER RALEIGH (1552-1618)
The Lie

HAPPY RETURN

From the dull confines of the drooping West,
To see the day spring from the pregnant East,
Ravisht in spirit, I come, nay more, I flie
To thee, blest place of my Nativitie!

Thus, thus with hallowed foot I touch the ground,
With thousand blessings by thy Fortune crown'd.
O fruitfull Genius! that bestowest here
An everlasting plenty, yeere by yeere.
O Place! O People! Manners! fram'd to please
All Nations, Customs, Kindreds, Languages!
I am a free-born Roman; suffer then,
That I amongst you live a Citizen.
London my home is; though by hard fate sent
Into a long and irksome banishment;
Yet since cal'd back; henceforward let me be,
O native countrey, repossest by thee!
For, rather than Ile to the West return,
Ile beg of thee first here to have mine Urn.
Weak I am grown, and must in short time fall;
Give thou my sacred Reliques Buriall.

ROBERT HERRICK (1591-1674)
Hesperides

FAREWELL TO WITS AND WOMEN

Come, spur away,
I have no patience for a longer stay;
    But must go down
And leave the chargeable noise of this great town.
    I will the country see,
    Where old simplicity,
    Though hid in grey,
    Doth look more gay
Than foppery in plush and scarlet clad.
    Farewell, you City wits, that are
    Almost at civil war;
'Tis time that I grow wise, when all the world grows mad.

More of my days
I will not spend to gain an idiot's praise;
   Or to make sport
For some slight puisne[1] of the Inns of Court.
  Then worthy Stafford, say
  How shall we spend the day,
  With what delights
  Shorten the nights?
When from the tumult we are got secure;
  Where mirth with all her freedom goes,
    Yet shall no finger lose;
Where every word is thought, and every thought is pure.

   There from the tree
We'll cherries pluck, and pick the strawberry.
   And every day
Go see the wholesome country girls make hay;
  Whose brown hath lovelier grace
  Than any painted face
   That I do know
   Hyde Park can show.
Where I had rather gain a kiss than meet
  (Though some of them in greater state
    Might court my love with place)
The beauties of the Cheap and wives of Lombard Street.

   But think upon
Some other pleasures, these to me are none.
   Why do I prate
Of women, that are things against my fate?
  I never mean to wed
  That torture to my bed.
  My Muse is she
  My love shall be.

[1] A junior Judge

Let clowns get wealth and heirs; when I am gone,
  And the great bugbear, grisly death,
    Shall take this idle breath,
If I a poem leave, that poem is my son.

THOMAS RANDOLPH (1605-1635)
An Ode to Mr. Anthony Stafford to Hasten Him into the Country

LAST THOUGHTS OF DR. JOHNSON

As Johnson had now very faint hopes of recovery, and as Mrs. Thrale was no longer devoted to him, it might have been supposed that he would naturally have chosen to remain in the comfortable house of his beloved wife's daughter, and end his life where he began it. But there was in him an animated and lofty spirit, and however complicated diseases might depress ordinary mortals, all who saw him beheld and acknowledged the *invictum animum Catonis*. Such was his intellectual ardour even at this time, that he said to one friend, " Sir, I look upon every day to be lost, in which I do not make a new acquaintance "; and to another, when talking of his illness, " I will be conquered; I will not capitulate." And such was his love of London, so high a relish had he of its magnificent extent, and variety of intellectual entertainment, that he languished when absent from it, his mind having become quite luxurious from the long habit of enjoying the metropolis; and, therefore, although at Lichfield, surrounded with friends who loved and revered him, and for whom he had a very sincere affection, he still found that such conversation as London affords, could be found nowhere else. These feelings, joined, probably, to some flattering hopes of aid from the eminent physicians and surgeons in London, who kindly and generously attended him without accepting fees, made him resolve to return to the capital.

JAMES BOSWELL (1740-1795)
The Life of Dr. Johnson

VANITY CURED, LOVE AVOIDED

Johnson was much attached to London: he observed, that a man stored his mind better there than anywhere else; and that in remote situations a man's body might be feasted, but his mind was starved, and his faculties apt to degenerate, from want of exercise and competition. No place (he said) cured a man's vanity or arrogance, so well as London; for as no man was either great or good *per se*, but as compared with others not so good or great, he was sure to find in the metropolis many his equals, and some his superiors. He observed, that a man in London was in less danger of falling in love indiscreetly, than any where else; for there the difficulty of deciding between the conflicting pretensions of a vast variety of objects kept him safe. He told me that he had frequently been offered country preferment, if he would consent to take orders; but he could not leave the improved society of the capital, or consent to exchange the exhilarating joys and splendid decorations of public life, for the obscurity, insipidity, and uniformity of remote situations.

JAMES BOSWELL (1740-1795)
quoting Dr. Maxwell in *The Life of Dr. Johnson*

LAMB THE LONDONER

To return to myself (from whence my zeal for the Public good is perpetually causing me to digress), I will let thee, Reader, into certain more of my peculiarities. I was born (as you have heard), bred, and have passed most of my time, in a crowd. This has begot in me an entire affection for that way of life, amounting to an almost insurmountable aversion from solitude and rural scenes. This aversion was never interrupted or suspended, except for a few years in the younger part of my life, during a period in which I had fixed my affections upon a charming young woman. Every man, while the *passion* is upon him, is for a time at least addicted to groves and meadows and purling streams. During this short period of my existence, I contracted just enough familiarity with rural objects to understand tolerably well ever after the Poets, when they declaim in such passionate terms in favour of a country life.

For my own part, now the fit is long past, I have no hesitation in declaring, that a mob of happy faces crowding up at the pit door of Drury Lane Theatre just at the hour of five, give me ten thousand finer pleasures, than I ever received from all the flocks of *silly sheep*, that have whitened the plains of Arcadia or Epsom Downs.

This passion for crowds is no where feasted so full as in London. The man must have a rare recipe for melancholy, who can be dull in Fleet-street. I am naturally inclined to *hypochondria*, but in London it vanishes, like all other ills. Often when I have felt a weariness of distaste at home, have I rushed out into her crowded Strand, and fed my humour, till tears have wetted my cheek for inutterable sympathies with the multitudinous moving picture, which she never fails to present at all hours, like the shifting scenes of a skilful Pantomime.

The very deformities of London, which give distaste to others, from habit do not displease me. The endless succession of shops, where Fancy (miscalled Folly) is supplied with perpetual new gauds and toys, excite in me no puritanical aversion. I gladly behold every appetite supplied with its food proper. The obliging customer, and the obliged tradesmen—things which live by bowing, and things which exist but for homage, do not affect me with disgust; from habit I perceive nothing but urbanity, where other men, more refined, discover meanness. I love the very smoke of London, because it

has been the medium most familiar to my vision. I see
grand principles of honour at work in the dirty ring
which encompasses two combatants with fists, and
principles of no less eternal justice in the tumultuous
detectors of a pick-pocket. The salutary astonishment
with which an execution is surveyed, convinces me more
forcibly than an hundred volumes of abstract polity, that
the universal instinct of man, in all ages, has leaned to
order and good government. Thus an art of extracting
morality, from the commonest incidents of a town life,
is attained by the same well-natured alchemy, with which
the *Foresters of Arden* in a beautiful country

> Found tongues in trees, books in the running brooks,
> Sermons in stones, and good in everything.

Where has spleen her food but in London—humour,
interest, curiosity, suck at her measureless breasts without a possibility of being satiated. Nursed amid her
noise, her crowds, her beloved smoke—what have I been
doing all my life, if I have not lent out my heart with
usury to such scenes?

Reader, in the course of my peregrinations about the
great city, it is hard, if I have not picked up matter, which
may serve to amuse thee, as it has done me, a winter
evening long. When next we meet, I purpose opening
my budget—Till when, farewell.

CHARLES LAMB (1775-1834)
Essays of Elia

LONDON, 1802

O Friend! I know not which way I must look
For comfort, being, as I am, opprest
To think that now our life is only drest
For show; mean handy-work of craftsman, cook,

Or groom!—We must run glittering like a brook
In the open sunshine, or we are unblest;
The wealthiest man among us is the best:
No grandeur now in nature or in book

Delights us. Rapine, avarice, expense,
This is idolatry; and these we adore:
Plain living and high thinking are no more:

The homely beauty of the good old cause
Is gone; our peace, our fearful innocence,
And pure religion breathing household laws.

WILLIAM WORDSWORTH (1770-1850)
Poems in Two Volumes

THE COCKNEY—CURSED AND PRAISED

The true Cockney has never travelled beyond the purlieus
of the Metropolis, either in the body or the spirit. Prim-
rose-hill is the *Ultima Thule* of his most romantic desires;
Greenwich Park stands him in stead of the Vales of
Arcady. Time and space are lost to him. He is confined
to one spot, and to the present moment. He sees every
thing near, superficial, little, in hasty succession. The
world turns round, and his head with it, like a roundabout at a fair, till he becomes stunned and giddy with
the motion. Figures glide by as in a *camera obscura*.
There is a glare, a perpetual hubbub, a noise, a crowd
about him; he sees and hears a vast number of things,
and knows nothing. He is pert, raw, ignorant, conceited,
ridiculous, shallow, contemptible. His senses keep him
alive; and he knows, inquires, and cares for nothing
farther.

He meets the Lord Mayor's coach, and without
ceremony treats himself to an imaginary ride in it. He
notices the people going to court or to a city-feast, and

is quite satisfied with the show. He takes the wall of a Lord, and fancies himself as good as he. He sees an infinite quantity of people pass along the street, and thinks there is no such thing as life or a knowledge of character to be found out of London. " Beyond Hyde Park all is a desert to him." He despises the country, because he is ignorant of it, and the town, because he is familiar with it. He is as well acquainted with St. Paul's as if he had built it, and talks of Westminster Abbey and Poets' Corner with great indifference. The King, the House of Lords and Commons are his very good friends. He knows the members for Westminster or the City by sight, and bows to the Sheriffs or the Sheriff's men. He is hand and glove with the Chairman of some Committee. He is, in short, a great man by proxy, and comes so often in contact with fine persons and things, that he rubs off a little of the gilding, and is surcharged with a sort of second-hand, vapid, tingling, troublesome self-importance. His personal vanity is thus continually flattered and perked up into ridiculous self-complacency, while his imagination is jaded and impaired by daily misuse. Everything is vulgarised in his mind. Nothing dwells long enough on it to produce an interest; nothing is contemplated sufficiently at a distance to excite curiosity or wonder. Your true Cockney is your only true leveller. Let him be as low as he will, he fancies he is as good as anybody else.

*　　　*　　　*

It is a strange state of society (such as that in London) where a man does not know his next-door neighbour, and where the feelings (one would think) must recoil upon themselves, and either fester or become obtuse. Mr. Wordsworth, in the preface to his poem of the " Excursion," represents men in cities as so many wild beasts or evil spirits, shut up in cells of ignorance,

2

without natural affections, and barricaded down in sensuality and selfishness. The nerve of humanity is bound up, according to him, the circulation of the blood stagnates. And it would be so, if men were merely cut off from intercourse with their immediate neighbours, and did not meet together generally and more at large.

But man in London becomes, as Mr. Burke has it, a sort of " public creature." He lives in the eye of the world, and the world in his. If he witnesses less of the details of private life, he has better opportunities of observing its larger masses and varied movements. He sees the stream of human life pouring along the streets —its comforts and embellishments piled up in the shops —the houses are proofs of the industry, the public buildings of the art and magnificence of man; while the public amusements and places of resort are a centre and support for social feeling. A playhouse alone is a school of humanity, where all eyes are fixed on the same gay or solemn scene, where smiles or tears are spread from face to face, and where a thousand hearts beat in unison! Look at the company in a country theatre (in comparison) and see the coldness, the sullenness, the want of sympathy, and the way in which they turn round to scan and scrutinise one another.

In London there is a public; and each man is part of it. We are gregarious, and affect the kind. We have a sort of abstract existence; and a community of ideas and knowledge (rather than local proximity) is the bond of society and good-fellowship. This is one great cause of the tone of political feeling in large and populous cities. There is here a visible body-politic, a type and image of that huge Leviathan the State. We comprehend that vast denomination, the People, of which we see a tenth part daily moving before us; and by having our imaginations emancipated from petty interests and personal dependence, we learn to venerate ourselves as men, and to respect the rights of human nature. Therefore it is that the citizens and freemen of London and Westminster are patriots by prescription, philosophers and politicians by the right of their birth-place. In the country, men are no better than a herd of cattle or scattered deer. They have no idea but of individuals, none of rights or principles—and a king, as the greatest individual, is the highest idea they can form. He is " a species alone," and as superior to any single peasant as the latter is to the peasant's dog, or to a crow flying over his head. In London the king is but as one to a million (numerically speaking), is seldom seen, and then distinguished only from others by the superior graces of his person. A country 'squire or a lord of the manor is a greater man in his village or hundred!

WILLIAM HAZLITT (1778-1830)
The Plain Speaker

There is some confusion about the word Cockney. It is sometimes associated with the Kingdom of Cockaigne, "an imaginary country, the abode of luxury or idleness." The origin of Cockney, however, probably lies in the French *coquiné*, meaning pampered, which has given us our "cockered" for spoiled or petted. To the countryman the townsman was a cockered person or even a "softy" or milk-sop: this was the idea of a Cockney in Chaucer's time. The Cockney was also a term for a small or mis-shapen egg: so again, in the countryman's eye, it would be a term of contempt. This fits in with the luxury and idleness attributed to the land of Cockaigne. Hence the linking of Cockaigne with Cockney.

LONDON REMEMBERED IN SAMOA

I heard the pulse of the besieging sea
Throb far away all night. I heard the wind
Fly crying and convulse tumultuous palms.
I rose and strolled. The isle was all bright sand,
And flailing fans and shadows of the palm;
The heaven all moon and wind and the blind vault;
The keenest planet slain, for Venus slept.

The king, my neighbour, with his host of wives,
Slept in the precinct of the palisade;
Where single, in the wind, under the moon,
Among the slumbering cabins, blazed a fire,
Sole street-lamp and the only sentinel.
To other lands and nights my fancy turned—
To London first, and chiefly to your house,
The many-pillared and the well-beloved.
There yearning fancy lighted; there again
In the upper room I lay, and heard far off
The unsleeping city murmur like a shell;
The muffled tramp of the Museum guard
Once more went by me; I beheld again
Lamps vainly brighten the dispeopled street;
Again I longed for the returning morn,
The awakening traffic, the bestirring birds,
The consentaneous trill of tiny song
That weaves round monumental cornices
A passing charm of beauty. Most of all,
For your light foot I wearied, and your knock
That was the glad réveillé of my day.
ROBERT LOUIS STEVENSON (1850-1894)
Lines to Sidney Colvin

THE LONDONER, 1900

The long story of London has shown many changes but,
I think, none so great and abrupt as the change in life,
manners, and outlook of all classes which began on
4 August 1914, the day the first world war started.
Whether it is for better or worse only time can show.

This book is no glorification of the past but a recon-
struction, based on my experience, of the life lived by the
Little Man who crowded the streets, the trains, buses, and
trams; who applauded Irving and Ellen Terry, Dan
Leno and Marie Lloyd. He was always hard up but as

optimistic as Mr. Micawber. He was as obscure as the
other side of the moon, and the only time he got his name
into the papers was in the casualty list of the first world
war. I ought to know, for I was such a one myself.

This, then, is the London of the Little Man; it is a
London which is normally unnoticed by the professional
historian. The London of the first three generations from
the old board schools.

The Londoner I have in mind was God-fearing,
although he seldom went to church, patriotic, but he
seldom waved a flag. He was blessed with a humorous
cynicism and patient endurance, and his natural shrewd-
ness was mixed with a naiveté which made him an easy
victim of humbug. He was the man the New Journalism
was made for, and the gorgeous oleographs in the
Christmas number of Pear's Annual and other publica-
tions. The Thirty-Shilling Tailors sprang into existence
especially for him and the smart teashops did likewise.
He was the life-blood of the Palace of Varieties and the
respected gallery boy of the West End theatres. He was
hard-working, cheerful, and expected help from nobody,
which was lucky, for he certainly did not get any.
Shakespeare has said, " Security is mortals' chiefest
enemy." If this is true, how happy was the pre-1914
Londoner, for security to him was unknown. Of course
I mean economic security, for he had any amount of
physical security, since London was the safest city in the
world. He took his ease in hundreds of obscure little
taverns on Saturday night, and he did not suffer from
inhibitions, complexes and frustrations, so was a headache to nobody.

Rattle him out of bed early in the morning, keep his
nose to the grindstone for from eight to twelve hours a
day, give him a little six-roomed house and a wife and
children to go home to at night, and he was as happy as
we poor mortals can hope to be. Provided he managed
to pay his rent he was as safe in his little house as William

the First was in his Tower of London. Probably he was
much safer, and I suspect he loved his little castle much
more than William loved his great one.

Over one hundred thousand of these little houses were
wholly destroyed in the last war, and in many cases the
Londoners they sheltered went with them. The majority
of those little houses were not much loss, and as I see the
fine new blocks of flats arising on their sites I fervently
hope they will shelter the same sturdy spirits and modest
happiness, the same kind of people I have here presented
with affectionate care.

FREDERICK WILLIS (1885-   )
A Book of London Yesterdays

TWO VIEWS OF A POET LAUREATE

(I) ST. PANCRAS NIGHTS

So, if the penman sums my London days,
Let him but say that there were holy ways,
Dull Bloomsbury streets of dull brick mansions old
With stinking doors where women stood to scold
And drunken waits at Christmas with their horn
Droning the news, in snow, that Christ was born;
And windy gas lamps and the wet roads shining
And that old carol of the midnight whining,
And that old room above the noisy slum
Where there was wine and fire and talk with some
Under strange pictures of the wakened soul
To whom this earth was but a burnt-out coal.

O Time, bring back those midnights and those friends,
Those glittering moments that a spirit lends,
That all may be imagined from the flash,
The cloud-hid god-game through the lightning gash;
Those hours of stricken sparks from which men took
Light to send out to men in song or book;

Those friends who heard St. Pancras' bells strike two,
Yet stayed until the barber's cockerel crew,
Talking of noble styles, the Frenchman's best,
And thought beyond great poets not expressed,
The glory of mood where human frailty failed,
The forts of human light not yet assailed,

Till the dim room had mind and seemed to brood,
Binding our wills to mental brotherhood;
Till we became a college, and each night
Was discipline and manhood and delight;
Till our farewells and winding down the stairs
At each grey dawn had meaning that Time spares
That we, so linked, should roam the whole world round
Teaching the ways our brooding minds had found,
Making that room our Chapter, our one mind
Where all that this world soiled should be refined.

Often at night I tread those streets again
And see the alleys glimmering in the rain,
Yet now I miss that sign of earlier tramps,
A house with shadows of plane-boughs under lamps,
The secret house where once a beggar stood,
Trembling and blind, to show his woe for food.
And now I miss that friend who used to walk
Home to my lodgings with me, deep in talk,
Wearing the last of night out in still streets
Trodden by us and policemen on their beats
And cats, but else deserted; now I miss
That lively mind and guttural laugh of his
And that strange way he had of making gleam,
Like something real, the art we used to dream.

JOHN MASEFIELD (1878-   )
Biography

(2) A GOOD PLACE TO LEAVE

O London Town's a fine town, and London sights are
    rare,
And London ale is right ale, and brisk's the London air,
And busily goes the world there, but crafty grows the
    mind,
And London Town of all towns I'm glad to leave behind.

Then hey for croft and hop-yard, and hill, and field, and
    pond,
With Bredon Hill before me and Malvern Hill beyond,
The hawthorn white i' the hedgerow, and all the spring's
    attire
In the comely land of Teme and Lugg, and Clent, and
    Clee, and Wyre!

Oh London girls are brave girls, in silk and cloth o' gold,
And London shops are rare shops, where gallant things
    are sold,
And bonnily clinks the gold there, but drowsily blinks
    the eye,
And London Town of all towns I'm glad to hurry by.

Then, hey for covert and woodland, and ash and elm and
    oak,
Tewkesbury inns, and Malvern roofs, and Worcester
    chimney smoke,
The apple trees in the orchard, the cattle in the byre,
And all the land from Ludlow town to Bredon church's
    spire.

EARLY MORNING SPECIAL

Most Londoners get their morning papers delivered by a newsagent, but many still patronise the street-sellers on their way to the office. It is a hard life for the newsvendors in rough weather and it has produced hardy as well as popular types, and many well-known "characters".

WINGS OVER THE CITY

The poet John Davidson wrote, "Afloat upon ethereal tides St. Paul's above the City rides." Now the helicopter rides over all, but still Wren's great Cathedral dominates even the massive new office-buildings erected where the bombs had blasted great gaps in London's fabric.

OXFORD STREET

Oxford Street, named after Queen Anne's statesman, Robert Harley, First Earl of Oxford, runs from the Marble Arch to St. Giles's Church. Largely occupied by Department Stores and catering especially for women, it is sometimes called "The Ladies' Mile."

Oh London tunes are new tunes, and London books are
  wise,
And London plays are rare plays, and fine to country
  eyes,
Wretchedly fare the most there, and happily fare the few,
And London Town of all towns I'm glad to hurry
  through.

So hey for the road, the west road, by mill and forge and
  fold,
Scent of the fern and song of the lark by brook, and field,
  and wold,
To the comely folk at the hearth-stone and the talk beside
  the fire,
In the hearty land, where I was bred, my land of heart's
  desire!

JOHN MASEFIELD (1878-   )
London Town

History

LONDON—NEW TROY

As the Roman writers, to glorify the city of Rome, derive the original thereof from gods and demi-gods, by the Trojan progeny, so Geoffrey of Monmouth, the Welsh historian, deduceth the foundation of this famous city of London, for the greater glory thereof, and emulation of Rome, from the very same original. For he reporteth that Brute, lineally descended from the demi-god Aeneas, the son of Venus, daughter of Jupiter, about the year of the world 2855, and 1108 before the nativity of Christ, built this city near unto the river now called Thames, and named it Troynovant, or Trenovant. But herein, as Livy, the most famous historiographer of the Romans, writeth, antiquity is pardonable, and hath an especial privilege, by interlacing divine matters with human, to make the first foundation of cities more honourable, more sacred, and, as it were, of greater majesty.

King Lud (as the aforesaid Geoffrey of Monmouth noteth) afterwards not only repaired this city, but also increased the same with fair buildings, towers, and walls, and after his own name called it Caire-Lud, as Lud's town; and the strong gate which he built in the west part of the city he likewise, for his own honour, named Ludgate.

JOHN STOW (1525-1605)
Survey of London

LONDON'S ARMADA BEACONS, 1588

The sentinel on Whitehall gate looked forth into the
    night,
And saw o'erhanging Richmond Hill the streak of blood-
    red light;
Then bugle's note and cannon's roar the deathlike silence
    broke,
And with one start, and with one cry, the royal city
    woke.
At once on all her stately gates arose the answering
    fires;
At once the wild alarum clashed from all her reeling
    spires;
From all the batteries of the Tower pealed loud the voice
    of fear;
And all the thousand masts of Thames sent back a louder
    cheer;
And from the farthest wards was heard the rush of hurry-
    ing feet,
And the broad streams of pikes and flags rushed down
    each roaring street;

And broader still became the blaze, and louder still the
    din,
As fast from every village round the horse came spurring
    in:
And eastward straight from wild Blackheath the warlike
    errand went,
And roused in many an ancient hall the gallant squires
    of Kent.
Southward from Surrey's pleasant hills flew those
    bright couriers forth;

High on bleak Hampstead's swarthy moor they started
    for the north;
And on, and on, without a pause, untired they bounded
    still:
All night from tower to tower they sprang; they sprang
    from hill to hill.

LORD MACAULAY (1800-1859)
The Armada

THE BRIDGE AND THE CITY

Any one can perceive the historical fragrance of places
like Winchelsea and Montreuil, Ravenna and Rye. Once
on a time they were ports with the sea deep at their
quays; the sea made them great. Now they are far in-
land: in none of them will you hear on the roughest day
the sound of a wave. The sea gave and the sea has taken
away. Yet they survive, pensioned off as it were, and
living, in a modest way, a pensive and dignified life, like
the old soldiers at Chelsea. Long sequestered from the
hustle and racket of the central stream of urban progress,
they sit apart in their archaic clothes, quietly brood
in the sun and tell stories of their great youth to the
eager amateurs of the antique who come to converse with
them.

Yet their cases are not singular; only a little extreme.
The special causes that once made a site peculiarly good
for a town are always passing away and giving place to
causes which make some other site better. It is not the
sea alone that recedes. London herself, as well as Rye,
has long survived the state of things which caused her
to be exactly where she is. On London Bridge, as well as
on the ramparts of Montreuil, which once had the sea at
their feet, you may feast your fill upon thoughts about
the perishableness of the *raisons d'être* of cities. Your
mind may cast back to the earliest bodies of Continental

entrants into our island. Not liking to lose sight of
land, they would cross to England south of the
Thames, probably by that route, from Calais to Dover,
to which human frailty still assures primacy. But
their hearts would be set on the good things that they
had heard to be awaiting them north of the Thames,
the fat, flat, sunny cornlands of East Anglia, still
the teeming mother of the best English wheat. So
the thing they wanted to do, from the moment they
came ashore, was to find a ford where an army could
wade across the Thames, or a gut where they might
bridge it.

With his fancy warming to the work, the musing
person sees the newcomers feel their way westward along
the south bank of the Thames. They are constantly
thwarted. They cannot even get near the deep waters in
mid-stream. Miles of squelchy riverain marshland hold
them off. Now and then hope rises, where a spit of hard
gravel or chalk sticks out like a pier into the river
through the boggy alluvial clays of its south bank. The
leader marks down one of these piers at what is now
Gravesend, another at Greenhithe, another at Erith, and
two more at Woolwich and Greenwich. He wades out
from the tip of each spit, but soon finds he is swimming.
He ferries himself across in a native coracle to see if there
be any hope of throwing a bridge, for his host and its
baggage to cross. No, plague take it! Opposite each of
the piers jutting out from the south there is on the north
bank nothing but that endless clayey morass; a bridge
would have to be miles long. He reconnoitres the northern bank as well as he can and finds a couple of those
bony natural piers there too—one at Grays, as we call it,
another at what we name Purfleet. But none of these
piers jutting southward is opposite any of the piers
jutting northward. All no good. " Will Fortune never
come with both hands full ? " So, like the sick king, the
early invaders of Britain may reasonably have asked as

they groped and sounded their way along the river boundary of Kent.

And then at last Fortune did come full-handed. Out through the spongy alluvial clays on the southern side a ridge of hard sandy gravel projected northwards, carrying the explorers dry-shod to, at least, the edge of the open river. And right down to the water's edge, exactly opposite, upon the northern shore, there sloped, steep and dry, another bank or ridge of hard gravel. At last nature had vouchsafed the two abutments needed for a bridge. Along the crown of that southern ridge of gravel and over London Bridge to gain the northern ridge of gravel, a morning host of City clerks troops today. Though neither King William Street, E.C., nor the Borough High Street presents a gravelly appearance to these wayfarer's eyes, the site of the world's greatest city was thus determined some millions of years before, by a seeming caprice in the earth's distribution of gravel, sand, alluvium and Eocene clays.

When once the luck came, it came in abundance. A natural waist in the Thames, a geological invitation to the bridge-builder, was to be found at Battersea too, and an easy ford at Brentford. Still, the first bridgeable place was the thing. The lowest easy crossing over a great river is like the eldest son of a peer: everything goes to each of these two, though the one be only the first by a mile and the other the eldest by five minutes. Like Bristol and Norwich and Lincoln, Canterbury and York, Rochester, Chester and Exeter, London got her chance in life by being the first bridge town upon a river navigable by sea-going craft. Every one of that august company has its cathedral and bishop and great historical glories, although the original reason for its importance has long passed away or declined. Nearly all of them wear something now of that Chelsea pensioner look. More or less, the world has passed them by—a world they partly envy and partly disdain, feeling it ugly and

raw as compared with their fair, mellow selves, and yet
ruefully feeling, besides, that it seems in these vulgar
times to have more of a function than they—to be, as
the people   science say, more wholly organic.

C. E. MONTAGUE (1867-1928)
The Right Place

HOW LONDON GREW

" London! " It has the sound of distant thunder. Only
one other great capital has its might reverberating in
its name. Rome—Roma, however you say it, sounds like
the shout of legions or long waves breaking on the shore.
London with its equipoise of syllables seems to hold its
power, to impend, almost to threaten. To some it sounds
like a warning, to some like applause, but always distant,
distant. How the name rolls over the country calling up
the recruits! And how did it sound in alien ears, to the
generations of exiles who have sought shelter here
through the ages: the Dutch refugees who were given
the church of Austin Friars; the Huguenots driven out
by the Catholics, the Catholic *emigrés* fleeing from the
revolutionaries, the Communists fleeing from the
Republicans, all to settle and mingle in Soho; the
Italian liberators; the Russian revolutionaries fleeing
from the Czarists, the Czarists in turn fleeing from the
Bolsheviki; then the coming of the refugee Belgians in
their thousands. To them all the growl of London must
have softened to a purr.

If the name suggests thunder and its association of
darkness and vastness and the beauty of lightning,
something of that may be found in the inchoate, inter-
minable, soot-darkened mass of London itself, assembled
without plan or control, with its sudden apparitions of
grace and beauty springing so often out of its obstruction
and confusion. Unlike other royal capitals, the fe-

planning and ornamentation of the capital, so popular and pardonable an extravagance of continental monarchs, have not been practised here, and London owes little beyond its parks, and a few buildings to the Court. The genius of the people for half-measures and compromise and distrust of logic and symmetry has resulted in nearly all the finest things being half reluctantly displayed and rarely connected in an architectural effect. The winding of the river Thames creates curious topographical illusions by which St. Paul's and the Abbey seem constantly to be appearing and reappearing in the wrong places. Then, there are the weathering idiosyncrasies of Portland stone, of which the chief London buildings are made, which creates a world of shadows and high lights all of its own. These are the ever-salient factors that profoundly affect the form and complexion of London, adding mystery to all her qualities.

London differs organically from other ancient capitals. It has not the grand scale planning and uniform dignity of façade of the main part of Paris, nor the grandeur of stupendous building and flashing fountain that still is Rome, nor the wooded handsomeness and drilled impressiveness of Berlin, nor the gaiety of baroque and garden that was the old Vienna; nor has it anything like the historic highway that runs between the crowded " lands " of Edinburgh from its ancient castle to the shadowy palace of Holyrood, nor the surprise of Stockholm with its water front from which rises its new Town Hall, the most remarkable communal effort in architecture in our time. The character of London is its bulk and multitude, and the quality of London is its accidentalness. It never seems to have set out to be or to look like a capital.

Its relations with royalty have never been intimate. William the Conqueror built the Tower of London on its eastern edge to over-awe its citizens, and, unlike all other capital cities, it has never been the regular seat of the sovereign, who has always held his Court in West-minster. In no other capital city in the world has the king to ask permission of the civic ruler before he enters it, nor any where the king's soldiers may not march through its streets with fixed bayonets and drawn swords save with the City fathers' permission. The little ceremony at Temple Bar on every official royal visit, when the Lord Mayor and his Swordbearer with the Pearl Sword and Sheriffs wait at Child's Bank, has an historical significance that marks out London from all other capitals.

With the powerful City of London, with its privileges and charters always beside them and usually confronting them over questions of rights and funds and taxes, the sovereigns of England have never felt towards London as sovereigns of other states have felt towards their capitals. The Popes in Rome, Francis the First, Louis XIV, Napoleon and Louis Napoleon in Paris, Frederick the Great and the Hohenzollerns in Berlin, the Bavarian kings in Munich, the Bourbons in Madrid, the Czars in Moscow and St. Petersburg, all reformed their capitals after their own desire. It is impossible to imagine these cities without them. Once there was a grand possibility for London and a great man ready, but even Charles II failed in one of the few things he cared about, and Wren's plan for the rebuilding of London after the Great Fire remained on paper. The Hanoverian Georges had their hearts elsewhere until George the Regent and latterly the Fourth of the name helped London to something really spacious and fine, and the gracious urbane composition of Regent Street set London moving to a statelier measure. (And we of this generation have exchanged it for a mess of architectural pottage!) Queen Victoria, who reigned when England had reached to heights of unparalleled prosperity, had no particular love for London, nor taste for showiness in capitals, and the Prince Consort, who cared for Italian primitives before they were the fashion, and had enlightened ideas of the responsibilities of sovereigns in the advancement of the arts and the industries, died before he had the power to do more than hatch the Crystal Palace. The Tudors and the Stuarts sometimes had the power and the money and the taste to do what was fashionable in their day to give their capital a new fame for beauty. But what they did in that cause was mainly done at Windsor, Richmond, and Hampton Court and Greenwich, and so with the exception of the three parks, our peerless Westminster Hall with its angel hammerbeams, the Banqueting Hall in Whitehall, Holbein's Gateway to St. James's Palace, and Chelsea Hospital, London owes little to the taste and generosity of kings.

JAMES BONE (1872-1962)
The London Perambulator

THE PRINCES IN THE TOWER

It has been claimed that King Richard III has been grossly maligned by the writers serving Henry VII who needed to justify the latter's rebellion and overthrow of his crookback predecessor. Shakespeare, working under a Tudor Queen who was Henry VII's grand-daughter, accepted, doubtless in complete good faith, the tradition of Richard as a conscienceless murderer who did not stop at the slaughter of innocent children. He graced the hideous deed in the Tower with lines of characteristic beauty. It has been observed of Shakespeare that, in the profusion of his verbal bounty, he frequently gave gems to his small-part players. Dighton and Forrest, who do not figure in the play, are turned into first-class poets, whatever their achievements as assassins.

TYRREL: The tyrannous and bloody act is done—
The most arch deed of piteous massacre
That ever yet this land was guilty of.
Dighton and Forrest, whom I did suborn
To do this ruthless piece of butchery,
Albeit they were flesh'd villains, bloody dogs,
Melting with tenderness and mild compassion,

Wept like two children in their death's sad story.
" Lo, thus," quoth Dighton, " lay the gentle babes,"—
" Thus, thus," quoth Forrest, " girdling one another
Within their innocent alabaster arms:
Their lips were four red roses on a stalk,
Which in their summer beauty kiss'd each other.
A book of prayers on their pillow lay;
" Which once," quoth Forrest, " almost chang'd my
    mind;
But, O, the devil "—there the villain stopp'd;
When Dighton thus told on,—" We smothered
The most replenished sweet work of nature,
That from the prime creation e'er she fram'd."
Hence both are gone with conscience and remorse;
They could not speak; and so I left them both,
To bear this tidings to the bloody king:—
And here he comes.

    Enter KING RICHARD.

                    All health, my sovereign lord!
  KING RICHARD: Kind Tyrrel, am I happy in thy news?
  TYRREL: If to have done the thing you gave in charge
Beget your happiness, be happy then,
For it is done.
  KING RICHARD: But didst thou see them dead?
  TYRREL: I did, my lord.
  KING RICHARD: And buried, gentle Tyrrel?
  TYRREL: The chaplain of the Tower hath buried them;
But where, to say the truth, I do not know.
  KING RICHARD: Come to me, Tyrrel, soon at after
    supper,
When thou shalt tell the process of their death.
Meantime, but think how I may do thee good,
And be inheritor of thy desire.
Farewell till then.
  TYRREL: I humbly take my leave.

WILLIAM SHAKESPEARE (1564-1616)
Richard III

KING RICHARD II TAKEN TO THE TOWER

London. A street leading to the Tower.

Enter QUEEN *and* LADIES.

QUEEN: This way the king will come; this is the way
To Julius Caesar's ill-erected tower,
To whose flint bosom my condemned lord
Is doom'd a prisoner by proud Bolingbroke;
Here let us rest, if this rebellious earth
Have any resting for her true king's queen—
But soft, but see, or rather do not see,
My fair rose wither: yet look up, behold,
That you in pity may dissolve to dew,
And wash him fresh again with true-love tears.

Enter KING RICHARD *and* GUARDS.
Ah, thou, the model where old Troy did stand,
Thou map of honour, thou King Richard's tomb,
And not King Richard; thou most beauteous inn,
Why should hard-favour'd grief be lodg'd in thee,
When triumph is become an alehouse guest?

KING RICHARD: Join not with grief, fair woman, do
not so,
To make my end too sudden: learn, good soul,
To think our former state a happy dream;
From which awak'd, the truth of what we are
Shows us but this: I am sworn brother, sweet,
To grim Necessity; and he and I
Will keep a league till death. Hie thee to France,
And cloister thee in some religious house:
Our holy lives must win a new world's crown,
Which our profane hours here have stricken down.

QUEEN: What, is my Richard both in shape and mind
Transform'd and weaken'd? hath Bolingbroke depos'd
Thine intellect? hath he been in thy heart?
The lion dying thrusteth forth his paw,
And wounds the earth, if nothing else, with rage
To be o'erpower'd; and wilt thou, pupil-like,
Take thy correction mildly, kiss the rod,
And fawn on rage with base humility,
Which art a lion and a king of beasts?

KING RICHARD: A king of beasts, indeed; if aught but
    beasts,
I had been still a happy king of men.
Good sometime queen, prepare thee hence for France:
Think I am dead; and that even here thou takest,
As from my death-bed, thy last living leave.
In winter's tedious nights sit by the fire
With good old folks, and let them tell thee tales
Of woeful ages long ago betid:
And ere thou bid good night, to quit their griefs
Tell thou the lamentable tale of me,
And send the hearers weeping to their beds:
For why the senseless brands will sympathize
The heavy accent of thy moving tongue,
And in compassion weep the fire out;
And some will mourn in ashes, some coal-black,
For the deposing of a rightful king.

WILLIAM SHAKESPEARE (1564-1616)
Richard II

RALEIGH'S CELL IN THE TOWER

Sir Walter Raleigh, proud, tactless, disliked by Queen Elizabeth the
First and victimised by her successor on the throne, was typical of his
time in mixing foppery with endurance and adventures of the body
with the fine play of mind. Poet and explorer he languished in the

Tower, on a false charge of treason, from 1603-1615, and was executed in 1618. He was allowed books and paper during his imprisonment and there began his History of the World.

Here writ was the World's History by his hand
    Whose steps knew all the earth; albeit his world
    In these few piteous paces then was furl'd.
Here daily, hourly, have his proud feet spann'd
This smaller speck than the receding land
    Had ever shown his ships; what time he hurl'd
    Abroad o'er new-found regions spiced and pearl'd
His country's high dominion and command.

Here dwelt two spheres. The vast terrestrial zone
    His spirit traversed; and that spirit was
        Itself the zone celestial, round whose birth
        The planets played within the zodiac's girth;
    Till hence, through unjust death unfeared, did pass
His spirit to the only land unknown.

DANTE GABRIEL ROSSETTI (1828-82)
Poems

THE TRIAL OF KING CHARLES I

During his trial at Westminster Hall King Charles I was kept under guard at St. James's Palace. In reading the account and the comment in the Earl of Clarendon's *History of the Rebellion and the Civil Wars* it must be remembered that Clarendon was a strongly partisan historian, for whom Charles was the completely maligned hero of a dramatic tragedy.

From the time of the King's being come to St. James's, . . . his majesty was treated with more rudeness and barbarity than he had ever been before. No man was suffered to see or speak to him, but the soldiers who were his guard, some of whom sat up always in his bed-chamber, and drank, and took tobacco, as if they had been upon the court of guard; nor was he suffered to go into any other room, either to say his prayers, or to receive the ordinary benefits of nature, but was obliged to do both in their presence and before them: and yet they were so jealous of these their janizaries, that they might be wrought upon by the influence of this innocent prince, or by the remorse of their own conscience upon the exercise of so much barbarity, that they caused the guards to be still changed; and the same men were never suffered twice to perform the same monstrous duty.

When he was first brought to Westminster-hall, which was upon the twentieth of January, before their high court of justice, he looked upon them, and sat down, without any manifestation of trouble, never stirring his hat; all the impudent judges sitting covered, and fixing their eyes upon him, without the least show of respect. The odious libel, which they called a charge and impeachment, was then read by the clerk; which contained, " that he had been admitted king of England, and trusted with a limited power to govern according to law; and, by his oath and office, was obliged to use the power committed to him for the good and benefit of the people: but that he had, out of a wicked design to erect himself an illimited and tyrannical power, and to overthrow the rights and liberties of the people, traitorously levied war against the present parliament, and the people therein represented." And it was prayed, " that he might be put to answer to all the particulars, to the end that such an examination, trial, and judgment, might be had thereupon, as should be agreeable to justice."

Which being read, their president Bradshaw, after he had insolently reprehended the king " for not having stirred his hat, or shewed more respect to that high tribunal," told him, " that the parliament of England had appointed that court to try him for the several treasons, and misdemeanours, which he had committed against the kingdom during the evil administration of his government; and that, upon the examination thereof, justice might be done." And, after a great sauciness and impudence of talk, he asked the king, " what answers he had to make to that impeachment."

The king, without any alteration in his countenance by all that insolent provocation, told them, " he would first know of them, by what authority they presumed by force to bring him before them, and who gave them power to judge of his actions, for which he was accountable to none but God; though they had always been such as he need not be ashamed to own them before all the world." He told them, " that he was their king, they his subjects; who owed him duty and obedience: that no parliament had authority to call him before them; but that they were not the parliament, nor had any authority from the parliament to sit in that manner: that of all the persons who sat there, and took upon them to judge him, except those persons who being officers of the army he could not but know whilst he was forced to be amongst them, there were only two faces which he had ever seen before, or whose names were known to him." And, after urging, " their duty, that was due to him, and his superiority over them," by such lively reasons, and arguments, as were not capable of any answer, he concluded, " that he would not so much betray himself, and his royal dignity, as to answer anything they objected against him, which were to acknowledge their authority; though he believed that every one of themselves, as well as the spectators, did, in their own consciences, absolve him from all the material things which were objected against him."

Bradshaw advised him, in a very arrogant manner, " not to deceive himself with an opinion that anything he had said would do him any good: that the parliament knew their own authority, and would not suffer it to be called in question or debated ": therefore wished him, " to think better of it, against he should be next brought

TRAFALGAR SQUARE: THE FOUNTAINS

It has been unkindly said that "Civil Servants play from ten to five, like the fountains in Trafalgar Square." That is hardly an accurate comparison now that the fountains, designed by Barry in 1845, play late at night and are lit up to show it, especially at Christmas.

ORANGES AND LEMONS

In 1920 the Rev. W. Pennington-Bickford started an annual children's service at St. Clement Danes to bring the old rhyme about the bells of St. Clement's saying "Oranges and Lemons" into the life of the local children. So the bells ring out in March and the gifts are made.

RAIN BY THE RIVER

London is in a fairly dry corner of England, but it has its downpours when a descent to the Underground (Blackfriars Station in this case) is a natural escape. Blackfriars Bridge on the left was built as a tollbridge in 1770 and so much expanded early in this century that it is Britain's broadest river-bridge, a precious link between the City and South London.

thither, and that he would answer directly to his charge; otherwise, he could not be so ignorant, as not to know what judgment the law pronounced against those who stood mute, and obstinately refused to plead." So the guard carried his majesty back to St. James's; where they treated him as before.

There was an accident happened that first day, which may be fit to be remembered. When all those who were commissioners had taken their places, and the king was brought in, the first ceremony was, to read their commission; which was the ordinance of parliament for the trial; and then the judges were all called, every man answering to his name as he was called, and the president being first called and making answer, the next who was called being the general, Lord Fairfax, and no answer being made, the officer called him the second time, when there was a voice heard that said, "he had more wit than to be there"; which put the court into some disorder, and somebody asking, who it was, there was no answer but a little murmuring. But, presently, when the impeachment was read, and that expression used, of " all the good people of England," the same voice in a louder tone answered, " No, nor the hundredth part of them ": upon which, one of the officers bid the soldiers give fire into that box whence those presumptuous words were uttered.

But it was quickly discerned that it was the general's wife, the Lady Fairfax, who had uttered both those sharp sayings; who was presently persuaded or forced to leave the place, to prevent any new disorder. She was of a very noble extraction, one of the daughters and heirs of Horace Lord Vere of Tilbury; who, having been bred in Holland, had not that reverence for the church of England, as she ought to have had, and so had unhappily concurred in her husband's entering into rebellion, never imagining what misery it would bring upon the kingdom; and now abhorred the work in hand as

much as anybody could do, and did all she could to
hinder her husband from acting any part in it. Nor did
he ever sit in that bloody court, though out of the
stupidity of his soul he was throughout overwitted by
Cromwell, and made a property to bring that to pass
which could very hardly have been otherwise effected.

As there was in many persons present at that woeful
spectacle a real duty and compassion for the king, so
there was in others so barbarous and brutal a behaviour
towards him, that they called him tyrant and murderer;
and one spit in his face; which his majesty, without expressing any trouble, wiped off with his handkerchief.

The several unheard of insolences which this excellent
prince was forced to submit to, at the other times he was
brought before that odious judicatory, his majestic
behaviour under so much insolence, and resolute insisting upon his own dignity, and defending it by manifest
authorities in the law, as well as by the clearest deductions
from reason, the pronouncing that horrible sentence
upon the most innocent person in the world, the execution of that sentence by the most execrable murder that
was ever committed since that of our blessed Saviour,
and the circumstances thereof; the application and interposition that was used by some noble persons to prevent
that woeful murder, and the hypocrisy with which that
interposition was eluded, the saint-like behaviour of that
blessed martyr, and his Christian courage and patience
at his death, are all particulars so well known, and have
been so much enlarged upon in a treatise peculiarly writ
to that purpose, that the farther mentioning it in this
place would but afflict and grieve the reader, and make
the relation itself odious as well as needless; and therefore no more shall be said here of that lamentable
tragedy, so much to the dishonour of the nation, and the
religion professed by it.

EDWARD HYDE, FIRST EARL OF CLARENDON (1609-1674)
History of the Rebellion and Civil Wars

THE GREAT FIRE, 1666

September 2nd, 1666 (*Lord's Day*). Some of our maids sitting up late last night to get things ready against our feast today, Jane called us up about three in the morning, to tell us of a great fire they saw in the City. So I rose, and slipped on my night-gown, and went to her window; and thought it to be on the back-side of Mark Lane at the farthest; but, being unused to such fires as followed, I thought it far enough off; and so went to bed again, and to sleep. About seven rose again to dress myself, and there looked out at the window, and saw the fire not so much as it was, and further off. So to my closet to set things to rights, after yesterday's cleaning.

By and by Jane comes and tells me that she hears that above 300 houses have been burned down tonight by the fire we saw, and that it is now burning down all Fish Street, by London Bridge. So I made myself ready presently, and walked to the Tower; and there got up upon one of the high places, Sir J. Robinson's little son going up with me; and there I did see the houses at that end of the bridge all on fire, and an infinite great fire on this and the other side the end of the bridge; which, among other people, did trouble me for poor little Michell and our Sarah on the bridge. So down, with my heart full of trouble, to the Lieutenant of the Tower, who tells me that it began this morning in the King's baker's house in Pudding Lane, and that it hath burned down St. Magnus's Church and most part of Fish Street already. So I down to the water-side, and there got a boat, and through bridge, and there saw a lamentable fire.

Poor Michell's house, as far as the Old Swan, already burned that way, and the fire running further, that, in a very little time, it got as far as the Steele-yard, while I was there. Every body endeavouring to remove their goods, and flinging into the river, or bringing them into lighters that lay off; poor people staying in their houses as long as till the very fire touched them, and then running into boats, or clambering from one pair of stairs, by the waterside, to another. And, among other things, the poor pigeons, I perceive, were loth to leave their houses, but hovered about the windows and balconys, till they burned their wings, and fell down.

Having staid, and in an hour's time seen the fire rage every way; and nobody, to my sight, endeavouring to quench it, but to remove their goods, and leave all to the fire; and, having seen it get as far as the Steele-yard, and the wind mighty high, and driving it into the City; and everything, after so long a drought, proving combustible, even the very stones of churches; and, among other things, the poor steeple by which pretty Mrs. ——— lives, and whereof my old schoolfellow Elborough is parson, taken fire in the very top, and there burned till it fell down; I to White Hall, with a gentleman with me, who desired to go off from the Tower, to see the fire, in my boat; and there up to the King's closet in the Chapel, where people come about me, and I did give them an account dismayed them all, and word was carried in to the King.

Good hopes there was of stopping it at the Three Cranes above, and at the Buttolph's Wharf below bridge, if care be used; but the wind carries it into the City, so as we know not, by the water-side, what to do there. River full of lighters and boats taking in goods, and good goods swimming in the water; and only I observed that hardly one lighter or boat in three that had the goods of a house in, but there was a pair of Virginalls in it. Having seen as much as I could now, I away to

White Hall by appointment, and there walked to St. James's Park; and there met my wife, and Creed, and Wood, and his wife, and walked to my boat; and there upon the water again, and to the fire up and down, it still increasing, and the wind great. So near the fire as we could for smoke; and all over the Thames, with one's faces in the wind, you were almost burned with a shower of fire-drops. This is very true: so as houses were burned by these drops and flakes of fire, three or four, nay, five or six houses, one from another.

When we could endure no more upon the water, we to a little alehouse on the Bankside, over against the Three Cranes, and there staid till it was dark almost, and saw the fire grow; and, as it grew darker, appeared more and more; and in corners and upon steeples, and between churches and houses, as far as we could see up the hill of the City, in a most horrid, malicious, bloody flame, not like the fine flame of an ordinary fire. Barbary and her husband away before us. We staid till, it being darkish, we saw the fire as only one entire arch of fire from this to the other side of the bridge, and in a bow up the hill for an arch of above a mile long: it made me weep to see it. The churches, houses, and all on fire, and flaming at once; and a horrid noise the flames made, and the cracking of houses at their ruine.

So home with a sad heart, and there find every body discoursing and lamenting the fire; and poor Tom Hater come with some few of his goods saved out of his house, which was burned upon Fish Street Hill. I invited him to lie at my house, and did receive his goods; but was deceived in his lying there, the news coming every moment of the growth of the fire; so as we were forced to begin to pack up our own goods, and prepare for their removal; and did by moonshine, it being brave, dry, and moonshine and warm weather, carry much of my goods into the garden; and Mr. Hater and I did remove my money and iron chests into my cellar, as thinking that the safest place. And got my bags of gold into my office, ready to carry away, and my chief papers of accounts also there, and my tallies into a box by themselves. So great was our fear, as Sir W. Batten hath carts come out of the country to fetch away his goods this night. We did put Mr. Hater, poor man! to bed a little; but he got but very little rest, so much noise being in my house, taking down of goods.

September 7th. Up by five o'clock; and, blessed by God! find all well; and by water to Pane's Wharfe. Walked thence, and saw all the towne burned, and a miserable sight of Paul's church, with all the roofs fallen, and the body of the quire fallen into St. Fayth's; Paul's school also, Ludgate, and Fleet Street. My father's house, and the church, and a good part of the Temple the like. So to Creed's lodging, near the New Exchange, and there find him laid down upon a bed; the house all unfurnished, there being fears of the fire's coming to them. There borrowed a shirt of him, and washed. To Sir W. Coventry at St. James's, who lay without curtains, having removed all his goods; as the King at White Hall, and everybody had done, and was doing. He hopes we shall have no public distractions upon this fire which is what every body fears, because of the talk of the French having a hand in it. And it is a proper time for discontents; but all men's minds are full of care to protect themselves and save their goods: the Militia is in arms every where.

I home late to Sir W. Pen's, who did give me a bed, but without curtains or hangings, all being down. So here I went the first time into a naked bed, only my drawers on; and did sleep pretty well: but still both sleeping and waking had a fear of fire in my heart, that I took little rest. People do all the world over cry out of the simplicity of my Lord Mayor in generall; and more particularly in this business of the fire, laying it all upon him. A proclamation is come out for markets to be kept at Leadenhall and Mile-end Greene, and several other places about the town; and Tower Hill, and all churches to be set open to receive poor people.

SAMUEL PEPYS (1633-1703)
Diary

THE GREAT FIRE

Such was the rise of this prodigious fire,
Which in mean buildings first obscurely bred,
From thence did soon to open streets aspire,
And straight to palaces and temples spread.

The diligence of trades and noiseful gain,
And luxury, more late, asleep were laid;
All was the night's, and in her silent reign
No sound the rest of Nature did invade.

In this deep quiet, from what source unknown,
Those seeds of fire their fatal birth disclose;
And first, few scatt'ring sparks about were blown,
Big with the flames that to our ruin rose.

Then in some close-pent room it crept along,
And, smould'ring as it went, in silence fed;
Till th' infant monster, with devouring strong
Walked bodily upright with exalted head.

At length the crackling noise and dreadful blaze
Called up some waking lover to the sight;
And long it was ere he the rest could raise,
Whose heavy eyelids yet were full of night.

The next to danger, hot pursued by fate,
Half-clothed, half-naked, hastily retire;
And frighted mothers strike their breasts too late
For helpless infants left amidst the fire.

Their cries soon waken all the dwellers near;
Now murmuring noises rise in every street;
The more remote run stumbling with their fear,
And in the dark men justle as they meet.

A key of fire ran all along the shore,
And lightened all the river with a blaze;
The wakened tides began again to roar,
And wondering fish in shining waters gaze.

Old Father Thames raised up his reverend head,
But feared the fate of Simois would return;
Deep in his ooze he sought his sedgy bed,
And shrunk his waters back into his urn.

The Fire meantime walks in a broader gross;
To either hand his wings he opens wide;
He wades the streets, and straight he reaches cross,
And plays his longing flames on th' other side.

To every nobler portion of the town
The curling billows roll their restless tide;
In parties now they straggle up and down,
As armies unopposed for prey divide.

One mighty squadron with a side-wind sped
Through narrow lanes his cumbered fire does haste;
By powerful charms of gold and silver led,
The Lombard bankers and the Change to waste.

Another backward to the Tower would go,
And slowly eats his way against the wind;
But the main body of the marching foe
Against th' imperial palace is designed.

BIG BEN AND BOADICEA STATUE

One of the horses of the Boadicea statue by Thornycroft on the Embankment makes a galloping foreground for this close-up of Big Ben. The great clock, reached by 374 steps, came into operation in 1856. It was named after Sir Benjamin Hall, then Commissioner of Works.

THE HOUSES OF PARLIAMENT

The best view of the Houses of Parliament is obtainable across the river. The Victoria Tower is seen on the left and the Clock Tower with "Big Ben" on the right. After the fire of 1834 the Houses were rebuilt to Sir Charles Barry's neo-Gothic designs.

FLOWER SELLERS

A London flower-girl has been a conquering theatrical heroine since Bernard Shaw's Eliza became "My Fair Lady". Not all are so promoted, but the sellers remain great public favourites and their blossom-laden baskets bring welcome colour to the grey streets and buildings.

THE UNDERGROUND

There are seven great underground railways serving London and its suburbs, of which four are deeply-dug tubes and three are lines just below the surface. All are inter-connected. The rush-hour traffic tests their carrying capacity and the passengers' endurance to the utmost.

Those who have homes, when home they do repair,
To a last lodgings call their wand'ring friends;
Their short uneasy sleeps are broke with care,
To look how near their own destruction tends.

Those who have none, sit round where once it was,
And with full eyes each wonted room require;
Haunting the yet warm ashes of the place,
As murdered men walk where they did expire.

The most in fields like herded beasts lie down,
To dews obnoxious on the grassy floor;
And while their babes in sleep their sorrows drown,
Sad parents watch the remnants of their store.

JOHN DRYDEN (1631-1700)
Annus Mirabilis

BACK-DOOR DEPARTURE

The flight from London of the last of the Stuart Kings, the defeated
and despairing James II, was made on December 11, 1688. It was not
immediately successful. Bad weather held up his vessel and he was
soon in the hands of his enemies. But Prince William of Orange, soon
to be King William III, was glad to be rid of James without further
trouble. The fugitive had his escape made easy by negligence of the
guard. So James was sailing down the Thames to exile eleven days
later. Here is Lord Macaulay's description of the events.

The arrangements for the flight were promptly made: a
vessel was ordered to be in readiness at Gravesend: but
to reach Gravesend was not easy. The City was in a state
of extreme agitation. The slightest cause sufficed to
bring a crowd together. No foreigner could appear in
the streets without risk of being stopped, questioned, and
carried before a magistrate as a Jesuit in disguise. It was,
therefore, necessary to take the road on the south of the
Thames. No precautions which could quiet suspicion

3

was omitted. The King and Queen retired to rest as usual.

When the palace had been some time profoundly quiet, James rose and called a servant who was in attendance. " You will find," said the King, " a man at the door of the antechamber; bring him hither." The servant obeyed, and Lauzun was ushered into the royal bedchamber. " I confide to you," said James, " my Queen and my son; everything must be risked to carry them into France." Lauzun, with a truly chivalrous spirit, returned thanks for the dangerous honour which had been conferred on him, and begged permission to avail himself of the assistance of his friend Saint Victor, a gentleman of Provence, whose courage and faith had been often tried. The services of so valuable an assistant were readily accepted. Lauzun gave his hand to Mary; Saint Victor wrapped up in his warm cloak the ill-fated heir of so many Kings. The party stole down the back stairs, and embarked in an open skiff.

It was a miserable voyage. The night was bleak: the rain fell: the wind roared: the waves were rough: at length the boat reached Lambeth; and the fugitives landed near an inn, where a coach and horses were in waiting. Some time elapsed before the horses could be harnessed. Mary, afraid that her face might be known, would not enter the house. She remained with her child, cowering for shelter from the storm under the tower of Lambeth Church, and distracted by terror whenever the ostler approached her with his lantern. Two of her women attended her, one who gave suck to the Prince, and one whose office was to rock his cradle; but they could be of little use to their mistress; for both were foreigners who could hardly speak the English language, and who shuddered at the rigour of the English climate. The only consolatory circumstance was that the little boy was well, and uttered not a single cry.

At length the coach was ready. Saint Victor followed

it on horseback. The fugitives reached Gravesend safely, and embarked in the yacht which waited for them. They found there Lord Powis and his wife. Three Irish officers were also on board. These men had been sent thither in order that they might assist Lauzun in any desperate emergency; for it was thought not impossible that the captain of the ship might prove false; and it was fully determined that, on the first suspicion of treachery, he should be stabbed to the heart. There was, however, no necessity for violence. The yacht proceeded down the river with a fair wind; and Saint Victor, having seen her under sail, spurred back with the good news to White-hall.

On the morning of Monday, the tenth of December, the King learned that his wife and son had begun their voyage with a fair prospect of reaching their destination. About the same time a courier arrived at the palace with despatches from Hungerford. Had James been a little more discerning, or a little less obstinate, those despatches would have induced him to reconsider all his plans. The Commissioners wrote hopefully. The conditions proposed by the conqueror were strangely liberal. The King himself could not refrain from exclaiming that they were more favourable than he could have expected. He might indeed not unreasonably suspect that they had been framed with no friendly design: but this mattered nothing; for, whether they were offered in the hope that, by closing with them, he would lay the ground for a happy reconciliation, or, as is more likely, in the hope that, by rejecting them, he would exhibit himself to the whole nation as utterly unreasonable and incorrigible, his course was equally clear. In either case his policy was to accept them promptly and to observe them faithfully.

But it soon appeared that William had perfectly understood the character with which he had to deal, and, in offering those terms which the Whigs at Hungerford had censured as too indulgent, had risked nothing. The

solemn farce by which the public had been amused since
the retreat of the royal army from Salisbury was prolonged during a few hours. All the Lords who were still
in the capital were invited to the palace that they might
be informed of the progress of the negotiation which had
been opened by their advice. Another meeting of Peers
was appointed for the following day. The Lord Mayor
and the Sheriffs of London were also summoned to attend
the King. He exhorted them to perform their duties
vigorously, and owned that he had thought it expedient
to send his wife and child out of the country, but assured
them that he would himself remain at his post.

While he uttered this unkingly and unmanly falsehood, his fixed purpose was to depart before daybreak.
Already he had entrusted his most valuable moveables
to the care of several foreign Ambassadors. His most
important papers had been deposited with the Tuscan
minister. But before the flight there was still something
to be done. The tyrant pleased himself with the thought
that he might avenge himself on a people who had been
impatient of his despotism by inflicting on them at
parting all the evils of anarchy. He ordered the Great
Seal and the writs for the new Parliament to be brought
to his apartment. The writs which could be found he
threw into the fire. Those which had been already sent
out he annulled by an instrument drawn up in legal form.
To Feversham he wrote a letter which could be understood only as a command to disband the army.

Still, however, the King concealed his intention of
absconding even from his chief ministers. Just before he
retired he directed Jeffreys to be in the closet early on the
morrow; and, while stepping into bed, whispered to
Mulgrave that the news from Hungerford was highly
satisfactory. Everybody withdrew except the Duke of
Northumberland. This young man, a natural son of
Charles the Second by the Duchess of Cleveland, commanded a troop of Life Guards, and was a Lord of the

Bedchamber. It seems to have been then the custom of the court that, in the Queen's absence, a Lord of the Bedchamber should sleep on a pallet in the King's room; and it was Northumberland's turn to perform this duty.

At three in the morning of Tuesday the eleventh of December, James rose, took the Great Seal in his hand, laid his commands on Northumberland not to open the door of the bedchamber till the usual hour, and disappeared through a secret passage; the same passage probably through which Huddleston had been brought to the bedside of the late king. Sir Edward Hales was in attendance with a hackney coach. James was conveyed to Millbank, where he crossed the Thames in a small wherry. As he passed Lambeth he flung the Great Seal into the midst of the stream, where, after many months, it was accidentally caught by a fishing net and dragged up.

At Vauxhall he landed. A carriage and horses had been stationed there for him; and he immediately took the road towards Sheerness, where a hoy belonging to the Custom House had been ordered to await his arrival.

LORD MACAULAY (1800-1859)
The History of England

THE GORDON RIOTS

London has had fewer outbreaks of violence than many other capitals, but the Gordon Riots of 1780 were hugely destructive and seriously menaced life and property for some days. The primary cause was the anger of the Protestant Association, whose President was Lord George Gordon, with the removal of Catholic disabilities. Lord George, who was Member of Parliament for Inverness, endeavoured to pacify the mob that petitioned Parliament and made large processions with the cry of " No Popery." But the crowds would not be appeased and were joined by gangs of poverty-stricken folk and desperate criminal types who saw a chance of looting by a general over-throw of law and order. They were not crushed by the troops until they had burned Newgate and Bridewell prisons and several private houses of prominent lawyers. Lord George was accused of treason, but acquitted.

He then adopted the Jewish religion and engaged in writing violent letters which landed him in jail for libel. He died of a fever at the age of thirty-two while still a prisoner. The "No Popery" riots were graphically described by Dickens in *Barnaby Rudge*.

As the day crept on, still more unusual sights were witnessed in the streets. The gates of the King's Bench and Fleet Prisons being opened at the usual hour, were found to have notices affixed to them, announcing that the rioters would come that night to burn them down. The wardens, too well knowing the likelihood there was of this promise being fulfilled, were fain to set their prisoners at liberty, and give them leave to move their goods; so all day such of them as had any furniture were occupied in conveying it, some to this place, some to that, and not a few to the broker's shops, where they gladly sold it for any wretched price those gentry chose to give. There were some broken men among these debtors who had been in jail so long, and were so miserable and destitute of friends, so dead to the world, and utterly forgotten and uncared for, that they implored their jailers not to set them free, and to send them, if need were, to some other place of custody. But they, refusing to comply, lest they should incur the anger of the mob, turned them into the streets, where they wandered up and down, hardly remembering the ways untrodden by their feet so long, and crying—such abject things those rotten-hearted jails had made them—as they slunk off in their rags, and dragged their slipshod feet along the pavement.

Even of the three hundred prisoners who had escaped from Newgate, there were some—a few, but there were some—who sought their jailers out and delivered themselves up; preferring imprisonment and punishment to the horrors of such another night as the last. Many of the convicts, drawn back to their old place of captivity by some indescribable attraction, or by a desire to exult over it in its downfall and glut their revenge by seeing it in ashes, actually went back in broad noon, and loitered about the cells. Fifty were retaken at one time on this next day, within the prison walls; but their fate did not deter others, for there they went in spite of everything and there they were taken in twos and threes, twice or thrice a day, all through the week. Of the fifty just mentioned, some were occupied in endeavouring to rekindle the fire; but in general they seemed to have no object in view but to prowl and lounge about the old place: being often found asleep in the ruins, or sitting talking there, or even eating and drinking, as in a choice retreat.

Besides the notices on the gates of the Fleet and the King's Bench, many similar announcements were left, before one o'clock at noon, at the houses of private individuals; and further, the mob proclaimed their intention of seizing on the Bank, the Mint, the Arsenal at Woolwich, and the Royal Palaces. The notices were seldom delivered by more than one man, who, if it were at a shop, went in and laid it, with a bloody threat perhaps, upon the counter; or if it were at a private house, knocked at the door, and thrust it in the servant's hand. Notwithstanding the presence of the military in every quarter of the town, and the great force in the Park, these messengers did their errands with impunity all through the day. So did two boys who went down Holborn alone, armed with bars taken from the railings of Lord Mansfield's house, and demanded money for the rioters. So did a tall man on horseback who made a collection for the same purpose in Fleet Street, and refused to take anything but gold.

A rumour had now got into circulation, too, which diffused a greater dread all through London, even than these publicly announced intentions of the rioters, though all men knew that if they were successfully effected, there must ensue a national bankruptcy and

general ruin. It was said that they meant to throw the
gates of Bedlam open, and let all the madmen loose. This
suggested such dreadful images to the people's minds,
and was indeed an act so fraught with new and un-
imaginable horrors in the contemplation, that it beset
them more than any loss or cruelty of which they could
foresee the worst, and drove many sane men nearly mad
themselves.

So the day passed on: the prisoners moving their
goods: people running to and fro in the streets, carrying
away their property; groups standing in silence round
the ruins; all business suspended; and the soldiers disposed as has been already mentioned, remaining quite
inactive. So the day passed on, and dreaded night drew
near again.

At last, at seven o'clock in the evening, the Privy
Council issued a solemn proclamation that it was now
necessary to employ the military, and that the officers
had most direct and effectual orders, by an immediate
exertion of their utmost force, to repress the disturbances;
and warning all good subjects of the King to keep themselves, their servants and apprentices, within doors that
night. There was then delivered out to every soldier on
duty, thirty-six rounds of powder and ball; the drums
beat; and the whole force was under arms at sunset.

The City authorities, stimulated by these vigorous
measures, held a Common Council; passed a vote thank-
ing the military associations who had tendered their aid
to the civil authorities; accepted it; and placed them
under the direction of the two sheriffs. At the Queen's
palace, a double guard, the yeomen on duty, the groom-
porters, and all other attendants, were stationed in the
passages and on the staircases at seven o'clock, with
strict instructions to be watchful on their posts all night;
and all the doors were locked. The gentlemen of the
Temple, and the other Inns, mounted guard within their
gates, and strengthened them with the great stones of

the pavement, which they took up for the purpose. In Lincoln's Inn, they gave up the hall and commons to the Northumberland Militia, under the command of Lord Algernon Percy; in some few of the city wards, the burgesses turned out, and without making a very fierce show, looked brave enough. Some hundreds of stout gentlemen threw themselves, armed to the teeth, into the halls of the different companies, double-locked and bolted all the gates, and dared the rioters (among themselves) to come on at their peril.

These arrangements being all made simultaneously, or nearly so, were completed by the time it got dark; and then the streets were comparatively clear, and were guarded at all the great corners and chief avenues by the troops: while parties of the officers rode up and down in all directions, ordering chance stragglers home, and admonishing the residents to keep within their houses, and, if any firing ensued, not to approach the windows. More chains were drawn across such of the thorough-fares as were of a nature to favour the approach of a great crowd, and at each of these points a considerable force was stationed. All these precautions having been taken, and it being now quite dark, those in command awaited the result in some anxiety: and not without a hope that such vigilant demonstrations might of them-selves dishearten the populace, and prevent any new outrages.

But in this reckoning they were cruelly mistaken, for in half an hour or less, as though the setting in of night had been their preconcerted signal, the rioters having previously, in small parties, prevented the lighting of the street lamps, rose like a great sea; and that in so many places at once, and with such inconceivable fury, that those who had the direction of the troops knew not, at first, where to turn or what to do. One after another, new fires blazed up in every quarter of the town, as though it were the intention of the insurgents to wrap

the city in a circle of flames, which, contracting by
degrees, should burn the whole to ashes; the crowd
swarmed and roared in every street; and none but rioters
and soldiers being out of doors, it seemed to the latter as
if all London were arrayed against them, and they stood
alone against the town.

In two hours, six-and-thirty fires were raging—six-
and-thirty great conflagrations. Among them the
Borough Clink in Tooley Street, the King's Bench, the
Fleet, and the New Bridewell. In almost every street
there was a battle; and in every quarter the muskets of
the troops were heard above the shouts and tumult of
the mob. The firing began in the Poultry, where the
chain was drawn across the road, where nearly a score of
people were killed on the first discharge. Their bodies
having been hastily carried into St. Mildred's Church
by the soldiers, the latter fired again, and following fast
upon the crowd, who began to give way when they saw
the execution that was done, formed across Cheapside,
and charged them at the point of the bayonet.

The streets were now a dreadful spectacle. The shouts
of the rabble, the shrieks of women, the cries of the
wounded, and the constant firing, formed a deafening
and an awful accompaniment to the sights which every
corner presented. Wherever the road was obstructed
by the chains, there the fighting and the loss of life were
greatest; but there was hot work and bloodshed in
almost every leading thoroughfare.

CHARLES DICKENS (1812-1870)
Barnaby Rudge

WESTMINSTER HALL:

WARREN HASTINGS IMPEACHED

In the mean time, the preparations for the trial had
proceeded rapidly; and on the thirteenth of February,

1788, the sittings of the Court commenced. There have been spectacles more dazzling to the eye, more gorgeous with jewellery and cloth of gold, more attractive to grown-up children, than that which was then exhibited at Westminster; but, perhaps, there never was a spectacle so well calculated to strike a highly cultivated, a reflecting, an imaginative mind. All the various kinds of interest which belong to the near and to the distant, to the present and to the past, were collected on one spot, and in one hour. All the talents and all the accomplishments which are developed by liberty and civilisation were now displayed, with every advantage that could be derived both from co-operation and from contrast. Every step in the proceedings carried the mind either backward, through many troubled centuries, to the days when the foundations of our constitution were laid; or far away over boundless seas and deserts, to dusky nations living under strange stars, worshipping strange gods, and writing strange characters from right to left. The High Court of Parliament was to sit, according to forms handed down from the days of the Plantagenets, on an Englishman accused of exercising tyranny over the lord of the holy city of Benares, and over the ladies of the princely house of Oude.

The place was worthy of such a trial. It was the great hall of William Rufus, the hall which had resounded with acclamations at the inauguration of thirty kings, the hall which had witnessed the just sentence of Bacon and the just absolution of Somers, the hall where the eloquence of Strafford had for a moment awed and melted a victorious party inflamed with just resentment, the hall where Charles had confronted the High Court of Justice with the placid courage which has half redeemed his fame. Neither military nor civil pomp was wanting. The avenues were lined with grenadiers. The streets were kept clear by cavalry. The peers, robed in gold and ermine, were marshalled by the heralds and

Garter King-at-arms. The judges in their vestments of
state attended to give advice on points of law. Near a
hundred and seventy lords, three fourths of the Upper
House as the Upper House then was, walked in solemn
order from their usual place of assembling to the tribunal. The junior baron present led the way, George
Eliott, Lord Heathfield, recently ennobled for his
memorable defence of Gibraltar against the fleets and
armies of France and Spain. The long procession was
closed by the Duke of Norfolk, Earl Marshal of the realm,
by the great dignitaries, and by the brothers and sons of
the King. Last of all came the Prince of Wales, conspicuous by his fine person and noble bearing.

The grey old walls were hung with scarlet. The long
galleries were crowded by an audience such as has rarely
excited the fears or the emulation of an orator. There
were gathered together, from all parts of a great, free,
enlightened, and prosperous empire, grace and female
loveliness, wit and learning, the representatives of
every science and of every art. There were seated round
the Queen the fair-haired young daughters of the house
of Brunswick. There the Ambassadors of great Kings
and Commonwealths gazed with admiration on a spectacle which no other country in the world could present.
There Siddons, in the prime of her majestic beauty,
looked with emotion on a scene surpassing all the
imitations of the stage. There the historian of the
Roman Empire thought of the days when Cicero pleaded
the cause of Sicily against Verres, and when, before a
senate which still retained some show of freedom,
Tacitus thundered against the oppressor of Africa.

There were seen, side by side, the greatest painter and
the greatest scholar of the age. The spectacle had allured
Reynolds from that easel which has preserved to us the
thoughtful foreheads of so many writers and statesmen,
and the sweet smiles of so many noble matrons. It had
induced Parr to suspend his labours in that dark and

profound mind from which he had extracted a vast treasure of erudition, a treasure too often buried in the earth, too often paraded with injudicious and inelegant ostentation, but still precious, massive, and splendid. There appeared the voluptuous charms of her to whom the heir of the throne had in secret plighted his faith. There too was she, the beautiful mother of a beautiful race, the Saint Cecilia whose delicate features, lighted up by love and music, art has rescued from the common decay. There were the members of that brilliant society which quoted, criticized, and exchanged repartees, under the rich peacock-hangings of Mrs. Montague. And there the ladies whose lips, more persuasive than those of Fox himself, had carried the Westminster election against palace and treasury, shone round Georgiana Duchess of Devonshire.

LORD MACAULAY (1800-1859)
Essays

The trial before the members of the House of Lords dragged on for nearly eight years and naturally interest waned. But there was a final and fashionable gathering in Westminster Hall to see Hastings bow respectfully and retire on his acquittal in the spring of 1795.

ENTER QUEEN VICTORIA

On June 18, the King was visibly sinking. The Archbishop of Canterbury was by his side, with all the comforts of the church. Nor did the holy words fall upon a rebellious spirit; for many years his Majesty had been a devout believer. " When I was a young man," he once explained at a public banquet, " as well as I can remember I believed in nothing but pleasure and folly—nothing at all. But when I went to sea, got into a gale, and saw the wonders of the mighty deep, then I believed; and I have been a sincere Christian ever since." It was the anniversary of the Battle of Waterloo, and the dying man remembered it. He should be glad to live, he said, over that day; he would never see another sunset. " I hope your Majesty may live to see many," said Dr. Chambers. " Oh! that's quite another thing, that's quite another thing," was the answer. One other sunset he did live to see; and he died in the early hours of the following morning. It was June 20, 1837.

When all was over, the Archbishop and the Lord Chamberlain ordered a carriage, and drove post-haste from Windsor to Kensington. They arrived at the Palace at five o'clock, and it was only with considerable difficulty that they gained admittance. At six the Duchess woke up her daughter, and told her that the Archbishop of Canterbury and Lord Conyngham were there, and wished to see her. She got out of bed, put on her dressing-gown, and went, alone, into the room where the messengers were standing. Lord Conyngham fell on his knees, and officially announced the death of the King; the Archbishop added some personal details. Looking at the bending, murmuring dignitaries before her, she knew that she was Queen of England. " Since it has pleased Providence," she wrote that day in her journal, " to place me in this station, I shall do my utmost to fulfil my duty towards my country; I am very young, and perhaps in many, though not in all things, inexperienced, but I am sure, that very few have more real good will and more real desire to do what is fit and right than I have."

But there was scant time for resolutions and reflections. At once, affairs were thick upon her. Stockmar came to breakfast, and gave some good advice. She wrote a letter to her uncle Leopold, and a hurried note to her sister Feodora. A letter came from the Prime Minister, Lord Melbourne, announcing his approaching arrival. He came at nine, in full court dress, and kissed her hand. She saw him alone, and repeated to him the lesson which, no doubt, the faithful Stockmar had taught her at breakfast, " It has long been my intention to retain your Lordship and the rest of the present Ministry at the head of affairs "; whereupon Lord Melbourne again kissed her hand and shortly after left her. She then wrote a letter of condolence to Queen Adelaide. At eleven, Lord Melbourne came again; and at half past eleven she went downstairs into the red saloon to hold her first Council The great assembly of lords and notables, bishops, generals, and Ministers of State, saw the doors thrown open and a very short, very slim girl in deep plain mourning come into the room alone and move forward to her seat with extraordinary dignity and grace; they saw a countenance, not beautiful, but prepossessing—fair hair, blue prominent eyes, a small curved nose, an open mouth revealing the upper teeth, a tiny chin, a clear complexion, and, over all, the strangely mingled signs of innocence, of gravity, of youth, and of composure; they heard a high unwavering voice reading aloud with perfect clarity; and then, the ceremony over, they saw the small figure rise and, with the same consummate grace, the same amazing dignity, pass out from among them, as she had come in, alone.

GILES LYTTON STRACHEY (1880-1932)
Queen Victoria

CONFUSION AT THE ABBEY

The faultless preparation of royal ceremonials nowadays is in strong contrast with the carelessness shown by the responsible officials and dignitaries at the Coronation of Queen Victoria, as reported by Charles Greville.

The Queen looked very diminutive, and the effect of the procession itself was spoilt by being too crowded; there was not interval enough between the Queen and the Lords and others going before her. The Bishop of London

(Blomfield) preached a very good sermon. The different actors in the ceremonial were very imperfect in their parts, and had neglected to rehearse them. Lord John Thynne, who officiated for the Dean of Westminster, told me that nobody knew what was to be done except the Archbishop and himself (who had rehearsed), Lord Willoughby (who is experienced in these matters), and the Duke of Wellington, and consequently there was a continual difficulty and embarrassment, and the Queen never knew what she was to do next.

They made her leave her chair and enter into St. Edward's Chapel before the prayers were concluded, much to the discomfiture of the Archbishop. She said to John Thynne, " Pray tell me what I am to do, for they don't know "; and at the end, when the orb was put into her hand, she said to him, " What am I to do with it? " " Your Majesty is to carry it, if you please, in your hand." " Am I? " she said; " it is very heavy." The ruby ring was made for her little finger instead of the fourth, on which the rubric prescribes that it should be put. When the Archbishop was to put it on, she extended the former, but he said it must be on the latter. She said it was too small, and she could not get it on. He said it was right to put it there, and, as he insisted, she yielded, but had first to take off her other rings, and then this was forced on, but it hurt her very much, and as soon as the ceremony was over she was obliged to bathe her finger in iced water in order to get it off.

The noise and confusion were very great when the medals were thrown about by Lord Surrey, everybody scrambling with all their might and main to get them, and none more vigorously than the Maids of Honour. There was a great demonstration of applause when the Duke of Wellington did homage. Lord Rolle, who is between eighty and ninety, fell down as he was getting up the steps of the throne. Her first impulse was to rise, and afterwards when he came again to do homage she

said, " May I not get up and meet him? " and then rose
from the throne and advanced down one or two of the
steps to prevent his coming up, an act of graciousness
and kindness which made a great sensation. It is, in fact,
the remarkable union of navieté, kindness, nature, good
nature, with propriety and dignity, which makes her so
admirable and so endearing to those about her, as she
certainly is.

CHARLES GREVILLE (1794-1865)
Diary

QUEEN VICTORIA MEETS AUTHORS

Chelsea, March 11, 1869.

Dear Jean— . . . " Interview " took place this day gone a
week; nearly a week before that, the Dean and Deaness
(who is called Lady Augusta Stanley, once Bruce, an active
hand and busy little woman) drove up here in a solemnly
mysterious, though half quizzical manner, invited me
for Thursday, 4th, 5 p.m.:—must come, a very " high or
indeed highest person has long been desirous," etc., etc.
I saw well enough it was the Queen incognita; and
briefly agreed to come. " Half-past 4 COME you! "
and then went their ways.

Walking up at the set time, I was then ushered into a
long drawing-room in their monastic edifice. I found no
Stanley there; only at the farther end, a tall old Gearpole
of a Mrs. Grote—the most wooden woman I know in
London or the world, who thinks herself very clever;
etc.—the sight of whom taught me to expect others; as
accordingly, in a few minutes, fell out. Grote and wife,
Sir Charles Lyell and ditto, Browning and myself, were
I saw to be our party.

The Stanley's and we were all in a flow of talk, and
some flunkies had done setting coffee-pots, tea-cups of

sublime patterns, when Her Majesty, punctual to a minute, glided softly in, escorted by her Dame in Waiting
(a Dowager Duchess of Athol) and by the Princess Louise,
decidedly a very pretty young lady, and clever too, as I
found in speaking to her afterwards.

The Queen came softly forward, a kindly little smile
on her face; gently shook hands with all three women,
gently acknowledged with a nod the silent deep bow of
us male monsters; and directly in her presence everybody
was as if at ease again. She is a comely little lady, with a
pair of kind, clear, and intelligent grey eyes; still looks
plump and almost young (in spite of one broad wrinkle
that shows in each cheek occasionally); has a fine low
voice; soft indeed her whole manner is and melodiously
perfect; it is impossible to imagine a politer little
woman—nothing the least imperious; all gentle, all
sincere-looking; unembarrassing, rather attractive even;
—makes you feel too (if you have sense in you) that she is
Queen.

After, a little word to each of us in succession as we
stood,—to me it was, " Sorry you did not see my
Daughter," Princess of Prussia (or, " she sorry," perhaps?) which led us into Potsdam, Berlin, etc., for an
instant or two; to Sir Charles Lyell I heard her say,
" Gold in Sutherland," but quickly and delicately cut him
short in responding; to Browning, " Are you writing
anything? " (he has just been publishing the absurdest of
things!); to Grote I did not hear what she said; but it
was touch and go with everybody; Majesty visibly
without interest or nearly so of her own.

This done, coffee (very black and muddy) was handed
round; Queen and three women taking seats in opposite
corners, Mrs. Grote in a chair intrusively close to
Majesty, Lady Lyell modestly at the diagonal corner;
we others obliged to stand, and hover within call. Coffee
fairly done, Lady Augusta called me gently to " Come
and speak with Her Majesty." I obeyed, first asking, as

an old and infirmish man, Majesty's permission to sit,
which was graciously conceded. Nothing of the least
significance was said, nor indeed; however, my bit of
dialogue went very well. " What part of Scotland I
came from? " " Dumfries-shire (where Majesty might
as well go some time); Carlisle, i.e. Caer-Lewal, a place
about the antiquity of King Solomon (according to
Milton, whereat Majesty smiled); Border-Ballads (and
even old Jamie Pool slightly alluded to,—not by name!);
Glasgow, and even Grandfather's ride thither,—ending
in mere psalms, and streets vacant at half-past nine p.m.;
—hard sound and genuine Presbyterian root of what had
now shot up to be such a monstrous ugly cabbage-tree
and Hemlock-tree! ", all which her Majesty seemed to
take rather well.

Whereupon Mrs. Grote rose, and good-naturedly
brought forward her Husband to her own chair, cheek
by jowl with Her Majesty, who evidently did not care a
straw for him, but kindly asked " Writing anything? "
and one heard " Aristotle, now that I have done with
Plato," etc., etc.—but only for a minimum of time.
Majesty herself (I think apropos of some question of my
shaking hand) said something about her own difficulty
in writing by dictation, which brought forward Lady
Lyell and husband, naturally used to the operation—
after which, talk becoming trivial, Majesty gracefully
retired—Lady Augusta with her—and in ten minutes
more, returned to receive our farewell bows; which, too,
she did very prettily; and sailed out as if moving on
skates, and bending her head towards us with a smile.
By the Underground Railway I was home before seven,
and out of the adventure, with only a headache of little
moment.

THOMAS CARLYLE (1795-1881)
Letter to Mrs. Aitken, Dumfries

AFTER THE JUBILEE, 1935

The arches are down, the standards down, the flags have
 gone to store,
The pageants are done, and all the fun, and ceased the
 nightly roar,
And king and peasant must back to work, back to desk
 and plough,
There's no more time for rhythm and rhyme but that of
 the engines now.
But the tabard and gloves and the golden mail of Edward
 the Splendid Prince
Still guard his tomb as they've guarded it, all these
 centuries since;
Since the Pilgrimage met at the Southwark Inn, from
 cloister, hovel and hall,
And Chaucer rode at the Bath Wife's side, and watched,
 and smiled at it all.

Guards and Lancers, dragoons, hussars, they rode the
 streets in state,
Gold and scarlet and helm and plume that never were
 seen of late,
In the days of mud-coloured soldiery, and death that
 drops in the night;
They were seen, they are gone, like a glimpse of the past,
 they are hidden from the light;
But none can rob us of Nelson's hat, or his star or his
 armless sleeve
Where the clouds fly past and the birds fly round, morn-
 ing and noon and eve:
And Wellington's horse stands proud on its base that
 Alfred Stevens made
Though the poison gas has reeked in the air and the
 deathless charges fade.

The problems press on the statesmen, they never know
 where to turn,
They never can look to East or West but something seems
 to burn,
A spark or a glow or an angry blaze that threatens at
 once to spread
Like a prairie fire for a thousand miles and envelop a
 thousand dead;
Yet were there no perils ere we were born, are we the first
 to shrink
From a vision of last disasters and a world gone over the
 brink?
Sidney died at Zutphen and Raleigh lies at the Tower
And Drake went down with the shot at his feet when
 England was in flower.

The streets swarm out and the woods are cut and the
 fields go down to grass
And all the ills that Cobbett cursed have grimly come to
 pass;
We struggle and struggle in webs of Fate, we strive to
 save the soul,
Soul and body and sense and dream in a world beyond
 control—
And the brave are all bewildered, and the cowards content
 to be sad,
But Shakespeare laughed with such knowledge of life as
 no man ever had.
And still, whatever the chemists may brew, and the men
 who add the sums,
Though the mean malign and the pampered pine, there
 are flags in the heart of the slums.

SIR JOHN SQUIRE (1884-1959)
Selected Poems

Characters

MR. JUSTICE SHALLOW

FALSTAFF: . . . I do see the bottom of Justice Shallow. Lord, Lord, how subject we old men are to this vice of lying! This time starved justice hath done nothing but prate to me of the wildness of his youth, and the feats he hath done about Turnbull-street; and every third word a lie, duer paid to the hearer than the Turk's tribute. I do remember him at Clement's inn, like a man made after supper of a cheese-paring; when a' was naked, he was, for all the world, like a fork'd radish, with a head fantastically carved upon it with a knife; a' was so forlorn, that his dimensions to any thick sight were invisible: a' was the very genius of famine; yet lecherous as a monkey, and the whores call'd him mandrake: a' came ever in the rearward of the fashion; and sung those tunes to the overscutch'd huswives that he heard the carmen whistle, and sware they were his Fancies or his Good-nights.

And now is this Vice's dagger become a squire, and talks as familiarly of John o' Gaunt as if he had been sworn brother to him; and I'll be sworn a' ne'er saw him but once in the Tilt-yard; and then he burst his head for crowding among the marshal's men. I saw it, and told John o' Gaunt he beat his own name; for you might have thrust him and all his apparel into an eel-skin; the case of a treble hautboy was a mansion for him, a court: —and now has he land and beefs. Well, I'll be acquainted with him, if I return; and it shall go hard but I'll make him a philosopher's two stones to me: if the young dace be a bait for the old pike, I see no reason, in the law of nature, but I may snap at him. Let time shape, and there an end.

WILLIAM SHAKESPEARE (1564-1616)
Henry IV, Part II

RAKE'S PROGRESS, JACOBEAN

Happily it will be blown abroad, that you and your shoal of gallants swam through such an ocean of wine, that you danced so much money out at heels, and that in wild-fowl there flew away thus much; and I assure you to have the bill of your reckoning lost of purpose, so that it may be published, will make you to be held in dear estimation: only the danger is, if you owe money, and that your revealing gets your creditors by the ears; for then, look to have a peal of ordnance thundering at your chamber-door the next morning. But if either your tailor, mercer, haberdasher, silkman, cutter, linen-draper or sempster, stand like a guard of Switzers about your lodging, watching your uprising, or, if they miss of that, your down-lying in one of the Counters; you have no means to avoid the galling of their small-shot than by sending out a light-horseman to call your poticary to your aid, who, encountering this desperate band of your creditors only with two or three glasses in his hand, as though that day you purged, is able to drive them all to their holes like so many foxes; for the name of taking physic is a sufficient *quietus est* to any endangered gentlemen, and gives an acquittance, for the time, to them all; though the twelve companies stand with their hoods to attend your coming forth, and their officers with them.

I could now fetch you about noon, the hour which I prescribed you before to rise at, out of your chamber, and carry you with me into Paul's churchyard; where, planting yourself in a stationer's shop, many instructions are to be given you, what books to call for, how to censure of new books, how to mew at the old, how to look in your tables and inquire for such and such Greek, French, Italian, or Spanish authors, whose names you have there, but whom your mother for pity would not give you so much wit as to understand. From thence you should blow yourself into the tobacco-ordinary, where you are likewise to spend your judgement, like a quacksalver, upon that mystical wonder, to be able to discourse whether your cane or your pudding[1] be sweetest, and which pipe has the best bore, and which burns black, which breaks in the burning, etc. Or, if you itch to step into the barber's, a whole dictionary cannot afford more words to set down notes what dialogues you are to maintain, whilst you are doctor of the chair there. After your shaving, I could breathe you in a fence-school; in both which I could weary you, by shewing you more tricks than are in five galleries, or fifteen prizes. And, to close up the stomach of this feast, I could make Cockney's, whose fathers have left them well, acknowledge themselves infinitely beholden to me, for teaching them by familiar demonstration how to spend their patrimony, and to get themselves names, when their fathers are dead and rotten.

THOMAS DEKKER (1570?-1632)
The Gull's Hornbook

PEPYS AT CLAPHAM

This day died Mr. Samuel Pepys, a very worthy, industrious and curious person, none in England exceeding him in knowledge of the navy, in which he had passed through all the most considerable offices, Clerk of the Acts and Secretary of the Admiralty, all which he performed with great integrity. When King James II

[1] Cane and pudding were species of tobacco

went out of England, he laid down his office, and would serve no more; but withdrawing himself from all public affairs, he lived at Clapham with his partner, Mr. Hewer, formerly his clerk, in a very noble house and sweet place, where he enjoyed the fruit of his labours in great prosperity. He was universally beloved, hospitable, generous, learned in many things, skilled in music, a very great cherisher of learned men of whom he had the conversation. His library and collection of other curiosities were of the most considerable, the models of ships especially. Besides what he published of an account of the navy, as he found and left it, he had for divers years under his hand the History of the Navy, or Navalia, as he called it; but how far advanced, and what will follow of his, is left, I suppose, to his sister's son, Mr. Jackson, a young gentleman, whom Mr. Pepys had educated in all sorts of useful learning, sending him to travel abroad, from whence he returned with extraordinary accomplishments, and worthy to be heir. Mr. Pepys had been for near forty years so much my particular friend, that Mr. Jackson sent me complete mourning, desiring me to be one to hold up the pall at his magnificent obsequies; but my indisposition hindered me from doing him this last office.

JOHN EVELYN (1620-1706)
Diary

LADIES OF THE COURT

Ever since Evah was tempted, and the serpent prevailed with her, women have took upon them both the person of the tempted and the tempter. They tempt to be tempted, and not one of them, except she be tempted, but thinks herself contemptible. Unto the greatness of their great-grand-mother Evah they seek to aspire, in being tempted and tempting. If not to tempt and be

thought worthy to be tempted, why dye they and diet
their faces with so many drugs as they do, as it were to
correct God's workmanship, and reprove Him as a
bungler, and one that is not his craftsmaster? Why
ensparkle they their eyes with spiritualized distillations?
Why tip they their tongues with *aurum potabile*? Why
fill they age's frets with fresh colours? Even as roses and
flowers in winter are preserved in close houses under
earth, so preserve they their beauties by continual lying
in bed.

Just to dinner they will arise, and after dinner go to bed
again, and lie until supper. Yea, sometimes (by no sick-
ness occasioned) they will lie in bed three days together:
provided every morning before four o'clock, they have
their broths and their cullises, with pearl and gold
sodden in them. If haply they break their hours and
rise more early to go a banqueting, they stand practising
half a day with their looking-glasses, how to pierce and
to glance and look alluringly amiable. Their feet are
not so well framed to the measures, as are their eyes to
move and bewitch. Even as angels are painted in Church-
windows with glorious golden fronts beset with sunbeams, so beset they their foreheads on either side with
glorious borrowed gleamy bushes; which, rightly
interpreted, should signify beauty to sell, since a bush is
not else hanged forth but to invite men to buy. And in
Italy, when they set any beast to sale, they crown his
head with garlands, and bedeck it with gaudy blossoms,
as full as ever it may stick.

Their heads, with their top and top-gallant lawn baby-
caps, and snow-resembled silver curlings, they make a
plain puppet stage of. Their breasts they embusk up on
high, and their round roseate buds immodestly lay
forth to show at their hands there is fruit to be hoped.
In their curious antic-woven garments, they imitate
and mock the worms and adders that must eat them.
They shew the swellings of their mind, in the swellings

and plumpings out of their apparel. Gorgeous ladies of
the court, never was I admitted so near any of you, as to
see how you torture poor old Time with sponging,
pinning, and pouncing; but they say his sickle you have
burst in twain, to make your periwigs more elevated
arches of.

I dare not meddle with ye, since the philosopher that
too intently gazed on the stars, stumbled and fell into a
ditch; and many gazing too immoderately on our
earthly stars, fall in the end into the ditch of all un-
cleanness. Only this humble caveat let me give you by
the way, that you look the devil come not to you in the
likeness of a tailor or a painter; that however you disguise your bodies, you lay not on your colours so thick
that they sink into your souls; that your skins being too
white without, your souls be not all black within.

It is not your pinches, your purls, your flowery
jaggings, superfluous interlacings, and puffings up, that
can any way offend God, but the puffing up of your
souls, which therein you express. For as the biting of a
bullet is not that which poisons the bullet, but the lying
of the gunpowder in the dint of the biting; so it is not
the wearing of costly burnished apparel that shall be
objected unto you for sin, but the pride of your hearts,
which (like the moth) lies closely shrouded amongst the
threads of that apparel. Nothing else is garish apparel
but pride's ulcer broken forth. How will you attire yourselves, what gown, what head-tire will you put on, when
you shall live in hell amongst hags and devils?

THOMAS NASHE (1567-1601)
Christ's Tears Over Jerusalem

A LEARNED CITY MAN

James Bovey, esq., was the youngest son of Andrew
Bovey, merchant, cash-keeper to Sir Peter Vanore, in

London. He was borne in the middle of Mincing Lane, in the parish of Saint Dunstan's in the East, London, *anno* 1622, May 7th, at six a clock in the morning. Went to schoole at Mercers Chapell, under Mr. Augur. At 9 sent into the Lowe Countreys; then returned, and perfected himselfe in the Latin and Greeke. At 14, travelled into France and Italie, Switzerland, Germany, and the Lowe Countreys. Returned into England at nineteen; then lived with one Hoste, a banquier, eight yeares, was his cashier eight or nine yeares. Then traded for himselfe twenty-seven till he was thirty-one; then maried the only daughter of William de Vischer, a merchant; lived eighteen yeares with her, then continued single. Left off trade at thirty-two, and retired to a countrey life, by reason of his indisposition, the ayre of the citie not agreing with him. Then in these retirements he wrote Active Philosophy, (a thing not donne before) wherein are enumerated all the Arts and Tricks practised in Negotiation, and how they were to be ballanced by counter-prudentiall rules.

Whilest he lived with Mr. Hoste, he kept the cash of the ambassadors of Spaine that were here; and of the farmers, called by them Assentistes, that did furnish the Spanish and Imperiall armies of the Low-Countreys and Germany; and also many other great cashes, as of Sir Theodore Mayern, etc.; his dealing being altogether in money-matters: by which meanes he became acquainted with the ministers of state both here and abroad. When he was abroad, his chiefe employment was to observe the affaires of state and their judicatures, and to take the politique surveys in the countreys he travelled thorough, more especially in relation to trade. He speakes the Low-Dutch, High-Dutch, French, Italian, Spanish and Lingua Franca, and Latin, besides his owne.

When he retired from business he studied the Lawe-Merchant, and admitted himselfe of the Inner Temple, London, about 1660. His judgment haz been taken in most of the great causes of his time in points concerning the Lawe-Merchant. As to his person he is about five foot high, slender, strait, haire exceeding black and curling at the end, a dark hazell eie, of a midling size, but the most sprightly that I have beheld. Browes and beard of the colour as his haire. A person of great temperance, and deepe thoughts, and a working head, never idle. From fourteen he had a candle burning by him all night, with pen, inke, and paper, to write downe thoughts as they came into his head; that so he might not loose a thought. Was ever a great lover of Naturall Philosophie. His whole life has been perplex't in lawe-suites, (which haz made him expert in humane affairs), in which he alwaies over-came. He had many lawe-suites with powerful adversaries; one lasted eighteen yeares. Red-haired men never had any kindnesse for him.

In all his travells he was never robbed. He has one sone, and one daughter who resembles him. From 14 he began to take notice of all prudentiall rules as came in his way, and wrote them downe, and so continued till this day, Sept. 28, 1680, being now in his 59th yeare. For his health he never had it very well, but indifferently, alweies a weake stomach, which proceeded from the agitation of the braine. His dyet was always fine diet: much chicken. He wrote a Table of all the Exchanges in Europe.

JOHN AUBREY (1626-1697)
Brief Lives

MR. AND MRS. SAMUEL PEPYS

May 11th, 1667. My wife being dressed this day in fair hair did make me so mad, that I spoke not one word to her, though I was ready to burst with anger. After that, Creed and I into the Park, and walked, a most pleasant evening, and so took coach, and took up my wife, and in my way home discovered my trouble to my wife for her white locks, swearing several times, which I pray God forgive me for, and bending my fist, that I would not endure it. She, poor wretch, was surprized with it, and made me no answer all the way home; but there we parted, and I to the office late, and then home, and without supper to bed, vexed.

May 12th (*Lord's day*). Up, and to my chamber, to settle some accounts there, and by and by down comes my wife to me in her night-gown, and we begun calmly, that, upon having money to lace her gown for second mourning, she would promise to wear white locks no more in my sight, which I, like a severe fool, thinking not enough, begun to except against, and made her fly out to very high terms and cry, and in her heat, told me of keeping company with Mrs. Knipp, saying, that if I would promise never to see her more—of whom she hath more reason to suspect than I had heretofore of Pembleton—she would never wear white locks more. This vexed me, but I restrained myself from saying any thing, but do think never to see this woman—at least, to have her here more; and so all very good friends as ever.

August 1st, *1667*. Dined at Sir W. Pen's, only with Mrs. Turner and her husband, on a venison pasty, that stunk like a devil. However, I did not know it till dinner was done. We had nothing but only this, and a leg of mutton, and a pullet or two. Mrs. Markham was here, with her great belly. I was very merry, and after dinner, upon a motion of the women, I was got to go to the play with them—the first I have seen since before the Dutch's coming upon our coast, and so to the King's house, to see " The Custome of the Country." The house mighty empty—more than ever I saw it—and an ill play.

After the play, we went into the house, and spoke with Knipp, who went abroad with us by coach to the Neat

Houses, in the way to Chelsy; and there, in a box in a tree[1], we sat and sang, and talked and eat; my wife out of humour, as she always is, when this woman is by. So, after it was dark, we home. Set Knipp down at home, who told us the story how Nell is gone from the King's house, and is kept by my Lord Buckhurst. Home, the gates of the City shut, it being so late: and at Newgate we find them in trouble, some thieves having this night broke open prison. So we through, and home; and our coachman was fain to drive hard from two or three fellows, which he said were rogues, that he met at the end of Bluebladder Street, next Cheapside. So set Mrs. Turner home, and then we home, and I to the Office a little; and so home and to bed, my wife in an ill humour still.

January 12th, 1668-9. This evening I observed my wife mighty dull, and I myself was not mighty fond, because of some hard words she did give me at noon, out of a jealousy at my being abroad this morning, which, God knows, it was upon the business of the Office unexpectedly: but I to bed, not thinking but she would come after me. But waking by and by, out of a slumber, which I usually fall into presently after my coming into the bed, I found she did not prepare to come to bed, but got fresh candles, and more wood for her fire, it being mighty cold, too. At this being troubled, I after a while prayed her to come to bed; so, after an hour or two, she silent, and I now and then praying her to come to bed, she fell out into a fury, that I was a rogue, and false to her. I did, as I might truly, deny it, and was mightily troubled, but all would not serve.

At last, about one o'clock, she came to my side of the bed, and drew my curtaine open, and with the tongs red hot at the ends, made as if she did design to pinch me with them, at which, in dismay, I rose up, and with a

---

[1] A summer house in the branches

few words she laid them down; and did by little and little, very sillily, let all the discourse fall; and about two, but with much seeming difficulty, come to bed, and there lay well all night, and long in bed talking together, with much pleasure, it being, I know, nothing but her doubt of my going out yesterday, without telling her of my going, which did vex her, poor wretch! last night, and I cannot blame her jealousy, though it do vex me to the heart.

SAMUEL PEPYS (1633-1703)
Diary

KING'S ENEMY, BUT NO PURITAN

Henry Martin, esq., son and heir of Sir Henry Martin, knight, Judge of the Arches, was of the university; travelled France, but never Italie. His father found out a rich wife for him, whom he married something unwillingly. He was a great lover of pretty girles, to whom he was so liberall that he spent the greatest part of his estate. When he had found out a maried woman that he liked (and he had his emissaries, male and female, to looke out) he would contrive such or such a good bargain, 20 or 30 li. per annum under rent, to have her neer him. He lived from his wife a long time. If I am not mistaken shee was sometime distempered by his unkindnesse to her.

King Charles I had complaint against him for his wenching. It happened that Henry was in Hyde-park one time when his majestie was there, goeing to see a race. The king espied him, and sayd aloud, " Let that ugly rascall be gonne out of the parke, that whoremaster, or els I will not see the sport." So Henry went away patiently, *sed manebat alta mente repostum.*[1] That sarcasme raysed the whole countie of Berks against him

---

[1] But it remained in the depth of his mind

KEN WOOD: AN ADAM PARADISE

The mansion of Ken Wood, between Hampstead and Highgate, was built by Robert Adam for Lord Mansfield in the reign of George III. The house and the grounds of 200 acres, with superb lawns, lakes and woods, are open to the public.

KEN WOOD: WATER MUSIC

Backed by the remnants of the ancient Forest of Middlesex, the lake at Ken Wood is used as a setting for summer evening concerts. Many hundreds gather to enjoy the harmony of scene and sound. The London Symphony Orchestra is performing on this occasion.

PETTICOAT LANE

Petticoat Lane, just east of the City, is a popular name for what is
officially Middlesex Street. Its open market is a great attraction to
bargain-hunters. Since it is close to the Jewish area of Whitechapel
Sunday trading is allowed, the Sabbath being over.

(the king): he (Martin) was as far from a Puritane as light from darkness. Shortly after, (1641) he was chosen knight of the shire of that county, *nemine contradicente*, and proved a deadly enemy to the king.

He was a great and faithful lover of his countrey, and never gott a farthing by the Parliament. He was of an incomparable witt for reparte's; not at all covetous: humble, not at all arrogant, as most of them were; a great cultor of justice, and did always in the house take the part of the oppressed. *Anno* 1660 he was obnoxious for having been one of the late king's judges, and he was in very great danger to have suffred as the others did (he pleaded only the king's Act of Proclamation at Breda, which he shewd in his hand), but (as he was a witt himselfe) so the lord Falkland saved his life by witt, saying, " Gentlemen, yee talke here of makeing a sacrifice; it was the old lawe, all sacrifices were to be without spott or blemish; and now you are going to make an old rotten rascall a sacrifice." This witt tooke in the house, and saved his life. He was first a prisoner at the Tower; then at Windsore (removed from thence because he was an eie-sore to his majestie etc.); from thence to Chepstowe, where he is now (1680). During his imprisonment his wife reliefed him out of her joincture, but she dyed.

His stature was but midling; his habit moderate; his face not good. Sir Edward Baynton was wont to say that his company was incomparable, but that he would be drunke too soon.

His speeches in the house were not long, but wondrous poynant, pertinent, and witty. He was exceeding happy in apt instances. He alone haz sometimes turned the whole house. . . . A goodly member made a motion to have all profane and unsanctified persons expelled the Houses. H.M. stood up and moved that all the fooles might be putt out likewise, and then there would be a thin house. He was wont to sleep much in the house

4

(at least dog-sleepe). Alderman Atkins made a motion that such scandalous members as slept and minded not the business of the house, should be putt-out. H.M. starts up—" Mr. Speaker, a motion has been to turne out the Nodders; I desire the Noddees may also be turnd out."

JOHN AUBREY (1626-1697)
Brief Lives

EARLY VICTORIAN LADY

We continually hear of " the strain of modern life." If Thackeray was accurate, there is nothing new in this complaint.

" You are a professed misogynist, and hate the sex because, I suspect, you know very little about them," Mr. Pen continued, with an air of considerable self-complacency. " If you dislike the women in the country for being too slow, surely the London women ought to be fast enough for you. The pace of London life is enormous: how do people last at it, I wonder—male and female? Take a woman of the world—follow her course through the season: one asks how she can survive it? or if she tumbles into a sleep at the end of August, and lies torpid until the spring? She goes into the world every night, and sits watching her marriageable daughters dancing till long after dawn.

" She has a nursery of little ones, very likely, at home, to whom she administers example and affection; having an eye likewise to bread-and-milk, catechism, music and French, and roast leg of mutton at one o'clock. She has to call upon ladies of her own station, either domestically or in her public character, in which she sits upon Charity Committees, or Ball Committees, or Emigration Committees, or Queen's College Committees, and discharges I don't know what more duties of British stateswomanship. She very likely keeps a poor-visiting list; has conversations with the clergyman about soup or flannel, or proper religious teaching for the parish; and (if she lives in certain districts) probably attends early church. She has the newspapers to read, and, at least, must know what her husband's party is about, so as to be able to talk to her neighbour at dinner; and it is a fact that she reads every new book that comes out, for she can talk, and very smartly and well, about them all, and you see them all upon her drawing-room table.

" She has the cares of her household besides—to make both ends meet; to make the girls' milliner's bills appear not too dreadful to the father and paymaster of the family; to snip off, in secret, a little extra article of expenditure here and there, and convey it, in the shape of a banknote, to the boys at college or at sea; to check the encroachments of tradesmen and housekeepers' financial fallacies; to keep upper and lower servants from jangling with one another, and the household in order.

" Add to this, that she has a secret taste for some art or science—models in clay, makes experiments in chemistry, or plays in private on the violin-cello—(and I say, without exaggeration, many London ladies are doing this)—and you have a character before you such as our ancestors never heard of, and such as belongs entirely to our era and period of civilization."

W. M. THACKERAY (1811-1863)
Pendennis

TURNER'S LONDON BOYHOOD

Near the south-west corner of Covent Garden, a square brick pit or well is formed by a close-set block of houses, to the back windows of which it admits a few rays of light. Access to the bottom of it is obtained out of Maiden Lane, through a low archway and an iron gate; and if

you stand long enough under the archway to accustom
your eyes to the darkness you may see on the left hand a
narrow door, which formerly gave quiet access to a
respectable barber's shop, of which the front window,
looking into Maiden Lane, is still extant, filled, in this
year (1860), with a row of bottles, connected, in some
defunct manner, with a brewer's business. A more
fashionable neighbourhood, it is said, eighty years ago
than now—never certainly a cheerful one—wherein a
boy being born on St. George's day, 1775, began soon
after to take interest in the world of Covent Garden, and
put to service such spectacles of life as it afforded.

No knights to be seen there, nor, I imagine, many
beautiful ladies; their costume at least disadvantageous,
depending much on incumbency of hat and feather, and
short waists; the majesty of men founded similarly on
shoebuckles and wigs; impressive enough when Reynolds
will do his best for it; but not suggestive of much ideal
delight to a boy.

" Bello ovile dov' io dormii agnello": of things
beautiful, besides men and women, dusty sunbeams up
or down the street on summer mornings; deep furrowed
cabbage-leaves at the greengrocer's; magnificence of
oranges in wheelbarrows round the corner; and Thames'
shore within three minutes' race.

None of these things very glorious; the best, however,
that England, it seems, was then able to provide for a
boy of gift: who, such as they are, loves them—never,
indeed, forgets them. The short waists modify to the last
his visions of Greek ideal. His foregrounds had always a
succulent cluster or two of green-grocery at the corners.
Enchanted oranges gleam in Covent Gardens of the
Hesperides; and great ships go to pieces in order to
scatter chests of them on the waves. That mist of early
sunbeams in the London dawn crosses, many and many
a time, the clearness of Italian air; and by Thames'
shore, with its stranded barges and glidings of red sail,

dearer to us than Lucerne lake or Venetian lagoon—
by Thames' shore we will die.

With such circumstance round him in youth, let us
note what necessary effects followed upon the boy. I
assumed to have had Giorgione's sensibility (and more
than Giorgione's, if that be possible) to colour and form.
I tell you farther, and this fact you may receive trustfully,
that his sensibility to human affection and distress was
no less keen than even his sense for natural beauty—heart-
sight deep as eyesight.

Consequently, he attaches himself with the faithfullest
child-love to everything that bears an image of the place
he was born in. No matter how ugly it is—has it anything about it like Maiden Lane, or like Thames shore?
If so, it shall be painted for their sake. Hence, to the very
close of life, Turner could endure ugliness which no
one else, of the same sensibility, would have borne with
for an instant. Dead brick walls, blank square windows,
old clothes, market-womanly types of humanity—
anything fishy and muddy, like Billingsgate or Hungerford Market, had great attraction for him; black barges,
patched sails, and every possible condition of fog.

You will find these tolerations and affections guiding
or sustaining him to the last hour of his life; the notab-
lest of all such endurances being that of dirt. No
Venetian ever draws anything foul; but Turner devoted
picture after picture to the illustration of effects of
dinginess, smoke, soot, dust, and dusty texture; old
sides of boats, weedy roadside vegetation, dung-hills,
strawyards, and all the soilings and stains of every
common labour.

And more than this, he not only could endure, but
enjoyed and looked for litter, like Covent Garden wreck
after the market. His pictures are often full of it, from
side to side; their foregrounds differ from all others in
the natural way that things have of lying about in them.
Even his richest vegetation, in ideal work, is confused;

and he delights in shingles, debris, and heaps of fallen
stones. The last words he ever spoke to me about a
picture were in gentle exultation about his St. Gothard;
" that litter of stones which I endeavoured to represent."

The second great result of this Covent Garden training
was, understanding of and regard for the poor, whom the
Venetians, we saw, despised; whom, contrarily, Turner
loved, and more than loved—understood. He got no
romantic sight of them, but an infallible one, as he
prowled about the end of his lane, watching night
effects in the wintry streets; nor sight of the poor alone,
but of the poor in direct relations with the rich. He knew,
in good and evil, what both classes thought of, and how
they dealt with, each other.

Reynolds and Gainsborough, bred in country villages,
learned there the country boy's reverential theory of
" the squire," and kept it. They painted the squire and
the squire's lady as centres of the movements of the
universe, to the end of their lives. But Turner perceived
the younger squire in other aspects about his lane,
occurring prominently in its night scenery, as a dark
figure, or one of two, against the moonlight. He saw
also the working of city commerce, from endless ware-
house, towering over Thames, to the back shop in the
lane, with its stale herrings—highly interesting these
last; one of his father's best friends, whom he often
afterwards visited affectionately at Bristol, being a fish-
monger and glue-boiler; which gives us a friendly turn
of mind towards herring-fishing, whaling, Calais
poissardes, and many other of our choicest subjects in
after-life; all this being connected with that mysterious
forest below London Bridge on one side; and, on the other
with these masses of human power and national wealth
which weighs upon us, at Covent Garden here, with
strange compression, and crush us into narrow Hand
Court.

" That mysterious forest below London Bridge "—

better for the boy than wood of pine, or grove of myrtle.
How he must have tormented the watermen, beseeching
them to let him crouch anywhere in the bows, quiet as
a log, so only that he might get floated down there
among the ships, and round and round the ships, and
with the ships, and by the ships, and under the ships,
staring, and clambering;—these the only quite beautiful
things he can see in all the world, except the sky; but
these, when the sun is on their sails, filling or falling,
endlessly disordered by sway of tide and stress of anchor-
age, beautiful unspeakably; which ships also are inhabited by glorious creatures—red-faced sailors, with
pipes, appearing over the gunwales, true knights, over
their castle parapets—the most angelic beings in the
whole compass of London world. And Trafalgar
happening long before we can draw ships, we, nevertheless coax all current stories out of the wounded sailors,
do our best at present to show Nelson's funeral stream-
ing up the Thames; and vow that Trafalgar shall have
its tribute of memory some day. Which, accordingly, is
accomplished—once, with all our might, for its death;
twice, with all our might, for its victory; thrice, in
pensive farewell to the old Téméraire, and, with it, to
that order of things.

Now this fond companying with sailors must have
divided his time, it appears to me, pretty equally between
Covent Garden and Wapping (allowing for incidental
excursions to Chelsea on one side, and Greenwich on the
other), which time he would spend pleasantly, but not
magnificently, being limited in pocket-money, and
leading a kind of " Poor-Jack " life on the river.

JOHN RUSKIN (1819-1900)
Modern Painters

THE DRAPER RIDES

John Gilpin was a citizen
  Of credit and renown,
A train-band captain eke was he
  Of famous London town.

John Gilpin's spouse said to her dear:
  " Though wedded we have been
These twice ten tedious years, yet we
  No holiday have seen.

" Tomorrow is our wedding-day,
  And we will then repair
Unto the Bell at Edmonton
  All in a chaise and pair.

" My sister, and my sister's child,
  Myself, and children three,
Will fill the chaise; so you must ride
  On horseback after we."

He soon replied: " I do admire
  Of womankind but one,
And you are she, my dearest dear,
  Therefore it shall be done.

" I am a linen-draper bold,
  As all the world doth know,
And my good friend the calender[1]
  Will lend his horse to go."

[1] A calenderer or calender was one who pressed cloth in a machine and so was in Gilpin's line of business.

RIVERSIDE HELIPORT

A new London port for helicopters was opened opposite Battersea Power Station in 1959. The Power Station, conveniently fed with fuel by river barges, has been damned as a monstrosity and also praised by some modern architects as a fine piece of functional building.

THE PLAYERS OF PUDDLE DOCK

The innovation of a playhouse inside the City was thought of by the actor Bernard Miles. He triumphantly campaigned for funds and built his riverside Mermaid Theatre on a site known as Puddle Dock, with St. Paul's soaring behind it.

BUYING RAGS AND REMNANTS

The disposal of dust-bin contents is a major problem for local government. The individual collector who will pay for old bits and pieces is therefore a blessing to the Town Council and also to those who can sell their left-overs. Here is a rag-collector at work in Camberwell.

BOOKSTALL IN FARRINGDON STREET

London street markets sometimes offer goods of all kinds, as in Petticoat Lane. For the book-lover with an eye for a bargain, however, a special haunt is Farringdon Street which runs down to Ludgate Circus over the roofed-in course of the old Fleet river.

Quoth Mrs. Gilpin: " That's well said;
   And, for that wine is dear,
We will be furnished with our own,
   Which is both bright and clear."

John Gilpin kissed his loving wife;
   O'erjoyed was he to find
That, though on pleasure she was bent,
   She had a frugal mind.

The morning came, the chaise was brought,
   But yet was not allowed
To drive up to the door, lest all
   Should say that she was proud.

So three doors off the chaise was stayed,
   Where they did all get in;
Six precious souls, and all agog
   To dash through thick and thin!

Smack went the whip, round went the wheels,
   Were never folk so glad,
The stones did rattle underneath,
   As if Cheapside were mad.

John Gilpin at his horse's side
   Seized fast the flowing mane,
And up he got, in haste to ride,
   But soon came down again;

For saddle-tree scarce reached had he,
   His journey to begin,
When, turning round his head, he saw
   Three customers come in.

So down he came; for loss of time,
   Although it grieved him sore,
Yet loss of pence, full well he knew,
   Would trouble him much more.

'Twas long before his customers
    Were suited to their mind,
When Betty screaming came downstairs:
    " The wine is left behind! "

" Good lack! " quoth he, " yet bring it me,
    My leathern belt likewise,
In which I bear my trusty sword
    When I do exercise."

Now mistress Gilpin (careful soul!)
    Had two stone bottles found,
To hold the liquor that she loved,
    And keep it safe and sound.

Each bottle had a curling ear,
    Through which the belt he drew,
And hung a bottle on each side,
    To make his balance true.

Then, over all, that he might be
    Equipped from top to toe,
His long red cloak, well brushed and neat,
    He manfully did throw.

Now see him mounted once again
    Upon his nimble steed,
Full slowly pacing over the stones,
    With caution and good heed!

But, finding soon a smoother road
    Beneath his well-shod feet,
The snorting beast began to trot,
    Which galled him in his seat.

So, " Fair and softly," John he cried,
 But John he cried in vain;
The trot became a gallop soon,
 In spite of curb and rein.

So stooping down, as needs he must
 Who cannot sit upright,
He grasped the mane with both his hands,
 And eke with all his might.

His horse, who never in that sort
 Had handled been before,
What thing upon his back had got
 Did wonder more and more.

Away went Gilpin, neck or nought;
 Away went hat and wig!
He little dreamt, when he set out,
 Of running such a rig!

The wind did blow, the cloak did fly,
 Like streamer long and gay,
Till loop and button failing both,
 At last it flew away.

Then might all people well discern
 The bottles he had slung;
A bottle swinging at each side,
 As hath been said or sung.

The dogs did bark, the children screamed,
 Up flew the windows all;
And every soul cried out: " Well done! "
 As loud as he could bawl.

Away went Gilpin—Who but he?
 His fame soon spread around—
" He carries weight! " " He rides a race! "
 " 'Tis for a thousand pound! "

And still, as fast as he drew near,
   'Twas wonderful to view
How in a trice the turnpike men
   Their gates wide open threw.

And now, as he went bowing down
   His reeking head full low,
The bottles twain behind his back
   Were shattered at a blow.

Down ran the wine into the road,
   Most piteous to be seen,
Which made his horse's flanks to smoke
   As they had basted been.

But still he seemed to carry weight,
   With leathern girdle braced;
For all might see the bottle-necks
   Still dangling at his waist.

Thus all through merry Islington
   These gambols he did play,
And till he came unto the Wash
   Of Edmonton so gay.

And there he threw the wash about
   On both sides of the way
Just like unto a trundling mop,
   Or a wild goose at play.

At Edmonton his loving wife
   From the balcony spied
Her tender husband, wond'ring much
   To see how he did ride.

" Stop, stop, John Gilpin! Here's the house! "
    They all at once did cry;
" The dinner waits, and we are tired."
    Said Gilpin: " So am I! "

But yet his horse was not a whit
    Inclined to tarry there;
For why?—his owner had a house
    Full ten miles off, at Ware.

WILLIAM COWPER (1731-1800)
John Gilpin

Gilpin's return was no less precipitate; but he survived his holiday
outing.

MR. PODSNAP EXPLAINS

The majority of the guests were like the plate, and
included several heavy articles weighing ever so much.
But there was a foreign gentleman among them: whom
Mr. Podsnap had invited after much debate with himself
and there was a droll disposition, not only on the part of
Mr. Podsnap, but of everybody else, to treat him as if he
were a child who was hard of hearing.

" How Do You Like London? " Mr. Podsnap now
inquired from his station of host, as if he were adminis-
tering something in the nature of a powder or potion
to the deaf child; " London, Londres, London? "

The foreign gentleman admired it.

" You find it Very Large? " said Mr. Podsnap, spac-
iously.

The foreign gentleman found it very large.

" And Very Rich? "

The foreign gentleman found it, without doubt,
enormement riche.

" Enormously Rich, We say," returned Mr. Podsnap, in

a condescending manner. "Our English adverbs do Not terminate in Mong and We Pronounce the ' ch ' as if there were a ' t ' before it. We Say Ritch."

"Reetch," remarked the foreign gentleman.

"And Do you Find, Sir," pursued Mr. Podsnap, with dignity, "Many Evidences that Strike You, of our British Constitution in the Streets Of the World's Metropolis, London, Londres, London?"

The foreign gentleman begged to be pardoned, but did not altogether understand.

"The Constitution Britannique," Mr. Podsnap explained, as if he were teaching in an infant school. "We Say British, But You Say Britannique, You Know" (forgivingly, as if that were not his fault). "The Constitution, Sir."

The foreign gentleman said, "Mais, yees; I know eem."

A youngish sallowish gentleman in spectacles, with a lumpy forehead, seated in a supplementary chair at a corner of the table, here caused a profound sensation by saying, in a raised voice, "Esker," and then stopping dead.

"Mais oui," said the foreign gentleman, turning towards him. "Est-ce-que? Quoi donc?"

But the gentleman with the lumpy forehead having for the time delivered himself of all that he found behind his lumps, spake for the time no more.

"I Was Inquiring," said Mr. Podsnap, resuming the thread of his discourse, "Whether You Have Observed in our Streets as We should say, Upon our Pavvy as You would say, any Tokens——"

The foreign gentleman with patient courtesy entreated pardon; "But what was Tokenz?"

"Marks," said Mr. Podsnap; "Signs, you know, appearances—Traces."

"Ah! Of a Orse?" inquired the foreign gentleman.

"We call it Horse," said Mr. Podsnap, with forbearance. "In England, Angleterre, England, We Aspirate the 'H,' and We say 'Horse.' Only our Lower Classes Say 'Orse!'"

"Pardon," said the foreign gentleman; "I am alwiz wrong!"

"Our Language," said Mr. Podsnap, with a gracious consciousness of being always right, "is Difficult. Ours is a Copious Language, and Trying to Strangers. I will not pursue my Question."

But the lumpy gentleman, unwilling to give it up, again madly said, "Esker," and again spake no more.

"It merely referred," Mr. Podsnap explained, with a sense of meritorious proprietorship, "to Our Constitution, Sir. We Englishmen are Very Proud of our Constitution, Sir. It Was Bestowed Upon Us By Providence. No Other Country is so Favoured as This Country."

"And ozer countries?—" the foreign gentleman was beginning, when Mr. Podsnap put him right again.

"We do not say Ozer; we say Other: the letters are 'T' and 'H'; you say Tay and Aish, You Know" (still with clemency). "The sound is 'th'—'th!'"

"And other countries," said the foreign gentleman. "They do now?"

"They do, Sir," returned Mr. Podsnap, gravely shaking his head; "they do—I am sorry to be obliged to say it—as they do."

"It was a little particular of Providence," said the foreign gentleman, laughing; "for the frontier is not large."

"Undoubtedly," assented Mr. Podsnap; "But So it is. It was the Charter of the Land. This island was Blest, Sir, to the Direct Exclusion of such Other Countries as —as there may happen to be. And if we were all Englishmen present, I would say," added Mr. Podsnap, looking round upon his compatriots, and sounding solemnly with his theme, "that there is in the Englishman a combination of qualities, a modesty, an independence, a responsibility, a repose, combined with an absence of everything calculated to call a blush into the cheek of a young person, which one would seek in vain among the Nations of the Earth."

CHARLES DICKENS (1812-1870)
Our Mutual Friend

THE PREACHER DRAWS TEARS

I am just come from hearing the celebrated Mr. Spurgeon preach in the Music Hall of the Surrey Gardens. It was quite full; he told us from the pulpit that 9,000 people were present. The service was like the Presbyterian: Psalms, prayers, expounding a Psalm, and a sermon. He is certainly very remarkable, and undeniably a very fine character; not remarkable in person, in face rather resembling a smaller Macaulay, a very clear and powerful voice, which was heard through the whole hall; a manner natural, impassioned, and without affectation or extravagance; wonderful fluency and command of language, abounding in illustration, and very often of a very familiar kind, but without anything either ridiculous or irreverent. He gave me an impression of his earnestness and his sincerity; speaking without book or notes, yet his discourse was evidently very carefully prepared. The text was " Cleanse me from my secret sins," and he divided it into heads, the misery, the folly, the danger (and a fourth which I have forgotten) of secret sins, on all of which he was very eloquent and impressive. He preached for about three-quarters of an hour, and, to judge of the handkerchiefs and the audible sobs, with great effect.

CHARLES GREVILLE (1794-1865)
Diary

VICTORIAN—BOHEMIAN

British art either finds her peculiar nourishment in
melancholy, and loves to fix her abode in desert places;
or it may be her purse is but slenderly furnished, and she
is forced to put up with accommodation rejected by more
prosperous callings. Some of the most dismal quarters
of the town are colonized by her disciples and professors.
In walking through streets which may have been gay
and polite when ladies' chairmen jostled each other on
the pavement, and link-boys with their torches lighted
the beaus over the mud, who has not remarked the
artist's invasion of those regions once devoted to fashion
and gaiety? Centre windows of drawing-rooms are
enlarged so as to reach up into bedrooms—bedrooms
where Lady Betty has had her hair powdered, and where
the painter's north light now takes possession of the
place which her toilet-table occupied a hundred years
ago.

There are degrees in decadence: after the Fashion
chooses to emigrate, and retreats from Soho or Bloomsbury, let us say, to Cavendish Square, physicians come
and occupy the vacant houses, which still have a respectable look—the windows being cleaned, and the knockers
and plates kept bright, and the doctor's carriage rolling
round the square, almost as fine as the countess's, which
has whisked away her ladyship to other regions. A
boarding-house mayhap succeeds the physician, who has
followed after his sick folks into the new country; and
then Dick Tinto comes with his dingy brass plate, and
breaks in his north window, and sets up his sitters'
throne.

I love his honest moustache and jaunty velvet jacket,
his queer figure, his queer vanities, and his kind heart.
Why should he not suffer his ruddy ringlets to fall over

his shirt collar? Why should he deny himself his velvet? It is but a kind of fustian which costs him eighteen-pence a yard. He is naturally what he is, and breaks out into costume as spontaneously as a bird sings or a bulb bears a tulip. And as Dick, under yonder terrific appear-ance of waving cloak, bristling beard, and shadowy sombrero, is a good, kindly, simple creature, got up at a very cheap rate, so his life is consistent with his dress: he gives his genius a darkling swagger, and a romantic envelope, which, being removed, you find, not a bravo, but a kind, chirping soul; not a moody poet avoiding mankind for the better company of his own great thoughts, but a jolly little chap who has an aptitude for painting brocade gowns, bits of armour (with figures inside them), or trees and cattle, or gondolas and build-ings, or what not; an instinct for the picturesque, which exhibits itself in his works and outwardly on his person; beyond this, a gentle creature, loving his friends, his cups, feasts, merry-makings, and all good things.

The kindest folks alive I have found among those scowling whiskerandoes. They open oysters with their yataghans, toast muffins on their rapiers, and fill their Venice glasses with half-and-half. If they have money in their lean purses, be sure they have a friend to share it. What innocent gaiety, what jovial suppers on thread-bare cloths, and wonderful songs after; what pathos, merriment, humour, does not a man enjoy who frequents their company! Mr. Clive Newcome, who has long since shaved his beard, who has become a family man, and has seen the world in a thousand different phases, avers that his life as an art student at home and abroad was the pleasantest part of his whole existence.

W. M. THACKERAY (1811-1863)
The Newcomes

JOHN MILTON, SCHOOLMASTER

He now hired a lodging at the house of one Russel, a taylor in St. Bride's Church-yard, and undertook the education of John and Edward Philips, his sister's sons. Finding his rooms too little, he took a house and garden in Aldersgate-street, which was not then so much out of the world as it is now; and chose his dwelling at the upper end of a passage, that he might avoid the noise of the street. Here he received more boys, to be boarded and instructed.

Let not our veneration for Milton forbid us to look with some degree of merriment on great promises and small performance, on the man who hastens home, because his countrymen are contending for their liberty, and, when he reaches the scene of action, vapours away his patriotism in a private boarding-school. This is the period of his life from which all his biographers seem inclined to shrink. They are unwilling that Milton should be degraded to a school-master; but since it cannot be denied that he taught boys, one finds out that he taught for nothing, and another that his motive was only zeal for the propagation of learning and virtues; and all tell what they do not know to be true, only to excuse an act which no wise man will consider as in itself disgraceful. His father was alive; his allowance was not ample, and he supplied its deficiencies by an honest and useful employment.

It is told, that in the art of education he performed wonders; and a formidable list is given of the authors, Greek and Latin, that were read in Aldersgate-street, by youth between ten and fifteen or sixteen years of age. Those who tell or receive these stories, should consider that nobody can be taught faster than he can learn. The speed of the best horseman must be limited by the power of his horse. Every man, that has ever undertaken to instruct others, can tell what slow advances he has been able to make, and how much patience it requires to recall vagrant inattention, to stimulate sluggish indifference, and to rectify absurd misapprehension. . . .

He had taken a larger house in Barbican for the reception of scholars; but the numerous relations of his wife, to whom he generously granted refuge for a while, occupied his rooms. In time, however, they went away; and the " house again," says Philips, " now looked like a house of the Muses only, though the accession of scholars was not great. Possibly his having proceeded so far in the education of youth, may have been the occasion of his adversaries calling him pedagogue and schoolmaster; whereas it is well known he never set up for a publick school, to teach all the young fry of a parish; but only was willing to impart his learning and knowledge to relations, and the sons of gentlemen who were his intimate friends; and that neither his writings nor his way of teaching ever savoured in the least of pedantry."

Thus laboriously does his nephew extenuate what cannot be denied, and what might be confessed without disgrace. Milton was not a man who could become mean by a mean employment. This, however, his warmest friends seem not to have found; they therefore shift and palliate. He did not sell literature to all comers at an open shop; he was a chamber-milliner, and measured his commodities only to his friends.

DR. SAMUEL JOHNSON (1709-1784)
Lives of the Poets

It is surprising to find the profession of school-master regarded with such disdain. Even Dr. Johnson, while ably defending Milton from the humiliating apologies of his nephew, alludes to the calling as " mean." Our valuations have improved.

MR. GREWGIOUS, LAWYER OF STAPLE INN

Mr. Grewgious had been well selected for his trust, as a man of incorruptible integrity, but certainly for no other appropriate quality discernible on the surface. He was an arid, sandy man, who, if he had been put into a grinding-mill, looked as if he would have ground immediately into high-dried snuff. He had a scanty flat crop of hair, in colour and consistency like some very mangy yellow fur tippet; it was so unlike hair, that it must have been a wig, but for the stupendous improbability of anybody's voluntarily sporting such a head. The little play of feature that his face presented, was cut deep into it, in a few hard curves that made it more like work; and he had certain notches in his forehead, which looked as though Nature had been about to touch them into sensibility or refinement, when she had impatiently thrown away the chisel, and said: "I really cannot be worried to finish off this man; let him go as he is."

With too great length of throat at his upper end, and too much ankle-bone and heel at his lower; with an awkward and hesitating manner; with a shambling walk; and with what is called a near sight—which perhaps prevented his observing how much white cotton stocking he displayed to the public eye, in contrast with his black suit—Mr. Grewgious still had some strange capacity in him of making on the whole an agreeable impression. . . .

* * *

Behind the most ancient part of Holborn, London, where certain gabled houses some centuries of age still stand looking on the public way, as if disconsolately looking for the Old Bourne that has long run dry, is a little nook composed of two irregular quadrangles

called Staple Inn. It is one of those nooks, the turning
into which out of the clashing street, imparts to the
relieved pedestrian the sensation of having put cotton in
his ears, and velvet soles on his boots. It is one of those
nooks where a few smoky sparrows twitter in smoky
trees, as though they called to one another, " Let us play
at country," and where a few feet of garden-mould
and a few yards of gravel enable them to do that re-
freshing violence to their tiny understandings. Moreover, it is one of those nooks which are legal nooks;
and it contains a little Hall, with a little lantern in its
roof: to what obstructive purposes devoted, and at whose
expense, this history knoweth not.

In the days when Cloisterham took offence at the
existence of a railroad afar off, as menacing that sensitive
constitution, the property of us Britons: the odd fortune
of which sacred institution it is to be in exactly equal
degrees croaked about, trembled for, and boasted of,
whatever happens to anything, anywhere in the world:
in those days no neighbouring architecture of lofty
proportions had arisen to overshadow Staple Inn. The
westering sun bestowed bright glances on it, and the
south-west wind blew into it unimpeded.

Neither wind nor sun, however, favoured Staple Inn
one December afternoon towards six o'clock, when it was
filled with fog, and candles shed murky and blurred rays
through the windows of all its then-occupied sets of
chambers; notably from a set of chambers in a corner
house in the little inner quadrangle, presenting in black
and white over its ugly portal the mysterious inscription:

$$P$$
$$J \qquad T$$
$$1747$$

In which set of chambers, never having troubled his head
about the inscription, unless to bethink himself at odd
times on glancing up at it, that haply it might mean

Perhaps John Thomas, or Perhaps Joe Tyler, sat Mr. Grewgious writing by his fire.

Who could have told, by looking at Mr. Grewgious, whether he had ever known ambition or disappointment? He had been bred to the Bar, and had laid himself out for chamber practice; to draw deeds; " convey the wise it call," as Pistol says. But Conveyancing and he had made such a very indifferent marriage of it that they had separated by consent—if there can be said to be separation where there has never been coming together.

No. Coy Conveyancing would not come to Mr. Grewgious. She was wooed, not won, and they went their several ways. But an Arbitration being blown towards him by some unaccountable wind, and he gaining great credit in it as one indefatigable in seeking out right and doing right, a pretty fat Receivership was next blown into his pocket by a wind more traceable to its source. So, by chance, he has found his niche. Receiver and Agent now, to two rich estates, and deputing their legal business, in an amount worth having, to a firm of solicitors on the floor below, he had snuffed out his ambition (supposing him to have ever lighted it), and had settled down with his snuffers for the rest of his life under the dry vine and fig-tree of P.J.T., who planted in seventeen-forty-seven.

Many accounts and account-books, many files of correspondence, and several strongboxes, garnished Mr. Grewgious's room. They can scarcely be represented as having lumbered it, so conscientious and precise was their orderly arrangement. The apprehension of dying suddenly, and leaving one fact or one figure with any incompleteness or obscurity attaching to it, would have stretched Mr. Grewgious stone-dead any day.

CHARLES DICKENS (1812-1870)
The Mystery of Edwin Drood

Staple Inn, with its half-timbered façade, is the only specimen of Elizabethan domestic building left in London. It was built in 1586 as one of the nine Inns of Chancery. It was partly rebuilt in the eighteenth century and again in 1954. Ten years before that it had been severely damaged by a flying bomb. The Hall was reconstructed in 1955 with some material recovered from the bomb-shattered hall. Dr. Johnson lived there in 1759-60. The imaginary Mr. Grewgious was given by his creator rooms in the second court.

LONDON'S VICTIM

She was poor, but she was honest,
    Victim of the squire's whim:
First he loved her, then he left her,
    And she lost her honest name.

Then she ran away to London,
    For to hide her grief and shame;
There she met another squire,
    And she lost her name again.

See her riding in her carriage,
    In the Park and all so gay:
All the nibs and nobby persons
    Come to pass the time of day.

See the little old-world village
    Where her aged parents live,
Drinking the champagne she sends them;
    But they never can forgive.

In the rich man's arms she flutters,
    Like a bird with broken wing:
First he loved her, then he left her,
    And she hasn't got a ring.

PARK LANE

Where Mayfair ends and Hyde Park begins was a natural site for the great houses of the wealthiest Londoners, but these mansions have nearly all made way for hotels, offices, and blocks of flats. The luxurious Dorchester Hotel, on the right of the picture, was built in 1931.

KEATS HOUSE, HAMPSTEAD

John Keats lodged in Well Walk, Hampstead in 1817-1818 and later lived down the hill at Lawn Bank, now Keats House, Keats Grove. It became a Keats Museum in 1931, but retains the atmosphere of a home with the garden where his "Ode to a Nightingale" was written.

CUMBERLAND TERRACE

Regent's Park was laid out for the Prince Regent by the architect Nash who later designed the classical terraces which surround it. These suffered from destruction and decay during the war, but have since been restored in all their splendour of fresh-painted stucco.

See him in the splendid mansion,
  Entertaining with the best,
While the girl that he has ruined,
  Entertains a sordid guest.

See him in the House of Commons,
  Making laws to put down crime,
While the victim of his passions
  Trails her way through mud and slime.

Standing on the bridge at midnight,
  She says: " Farewell, blighted Love."
There's a scream, a splash—Good Heavens!
  What is she a-doing of?

Then they drag her from the river,
  Water from her clothes they wrang,
For they thought that she was drownded;
  But the corpse got up and sang:

" It's the same the whole world over,
  It's the poor that gets the blame,
It's the rich that gets the pleasure.
  Isn't it a blooming shame? "

ANONYMOUS

PROUD POLLY PERKINS

I am a broken-hearted milkman, in grief I'm arrayed,
Through keeping of the company of a young servant
    maid,
Who lived on board and wages the house to keep clean
In a gentleman's family near Paddington Green.

CHORUS
She was as beautiful as a butterfly
And as proud as a Queen
Was pretty little Polly Perkins of
Paddington Green.

She'd an ankle like an antelope and a step like a deer,
A voice like a blackbird, so mellow and clear,
Her hair hung in ringlets so beautiful and long,
I thought that she loved me, but I found I was wrong.

When I'd rattle in a morning and cry " milk below,"
At the sound of my milk-cans her face she would show
With a smile upon her countenance and a laugh in her
    eye,
If I thought she'd have loved me, I'd have laid down to
    die.

When I asked her to marry me she said " Oh! what
    stuff,"
And told me to " drop it, for she had quite enough
Of my nonsense "—at the same time I'd been very kind,
But to marry a milkman she didn't feel inclined.

" Oh, the man that has me must have silver and gold,
A chariot to ride in and be handsome and bold,
His hair must be curly as any watch spring,
And his whiskers as big as a brush for clothing."

The words that she uttered went straight through my
    heart,
I sobbed and I sighed, and straight did depart;
With a tear on my eyelid as big as a bean,
Bidding good-bye to Polly and Paddington Green.

In six months she married—this hard-hearted girl—
But it was not a Wi-count, and it was not a Nearl,
It was not a " Baronite," but a shade or two wuss,
It was a bow-legged conductor of a twopenny bus.

ANONYMOUS

COCKNEYS AND THEIR JOKES

A writer in the *Yorkshire Evening Post* is very angry indeed with my performances in this column. His precise terms of reproach are, " Mr. G. K. Chesterton is not a humourist: not even a Cockney humourist." I do not mind his saying that I am not a humourist—in which (to tell the truth) I think he is quite right. But I do resent his saying that I am not a Cockney.

That envenomed arrow, I admit, went home. If a French writer said to me, " He is no metaphysician: not even an English metaphysician," I could swallow the insult to my metaphysics, but I should feel angry about the insult to my country. So I do not urge that I am a humourist, but I do insist that I am a Cockney. If I were a humourist, I should certainly be a Cockney humourist; if I were a saint, I should certainly be a Cockney saint. I need not recite the splendid catalogue of Cockney saints who have written their names on our noble old City churches. I need not trouble you with the long list of the Cockney humourists who have discharged their bills (or failed to discharge them) in our noble old City taverns. We can weep together over the pathos of the Poor Yorkshireman, whose county has never produced some humour not intelligible to the rest of the world. And we can smile together when he says that somebody or other is " not even " a Cockney humourist like Samuel Johnson or Charles Lamb.

It is surely sufficiently obvious that all the best humour that exists in our language is Cockney humour. Chaucer

was a Cockney; he had his house close to the Abbey.
Dickens was a Cockney; he said he could not think without the London Streets. The London taverns heard
always the quaintest conversation, whether it was Ben
Jonson's at the Mermaid or Sam Johnson's at the Cock.
Even in our own time it may be noted that the most vital
and genuine humour is still written about London. Of
this type is the mild and humane irony which marks Mr.
Pett Ridge's studies of the small grey streets. Of this
type is the simple but smashing laughter of the best
tales of Mr. W. W. Jacobs, telling of the smoke and
sparkle of the Thames.

No; I concede that I am not a Cockney humourist. No;
I am not worthy to be. Some time, after sad and stren-
uous after-lives; some time, after fierce and apocalyptic
incarnations; in some strange world beyond the stars,
I may become at last a Cockney humourist. In that
potential paradise I may walk among the Cockney
humourists, if not an equal, at least a companion. I may
feel for a moment on my shoulder the hearty hand of
Dryden and thread the labyrinths of the sweet insanity
of Lamb. But that could only be if I were not only much
cleverer, but much better than I am. Before I reach that
sphere I shall have left behind, perhaps, the sphere that is
inhabited by angels, and even passed that which is
appropriated exclusively to the use of Yorkshiremen.

No; London is in this matter attacked upon its
strongest ground. London is the largest of the bloated
modern cities; London is the smokiest; London is the
dirtiest; London is, if you will, the most sombre;
London is, if you will, the most miserable. But London
is certainly the most amusing and the most amused. You
may prove that we have the most tragedy; the fact
remains that we have the most comedy, that we have the
most farce. We have at the very worst a splendid hypocrisy of humour. We conceal our sorrow behind a
screaming derision. You speak of people who laugh

through their tears; it is our boast that we only weep through our laughter. There remains always this great boast, perhaps the greatest boast that the most unhappy part of our population is also the most hilarious part. The poor can forget that social problem which we (the moderately rich) ought never to forget. Blessed are the poor; for they alone have not the poor always with them. The honest poor can sometimes forget poverty. The honest rich can never forget it.

I believe firmly in the value of all vulgar notions, especially of vulgar jokes. The vulgar comic papers are so subtle and true that they are even prophetic. If you really want to know what is going to happen to the future of our democracy, do not read the modern sociological prophecies, do not read even Mr. Wells's Utopias for this purpose, though you should certainly read them if you are fond of good honesty and good English. If you want to know what will happen, study the pages of Snaps or Patchy Bits as if they were the dark tablets graven with the oracles of the gods. For, mean and gross as they are, in all seriousness, they contain what is entirely absent from all Utopias and all the sociological conjectures of our time: they contain some hint of the actual habits and manifest desires of the English people. If we are really to find out what the democracy will ultimately do with itself, we shall surely find it, not in the literature which studies the people, but in the literature which the people studies.

G. K. CHESTERTON (1874-1936)
Selected Essays

THE POOTERS AT HOME

My dear wife Carrie and I have just been a week in our new house, "The Laurels," Brickfield Terrace, Holloway—a nice six-roomed residence, not counting basement, with a front breakfast-parlour. We have a little front garden; and there is a flight of ten steps up to the front door, which, by-the-by, we keep locked with the chain up. Cummings, Gowing, and our other intimate friends always come to the little side entrance, which saves the servant the trouble of going up to the front door, thereby taking her from her work. We have a nice little back garden which runs down to the railway. We were rather afraid of the noise of the trains at first, but the landlord said we should not notice them after a bit, and took £2 off the rent. He was certainly right; and beyond the cracking of the garden wall at the bottom, we have suffered no inconvenience.

After my work in the City, I like to be at home. What's the good of a home, if you are never in it? " Home, Sweet Home," that's my motto. I am always in of an evening. Our old friend Gowing may drop in without ceremony; so may Cummings, who lives opposite. My dear wife Caroline and I are pleased to see them, if they like to drop in on us. But Carrie and I can manage to pass our evenings together without friends. There is always something to be done: a tin-tack here, a Venetian blind to put straight, a fan to nail up, or part of a carpet to nail down—all of which I can do with my pipe in my mouth; while Carrie is not above putting a button on a shirt, mending a pillow-case, or practising the " Sylvia Gavotte " on our new cottage piano (on the three years' system), manufactured by W. Bilkson (in small letters), from Collard and Collard (in very large letters). It is also a great comfort to us to know that our boy Willie is getting on so well in the Bank at Oldham. We should like to see more of him. Now for my diary.

GEORGE GROSSMITH (1847-1912)
and WEEDON GROSSMITH (1854-1919)
The Diary of a Nobody

THE POOTERS AT THE MANSION HOUSE

April 30. Perfectly astounded at receiving an invitation for Carrie and myself from the Lord and Lady Mayoress to the Mansion House, to " meet the Representatives of Trades and Commerce." My heart beat like that of a schoolboy. Carrie and I read the invitation over two or three times. I could scarcely eat my breakfast. I said—and I felt it from the bottom of my heart—" Carrie darling, I was a proud man when I led you down the aisle of the church on our wedding day; that pride will be equalled, if not surpassed, when I lead my dear, pretty wife up to the Lord and Lady Mayoress at the Mansion House." I saw the tears in Carrie's eyes, and she said: " Charlie dear, it is I who have to be proud of you. And I am very, very proud of you. You have called me pretty; and as long as I am pretty in your eyes, I am happy. You, dear old Charlie, are not handsome, but you are good, which is far more noble." I gave her a kiss, and she said: " I wonder if there will be any dancing? I have not danced for years."

I cannot tell what induced me to do it, but I seized her round the waist and we were silly enough to be executing a wild kind of polka when Sarah entered, grinning, and said, " There is a man, mum, at the door who wants to know if you want any good coals." Most annoyed at this. Spent the evening in answering, and tearing up again, the reply to the Mansion House, having left word with Sarah if Gowing or Cummings called we were not at home. Must consult Mr. Perkupp how to answer the Lord Mayor's invitation.

May 1. Carrie said: " I should like to send mother the invitation to look at." I consented, as soon as I had answered it. I told Mr. Perkupp, at the office, with a feeling of pride, that we had received an invitation to the Mansion House; and he said, to my astonishment, that he himself gave in my name to the Lord Mayor's secretary. I felt this rather discounted the value of the invitation, but I thanked him; and in reply to me, he described how I was to answer it. I felt the reply was too simple; but of course, Mr. Perkupp knows best.

May 2. Sent my dress-coat and trousers to the little tailor's round the corner, to have the creases taken out. Told Gowing not to call next Monday, as we were going to the Mansion House. Sent similar note to Cummings.

May 3. Carrie went to Mrs. James, at Sutton, to consult about her dress for next Monday. While speaking incidentally to Spotch, one of our head clerks, about the Mansion House, he said: " Oh, I'm asked, but don't think I shall go." When a vulgar man like Spotch is asked I feel my invitation is considerably discounted. In the evening, while I was out, the little tailor brought round my coat and trousers, and because Sarah had not a shilling to pay for the pressing, he took them away again.

May 4. Carrie's mother returned the Lord Mayor's invitation, which was sent to her to look at, with apologies for having upset a glass of port over it. I was too angry to say anything.

May 5. Bought a pair of lavender kid-gloves for next Monday, and two white ties, in case one got spoiled in the tying.

May 6, Sunday. A very dull sermon, during which, I regret to say, I twice thought of the Mansion House reception tomorrow.

FLEET STREET

Named after the stream, now hidden underground, which ran from Hampstead to the Thames, Fleet Street has been called the "Street of Ink" and the "Street of Adventure". To the many men and women of the Press who work there it is simply known as "The Street".

A COFFEE-STALL IN KENNINGTON

The Coffee-bar, known as the "caff", has become a popular resort of young Londoners. But that kind of refreshment-house has not ended the life of the mobile coffee-stall at which those needing a warm drink can stop for tea, coffee, substantial sandwiches, and possibly an argument.

SUNSET AT WATERLOO BRIDGE

The first Waterloo Bridge was finished in 1817 but did not suffice the traffic of the motoring age and was demolished in 1937. It was replaced by Sir Giles Gilbert Scott's structure in concrete with Portland Stone slabs—an engineer's as well as architect's achievement.

BARGES GO RACING

The Thames barges add grace to haulage when, dark-winged in full sail, they have their own regatta and go racing to and from the mouth of the Medway, a matter of 45 miles. The prize is the Medway Challenge Cup and a flag of honour.

May 7. At nine o'clock Carrie swept into the room, looking like a queen. Never have I seen her look so lovely, or so distinguished. She was wearing a satin dress of sky-blue—my favourite colour—and a piece of lace, which Mrs. James lent her, round the shoulders, to give a finish. I thought perhaps the dress was a little too long behind and decidedly too short in front, but Mrs. James said it was *à la mode*. Mrs. James was most kind, and lent Carrie a fan of ivory with red feathers, the value of which she said, was priceless, as the feathers belonged to the Kachu eagle—a bird now extinct. I preferred the little white fan which Carrie bought for three-and-six at Shoolbred's, but both ladies sat on me at once.

We arrived at the Mansion House too early, which was rather fortunate, for I had an opportunity of speaking to his lordship, who graciously condescended to talk with me some minutes; but I must say I was disappointed to find he did not even know Mr. Perkupp, the principal.

I felt as if we had been invited to the Mansion House by one who did not know the Lord Mayor himself. Crowds arrived, and I shall never forget the grand sight. My humble pen can never describe it. I was a little annoyed with Carrie, who kept saying: " Isn't it a pity we don't know anybody ? "

Once she quite lost her head. I saw someone who looked like Franching, from Peckham, and was moving towards him when she seized me by the coat-tails, and said quite loudly: " Don't leave me," which caused an elderly gentleman, in a court-suit, and a chain round him, and two ladies, to burst out laughing. There was an immense crowd in the supper-room, and, my stars! it was a splendid supper—any amount of champagne.

Carrie made a most hearty supper, for which I was pleased; for I sometimes think she is not strong. There was scarcely a dish she did not taste. I was so thirsty, I could not eat much. Receiving a sharp slap on the shoulder, I turned, and, to my amazement, saw Farmerson, our ironmonger. He said, in the most familiar way: "This is better than Brickfield Terrace, eh?" I simply looked at him, and said coolly: "I never expected to see you here." He said, with a loud coarse laugh: "I like that—if you, why not me?" I replied: "Certainly." I wish I could have thought of something better to say. He said: "Can I get your good lady anything?" Carrie said: "No, I thank you," for which I was pleased. I said, by way of reproof to him: "You never sent today to paint the bath, as I requested." Farmerson said: "Pardon me, Mr. Pooter, no shop when we're in company, please."

Before I could think of a reply, one of the sheriffs, in full Court costume, slapped Farmerson on the back and hailed him as an old friend, and asked him to dine with him at his lodge. I was astonished. For full five minutes they stood roaring with laughter, and stood digging each other in the ribs. They kept telling each other they didn't look a day older. They began embracing each other and drinking champagne.

To think that a man who mends our scraper should know any member of our aristocracy! I was just moving with Carrie, when Farmerson seized me rather roughly by the collar, and addressing the sheriff, said: "Let me introduce my neighbour, Pooter." He did not even say "Mister." The sheriff handed me a glass of champagne. I felt, after all, it was a great honour to drink a glass of wine with him, and I told him so. We stood chatting for some time, and at last I said: "You must excuse me now if I join Mrs. Pooter." When I approached her, she said: "Don't let me take you away from friends. I am quite happy standing here alone in a crowd, knowing nobody!"

As it takes two to make a quarrel, and as it was neither the time nor the place for it, I gave my arm to Carrie, and said: "I hope my darling little wife will dance with me, if only for the sake of saying we had danced at the Mansion House as guests of the Lord Mayor." Finding the dancing after supper was less formal, and knowing how much Carrie used to admire my dancing in the days gone by, I put my arm round her waist and we commenced a waltz.

A most unfortunate accident occurred. I had got on a new pair of boots. Foolishly, I had omitted to take Carrie's advice; namely, to scratch the soles of them with the points of the scissors or to put a little wet on them. I had scarcely started when, like lightning, my foot slipped away and I came down, the side of my head striking the floor with such violence that for a second or two I did not know what had happened. I need hardly say that Carrie fell with me with equal violence, breaking the comb in her hair and grazing her elbow.

There was a roar of laughter, which was immediately checked when people found that we had really hurt ourselves. A gentleman assisted Carrie to a seat, and I expressed myself pretty strongly on the danger of having a plain polished floor with no carpet or drugget to prevent people slipping. The gentleman, who said his name was Darwitts, insisted on escorting Carrie to have a glass of wine, an invitation which I was pleased to allow Carrie to accept.

I followed, and met Farmerson, who immediately said, in his loud voice: " Oh, are you the one who went down? "

I answered with an indignant look.

With execrable taste, he said: " Look here, old man, we are too old for this game. We must leave these capers to the youngsters. Come and have another glass, that is more in our line."

Although I felt I was buying his silence by accepting, we followed the others into the supper-room.

Neither Carrie nor I, after our unfortunate mishap, felt inclined to stay longer. As we were departing,

Farmerson said: "Are you going? if so, you might give me a lift."

I thought it better to consent, but wish I had first consulted Carrie.

GEORGE GROSSMITH (1847-1912)
and WEEDON GROSSMITH (1854-1919)
The Diary of a Nobody

THE FORSYTES

John Galsworthy's novel *The Man of Property* was published in 1906: the author did not then expect to be the creator of a series which became world-famous. The Forsyte family were, however, firmly established when five stories were issued together under the title of *The Forsyte Saga* in 1922. They were accepted as a memorable picture of solid English and London prosperity at the level of the well-established bourgeoisie. The Forsytes were men and women of property, standing square against all "subversive" opinions and all menaces to their standards of behaviour as well as to their large possessions. Galsworthy wrote in explanation:

"If the upper middle class, with other classes, is destined to 'move on' into amorphism, here, pickled in these pages, it lies under glass for strollers in the wide and ill-arranged museum of Letters to gaze at. Here it rests, preserved in its own juice: The Sense of Property."

Now let us meet them as they appear at the beginning of *The Man of Property*. All living in good houses round Hyde Park, they meet to discuss an awkward situation. A Forsyte girl proposes to marry a man outside their circle, owner of an artistic temperament, a fellow who puts passion before possessions, one fit to be described as "a wild buccaneer."

Those privileged to be present at a family festival of the Forsytes have seen that charming and instructive sight— an upper middle class family in full plumage. But whosoever of these favoured persons has possessed the gift of psychological analysis (a talent without monetary value and properly ignored by the Forsytes), has witnessed a spectacle, not only delightful in itself, but illustrative of an obscure human problem. In plainer words, he has gleaned from a gathering of this family—

no branch of which had a liking for the other, between no three members of whom existed anything worthy of the name of sympathy—evidence of that mysterious concrete tenacity which renders a family so formidable a unit of society, so clear a reproduction of society in miniature. He has been admitted to a vision of the dim roads of social progress, has understood something of patriarchal life, of the swarmings of savage hordes, of the rise and fall of nations. He is like one who, having watched a tree grow from its planting—a paragon of tenacity, insulation, and success, amidst the deaths of a hundred other plants less fibrous, sappy, and persistent—one day will see it flourishing with bland, full foliage, in an almost repugnant prosperity, at the summit of its efflorescence.

On 15th June, 1886, about four of the afternoon, the observer who chanced to be present at the house of old Jolyon Forsyte in Stanhope Gate, might have seen the highest efflorescence of the Forsytes.

This was the occasion of an " at home " to celebrate the engagement of Miss June Forsyte, old Jolyon's grand-daughter, to Mr. Philip Bosinney. In the bravery of light gloves, buff waistcoats, feathers and frocks, the family were present—even Aunt Ann, who now but seldom left the corner of her brother Timothy's green drawing-room, where, under the ægis of a plume of dyed pampas grass in a light blue vase, she sat all day reading and knitting, surrounded by the effigies of three generations of Forsytes. Even Aunt Ann was there; her inflexible back and the dignity of her calm old face personifying the rigid possessiveness of the family idea.

When a Forsyte was engaged, married, or born, the Forsytes were present; when a Forsyte died—but no Forsyte had as yet died; they did not die; death being contrary to their principles, they took precautions against it, the instinctive precautions of highly vitalised persons who resent encroachment on their property.

About the Forsytes mingling that day with the crowd of other guests, there was a more than ordinarily groomed look, an alert, inquisitive assurance, a brilliant respectability, as though they were attired in defiance of something. The habitual sniff on the face of Soames Forsyte had spread through their ranks; they were on their guard.

The subconscious offensiveness of their attitude has constituted old Jolyon's " at home " the psychological moment of the family history and made it the prelude of their drama.

The Forsytes were resentful of something, not individually, but as a family; this resentment expressed itself in an added perfection of raiment, an exuberance of family cordiality, an exaggeration of family importance, and—the sniff Danger—so indispensable in bringing out the fundamental quality of any society, group, or individual—was what the Forsytes scented; the premonition of danger put a burnish on their armour. For the first time, as a family, they appeared to have an instinct of being in contact with some strange and unsafe thing.

Over against the piano a man of bulk and stature was wearing two waistcoats on his wide chest, two waistcoats and a ruby pin, instead of the single satin waistcoat and diamond pin of more usual occasions, and his shaven, square old face, the colour of pale leather, with pale eyes, had its most dignified look, above his satin stock. This was Swithin Forsyte. Close to the window, where he could get more than his fair share of fresh air, the other twin, James—the fat and the lean of it, old Jolyon called these brothers—like the bulky Swithin, over six feet in height, but very lean, as though destined from his birth to strike a balance and maintain an average, brooded over the scene with his permanent stoop; his grey eyes had an air of fixed absorption in some secret worry, broken at intervals by a rapid, shifting scrutiny of

surrounding facts; his cheeks, thinned by two parallel
folds, and a long, clean-shaven upper lip, were framed
within Dundreary whiskers. In his hands he turned and
turned a piece of china. Not far off, listening to a lady
in brown, his only son Soames, pale and well-shaved,
dark-haired, rather bald, had poked his chin up sideways,
carrying his nose with that aforesaid appearance of
" sniff," as though despising an egg which he knew he
could not digest. Behind him his cousin, the tall George,
son of the fifth Forsyte, Roger, had a Quilpish look on his
fleshy face, pondering one of his sardonic jests.

Something inherent to the occasion had affected them
all.

Seated in a row close to one another were three ladies—
Aunts Ann, Hester (the two Forsyte maids), and Juley
(short for Julia), who not in first youth had so far forgotten herself as to marry Septimus Small, a man of poor
constitution. She had survived him for many years.
With her elder and younger sister she lived now in the
house of Timothy, her sixth and youngest brother, on
the Bayswater Road. Each of these ladies held fans in
their hands, and each with some touch of colour, some
emphatic feather or brooch, testified to the solemnity of
the opportunity.

In the centre of the room, under the chandelier, as
became a host, stood the head of the family, old Jolyon
himself. Eighty years of age, with his fine, white hair,
his dome-like forehead. his little dark grey eyes, and an
immense white moustache, which dropped and spread
below the level of his strong jaw, he had a patriarchal
look, and in spite of lean cheeks and hollows at his
temples, seemed master of perennial youth. He held
himself extremely upright, and his shrewd eyes had lost
none of their clear shining. Thus he gave an impression
of superiority to the doubts and dislikes of smaller men.
Having had his own way for innumerable years, he had
earned a prescriptive right to it. It would never have

occurred to old Jolyon that it was necessary to wear a look of doubt or of defiance.

Between him and the four other brothers who were present, James, Swithin, Nicholas, and Roger, there was much difference, much similarity. In turn, each of these four brothers was very different from the other, yet they, too, were alike.

Through the varying features and expression of those five faces could be marked a certain steadfastness of chin, underlying surface distinctions, marking a racial stamp, too prehistoric to trace, too remote and permanent to discuss—the very hall-mark and guarantee of the family fortunes.

JOHN GALSWORTHY (1867-1933)
The Man of Property

THE BOOKSELLER

1923

I suppose that I really ought to put on record how I started the wonderful game of bookselling. I went to a jumble sale at Denmark Hill, Camberwell and for eight shillings I bought all the books they had. I spent all the next day (a Sunday) cleaning them up and on Monday morning I took them out in a nice clean sack, over to Charing Cross Road, and inside two hours I had sold out —and made a profit. I took twenty-four wonderful shillings. I have been doing very much the same for this year. Not always so lucky. Sometimes I've had to borrow two or three bob from my dad in order to pay my mother one pound a week, but I've never once owed my dad more than three days. I am very happy. I find Rider Haggard and Marie Corelli and Mrs. H. Wood to be the best of my sellers. I buy from barrows and I sell to shops. It's called " bookrunning " . . . only I don't run.

March, 1925

Slowly but surely I am getting around where I can buy books at very cheap prices. I make a lot of mistakes, but on the whole I do sell my stock. I have to walk miles to find books. I find that the better the borough the cleaner the books. If I go to a rummage sale in Tooting or Streatham I get clean books. If I go to Bethnal Green they are ever so grubby, but the price asked is much the same.

I buy books mostly Fridays and Saturdays. I clean them Sundays. I sell on Mondays and Tuesdays. What do I do Wednesdays and Thursdays? Well, I mostly go on Wednesdays to public Libraries to learn about books and their values and on Thursdays I have a day off and I go out autograph collecting. I have now spoken to Arnold Bennet four times and got his signature twice. His is a very worth while autograph to get, but he is not always in the mood to oblige. He can be very touchy. He suffers with bad head-aches. I know that he likes to hear saucy jokes and the twice I got his autograph I was able to tell him pretty good funny tales. He didn't laugh. I ain't never seen him really L A U G H—but he did grin.

This night as he waited for his car (it was a first night) he was for him a bit in a talkative mood and he told me a good tale. I best put this tale down before I go to sleep else I am sure to forget it. Arnold Bennet said, there was in a certain West End Club a cloak room attendant who possessed a very good memory and knew all the members of the club by sight. On one occasion a certain very noble gentleman handed over his overcoat to the attendant and was rather surprised that he didn't get a ticket for his coat, but said nothing. Later that evening the said noble bloke on leaving the club went back again to the attendant and was immediately handed over his correct overcoat. The noble gent then said to the attendant.

" How did you know it was my coat? "

" But I don't know if it's your coat sir," replied the attendant.

" Then why on earth did you give it to me? " asked the noble man.

" Because that's the coat you gave to me to mind! "

Mr. Bennet has a stammer. It spoils story telling—but he obviously told this one many times and it came out in his curious squeaky way almost pat. It's a jolly good tale. So far I've never yet been anywhere where I've yet had to get anyone to mind my coat because most places I sit on it to make me taller.

I suppose I ought to put here that in lots of ways Arnold Bennet is odd. He has a curious way of walking and one shoulder seems higher than the other. His hair looks odd. His face looks odd and he has an uncommonly shaped nose and teeth like a horse! He is a very great man for all his moods (he has head-aches that are most cruel to him). As long as I don't make myself a worry and perhaps speak 3 times a year to him real politely I think I can keep in his good books. I can't do anything for him (except make him smile) but he can do a jolly lot for ME. " Old Wives Tale " and " The Card " are his best novels and some stories of his read good. The most powerful living author—that's Mr. Bennet, and he came up the hard way. Staffordshire must be proud of him. I'm real sorry he ain't a fitter man. He is friends with E. M. Forster (I want this man's autograph!) and also of Eden Phillpotts (I've got his autograph). Tonight's meeting was at Court Theatre and " The Farmer's Wife " by E. Phillpotts was on. It could have been off for all I cared: I couldn't understand all of the lingo. But lots of people laughed, so I suppose half the audience know rustic language. I didn't laugh but I was satisfied for those 4 or 5 minutes with A.B. (as he waited for his car) made the journey worth while.

This is the first time I've been to the Court Theatre, as it's quite out of the way and when you get there, well, there is NO where else to go. I much prefer around Cambridge Circus 'cause then if you don't get autographs at one place in 15 minutes you can rush off to another theatre and perhaps be more lucky ... but where can you rush to after The Court? Nowhere! Near Victoria Station a well built lady asked if I had change for 6d. I had. I gave her 12 halfpennies. She said it was "No good." No Good for what? I asked her—and she didn't reply.

I am still bookselling—mostly by a sack of stock. I'm making a living. My mother's ceased to complain. My dad is pleased with me. I am pleased with myself. I am still H A P P Y.

FRED BASON (1907-   )
The Last Bassoon—A Diary

MR. SMEETH, LONDON CASHIER

His appearance was deceptive. He looked what he ought to have been, in the opinion of a few thousand hasty and foolish observers of this life, and what he was not—a grey drudge. They could easily see him as a drab ageing fellow for ever toiling away at figures of no importance, as a creature of the little foggy City street, of crusted inkpots and dusty ledgers and day books, as a typical troglodyte of this dingy and absurd civilisation. Angel Pavement and its kind, too hot and airless in summer, too raw in winter, too wet in spring, and too smoky in autumn, assisted by long hours of artificial light, by hasty breakfasts and illusory lunches, by walks in boots made of sodden cardboard and rides in germ-haunted buses, by fuss all day and worry at night, had blanched the whole man, had thinned his hair and turned it grey, wrinkled his forehead and the space at each side of his short grey moustache, put eyeglasses at one end of his nose and slightly sharpened and reddened the other end, and given him a prominent Adam's apple, drooping shoulders and a narrow chest, pains in his joints, a perpetual slight cough, and a hay-fevered look at least one week out of every ten.

Nevertheless, he was not a grey drudge. He did not toil hopelessly. On the contrary, his days at the office were filled with important and exciting events, all the more important and exciting because they were there in the light, for just beyond them, all round them, was the darkness in which lurked the one great fear, the fear that he might take part no longer in these events, that he might lose his job. Once he stopped being Twigg and Dersingham's cashier, what was he? He avoided the question by day, but sometimes at night, when he could not sleep, it came to him with all its force and dreadfully illuminated the darkness with little pictures of shabby and broken men, trudging round from office to office, haunting the Labour Exchanges and the newspaper rooms of Free Libraries, and gradually sinking into the workhouse and the gutter.

This fear only threw into brighter relief his present position. He had spent years making neat little columns of figures, entering up ledgers and then balancing them, but this was not drudgery to him. He was a man of figures. He could handle them with astonishing dexterity and certainty. In their small but perfected world, he moved with complete confidence and enjoyed himself. If you only took time and trouble enough, the figures would always work out and balance up, unlike life, which you could not possibly manipulate so that it would work out and balance up. Moreover, he loved the importance, the dignity, of his position. Thirty-five years had passed since he was an office boy, like Stanley, but a trifle smaller and younger; he was a boy from a poor home; and in those days a clerkship in the City still meant something, cashiers and chief clerks still wore silk hats, and to occupy a safe stool and receive your hundred and fifty a year was to have arrived. Mr. Smeeth was now a cashier himself and he was still enjoying his arrival. Somewhere at the back of his mind, that little office boy still lived, to mark the wonder of it. Going round to the bank, where he was known and respected and told it was a fine day or a wet day, was part of the routine of his work, but even now it was something more than that, something to be tasted by the mind and relished. The " Good-morning, Mr. Smeeth," of the bank cashiers at the counter still gave him a secret little thrill. And, unless the day had gone very badly indeed, he never concluded it, locking the ledger, the cash book, and the japanned box for petty cash, away in the safe and then filling and lighting his pipe, without being warmed by a feeling that he, Herbert Norman Smeeth, once a mere urchin, then office boy and junior clerk to Willoughby, Tyce and Bragg, then a clerk with the Imperial Trading Co., then for two War years a lance-corporal in the orderly room of the depot of the Middlesex Regiment, and now Twigg and Dersingham's cashier for the last ten years, had triumphantly arrived.

J. B. PRIESTLEY (1895-   )
Angel Pavement

MRS. SMEETH, CHILD OF LONDON

According to all the literary formulas, the wife of Mr. Smeeth should have been a grey and withered suburban drudge, a creature who had long forgotten to care for anything but a few household tasks, the welfare of her children, and the opinion of one or two chapel-going neighbours, a mere husk of womanhood, in whom Mr. Smeeth could not recognise the girl he had once courted. But Nature, caring nothing for literary formulas, had gone to work in another fashion, with Mrs. Smeeth. There was nothing grey and withered about her. She was only in her early forties, and did not look a day older than her age, by any standards. She was a good deal plumper than the girl Mr. Smeeth had married, twenty-two years before, but she was no worse for that. She still had a great quantity of untidy brown hair, a bright blue eye, rosy cheeks, and a ripe moist lip. She came of robust country stock, and perhaps that is why she had been able to conjure any amount of bad food into healthy and jolly womanhood.

By temperament, however, she was a real child of London, a daughter of Cockaigne. She adored oysters, fish and chips, an occasional bottle of stout or glass of port, cheerful gossip, hospitality, noise, jokes, sales, outings, comic songs, entertainments of any kind, in fact, the whole rattling and roaring, laughing and crying world of food and drink and bargaining and adventure and concupiscence. She liked to spend as much money as she could, but apart from that, would have been quite happy if the Smeeths had dropped to a lower social level. She never shared any of her husband's worries, and was indeed rather impatient of them, sometimes openly contemptuous, but she had no contempt, beyond that experienced by all deeply feminine natures for the male, for the man himself.

He had been her sweetheart, he was her husband; he had given her innumerable pleasures, had looked after her, had been patient with her, had always been fond of her; and she loved him and was proud of what seemed to her his cleverness. She knew enough about life to realise that Smeeth was a really good husband and that this was something to be thankful for. (North London does not form any part of that small hot-house world in which a good husband or wife is regarded as a bore, perhaps as an obstacle in the path of the partner's self-development.) Chastity for its own sake made no appeal to her, and she recognised with inward pleasure (though not with any outward sign) the glances that flirtatious and challenging males, in buses and shops and tea-rooms, threw in her direction.

If Mr. Smeeth had started any little games—as she frankly confessed—she would not have moaned and repined, but would have promptly " shown him " what she could do in that line. As it was, he did not require showing. He grumbled sometimes at her extravagance, her thoughtlessness, her rather slapdash housekeeping, but in spite of all that, in spite too of the fact that for two-and-twenty years they had been cooped up together in tiny houses, she still seemed to him an adorable person, at once incredible and delightful in the large, wilful, intriguing, mysterious mass of her femininity, the Woman among the almost indistinguishable crowd of mere women.

J. B. PRIESTLEY (1895-   )
Angel Pavement

Green Islands

EPSOM FOR INNOCENCE

Going to Epsom Downs for fresh air as well as for horse-racing is a historic London diversion. Epsom was famous for its curative waters at the Spa and also for indoor gaming in the salons. But Pepys found and enjoyed the airy and innocent Epsom.

"... and I could not find the way into any of the walks in the wood, which indeed are very pleasant, if I could have found them. At last got out of the wood again, and I, by leaping down the little bank, coming out of the wood, did sprain my right foot, which brought me great present pain, but presently, with walking, it went away for the present, and so the women and W. Hewer and I walked upon the Downes, where a flock of sheep was; and the most pleasant and innocent sight that ever I saw in my life— we find a shepherd and his little boy reading, far from any houses or sight of people, the Bible to him; so I made the boy read to me, which he did, with the forced tone that children do usually read, that was mighty pretty, and then I did give him something, and went to the father, and talked with him; and I find he had been a servant in my cozen Pepys's house, and told me what was become of their old servants. He did content himself mightily in my liking his boy's reading, and did bless God for him, the most like one of the old patriarchs that ever I saw in my life, and it brought those thoughts of the old age of the world in my mind for two or three days after."

SAMUEL PEPYS (1633-1703)
Diary

EPSOM FOR PLEASURE

Celia Fiennes, that wide-ranging traveller, disliked the source of the
Epsom waters and found the other amenities more agreeable.

The well is Large without Bason or Pavement, on the
bottom it is covered over with timber and is so darke you
Can scarce Look down into it for which Cause I do dislike it . . . There is a walk of trees by it, but not very
pleasant, there is a house built, in which the well is, and
that is paved with brick to walke in in the wet weather,
and where people have Carrawayes sweetmeates and the
tea etc, but it Look'd so dark and unpleasant, more Like
a Dungeon, that I would not Chuse to drinke it there, and
most people drink it at home.

A Coffee house and two roomes for gameing, and shops
for sweetmeates and fruite. Monday morning is their
day, the Company meete and then they have some Little
diversion, as raceing of boys or Rabbets or Piggs. In the
Evening the company meete in the Greenes, first in the
upper Green many steps up, where are Gentlemen
Bowling, Ladyes walking. There are Little Shopps and
a gameing or danceing roome, the same man at the
wells keepes it, sells Coffee there also. The Lower green
is not farr off—just in the heart of the town: it's a much
neater green and warmer. The whole side of this is a
very Large roome with Large sashe windows to the
green, with Cusheons in the windows and seates all along.
There are two hazards boards; at the End is a Milliner
and China Shop, this is belonging to the Great tavern or
Eateing house, and all the Length of this roome to the
street ward is a Piaza wall, and a row of trees Cutt and
platted together as the ffashion of the place.

CELIA FIENNES (1662-1741)
The Journeys of Celia Fiennes

EPSOM FOR VICTUALS

An account published in the reign of Queen Anne describes the worldly humours and luxuries of the Londoners' haunt in Surrey.

... the greatest Order that in such Cases can be expected (however to me it be a Rout) is preserv'd at the Gaming-Tables of every kind; where it is very diverting for a Stander-by to observe the different Humours and Passions of both Sexes, which discover themselves with less Art and Reserve at Play, than on any other Occasion. There you'll see a sparkish young Fellow of twenty-five, sitting right over a blooming Beauty of eighteen; but so intent on Gain and the Dice, that he never exchanges a Word of a Look with her: While a little lower you may smile at an old Hunks, that loves his Money as well as any in the City, yet losing it as fast as he plays, by having his Eyes wholly off his Cards, and fix'd on a green Girl of thirteen, that cares as little for any Man there, as he does for his Wife at home.

... The nearness of London does in like Manner afford it all the exotick Preparatives and Allurements to Luxury, whenever any is dispos'd to make a sumptuous Banquet, or to give a genteel Collation. You wou'd think your self in some enchanted Camp, to see the Peasants ride to every House with the choicest Fruits, Herbs, Roots and Flowers; with all Sorts of tame and wild Fowl, with the rarest Fish and Venison, and with every Kind of Butcher's Meat; among which Bansted-Down Mutton, is the most relishing Dainty. Thus, to see the fresh and artless Damsels of the Plain, either accompany'd by their amorous Swains, or aged Parents, striking their Bargains with the nice Court and City Ladies, who, like Queens in a Tragedy, display all their Finery on Benches before their Doors (where they hourly

censure, and are censur'd) and to observe, how the hand-
somest of each Degree equally admire, envy, and cozen
one another, is, to me, one of the chief Amusements of
the Place. The Ladies who are too lazy, or too stately;
but especially those that sit up late at Play, have their
Provisions brought to their Bed-side, where they conclude the Bargain; and then (perhaps after a Dish of
Chocolate) take t'other Nap, till what they have thus
bought is got ready for Dinner ...

JOHN TOLAND (1670-1722)
Description of Epsom (1711)

HAMPSTEAD IN 1815

A steeple issuing from a leafy rise,
   With farmy fields in front and sloping green,
   Dear Hampstead, is thy southern face serene,
Silently smiling on approaching eyes,
Within, thine ever-shifting looks surprise,
   Streets, hills and dells, trees overhead now seen,
   Now down below, with smoking roofs between,—
A village, revelling in varieties.
Then northward what a range—with heath and pond!
   Nature's own ground; woods that let mansions
      through
And cottaged vales with billowy fields beyond,
   And clump of darkening pines, and prospects blue,
And that clear path through all, where daily meet
Cool cheeks, and brilliant eyes, and morn-elastic feet!

LEIGH HUNT (1784-1859)
Poems

HAMPTON COURT IN 1840

A visit to Hampton Court Palace, is one of the bravest
pleasures that a party of happy friends can promise themselves. Especially is it calculated to charm the thousands

of pleasure-seekers from the dense and dusty vastness of London. It lies in a rich country; on the banks of the Thames,—there unmuddied by commerce, but flowing free and pure, amid the greenest meadows, scattered villas, and trees overhanging its clear waters, and adding to its glad aspect the richness of their beauty. From the swelling hills of Richmond, Esher, and St. George, the palace is seen standing aloft amid a wide sea of woodland foliage, like a little town in its extent.

Its ample and delightful gardens, bounded by the splendid masses of its lime-tree avenues; its ancient courts, with all their historic recollections; its accumulated paintings, the Cartoons of Raphael themselves being part of them—all are thrown open to the leisurely and perfect enjoyment of the public. There is no royal palace in England, excepting Windsor, which, after all, is to be compared to it, and this is, as it should be, given up to the use and refreshment of the people. It is the first step towards the national appropriation of public property. It is long since it was said, " The king has got his own again," and it is now fitting that the people should have their own again. Of all the palaces, the towers, the abbeys, and cathedrals, which have been raised with the wealth and ostensibly for the benefit of the people, none till lately have been freely open to the footsteps of the multitude. They have been jealously retained for the enjoyment of an exclusive few, or have been made engines to extort still further payment from those out of whose pockets they were raised. But the tolls at the doors of St. Paul's and the Tower have been relaxed; park after park in the metropolis has been thrown open; and now this charming old palace of Hampton Court has been made the daily resort of any, and of all, of the English people who choose to tread the pavements, and disport themselves in the gardens, and gaze on the works of art, which for ages were wont only to be accessible to the royal, the aristocratic, and the ecclesiastical dignitary and their retainers.

These are visible and unequivocal evidences of the growth of general intelligence, and of that popular influence and benefit which must spring out of it. Courts are no longer despotic because the people is no longer ignorant. The crown has resigned its lands into the hands of the people saying, give us what you deem fitting for the just maintenance of the regal dignity,—and the crown has had no cause to regret this surrender; while, on the other hand, it has given the people a right to use a bolder tone regarding those which were the royal lands and houses, woods and forests. The people can now say with an air of just authority, we demand to be admitted to the use and fruition of that for which we have given a noble equivalent. It is with this consciousness that we now walk about the courts, the gardens, the galleries, and painted chambers of Hampton Court; and there can be perhaps no instance cited where public property is more completely enjoyed by all classes of the community. The royal race have had their will of it from the days in which the last great English Cardinal built it, and presented it, as a most magnificent gift, to Harry VIII his master, till they abandoned it as an abode, for others which more engaged their fancies. A considerable portion of it has been since, and still is, given as residences to branches of the aristocracy, and lo! at length the very people have entered into possession of the rest.

And now, the great question is, how do they enjoy it? —How do they use their advantage? Do they feel the great delight of having got their own again? Do they act like rational masters and proprietors on their own estates, committing no injury and seeing none committed? A few facts will sufficiently answer these questions. Steam has in a great measure brought this delightful old palace into the very suburbs of London; and thrown it open to the thousands of its citizens. The

Southampton railway, passing within a short distance of it, has enabled almost all that please to be down at it in about an hour, and has given them a pleasant excursion at a cheap rate, through a delightful country, besides the luxury of fair gardens, on the banks of the Thames, and the contemplation of rich paintings when they get there. Have they availed themselves of these privileges? The palace has only been fairly thrown open this summer and for some time the fact was but little known—yet through spring and summer the resort thither has been constantly increasing; the average number of visitors on Sunday or Monday is now two thousand five hundred, and the amount of them for the month of August was thirty-two thousand!

And how have these swarms of Londoners of all classes behaved? With the exception of some scratches made on the panels of the grand staircase, for the discovery of the perpetrator of which an ominous placard is pasted on the door-post as you enter, offering five pounds reward, but of which slight injury no one can tell the date—the police, who are always on the spot, never having witnessed the doing of it since they were stationed there—I cannot learn that the slightest exhibition of what has been considered the English love of demolition, has been made. Never have I seen, at all times that I have been there, a more orderly or more well-pleased throng of people. I happened accidentally to be there on Whit-Monday, when, besides the railway, upwards of a dozen spring-vans, gaily adorned with ribbons, and blue and red hangings, had brought there their loads of servants and artisans, all with their sweethearts, and in fine spirits for a day's country frolic; and not less than two thousand people were wandering through the house and gardens, yet nothing could be more decorous than their behaviour.

Never, indeed, did I behold a scene which was more beautiful in my eyes, or which more sensibly affected me. Here were thousands of those whose fathers would have far preferred the brutal amusement of the bull-baiting or the cock-pit; who would have made holiday at the boxing-ring, or in guzzling beer in the lowest dens of debauch,—here were they, scattered in companies, and in family groups; fathers, mothers, brothers and sisters, old people, and children of all ages, strolling through the airy gardens, admiring the flowers, or resting on the benches, or watching the swarming shoals of gold and silver fish in the basin of the central fountain, and feeding them with crumbs of bun amid shouts of childish delight. Here were these poor people, set free from the fret and fume, the dust and sweat, and mental and bodily wear and tear of their city trades and domestic cares, well dressed, amongst their more wealthy neighbours, clean, and jocund from the sense of freedom and social affection, treading walks laid down only for royal feet, listening to the lapse of waters intended only for the ears of greatness and high-born beauty, though all constructed by the money of their forefathers; and here were they enjoying all these more than king or cardinal ever could do, beneath a sunny sky, that seemed to smile upon them as if itself rejoiced at the sight of so much happiness.

WILLIAM HOWITT (1792-1879)
Visits to Remarkable Places

THE COURT AT HAMPTON COURT

Close by those meads, for ever crown'd with flow'rs,
Where Thames with pride surveys his rising tow'rs,
There stands a structure of majestic frame,
Which from the neighb'ring Hampton takes its name.
Here Britain's statesmen oft the fall foredoom
Of foreign Tyrants and of Nymphs at home;
Here thou, great ANNA! whom three realms obey,
Dost sometimes counsel take—and sometimes Tea.

Hither the heroes and the nymphs resort,
To taste awhile the pleasures of a Court;
In various talk th' instructive hours they past,
Who gave the ball, or paid the visit last;
One speaks the glory of the British Queen,
And one describes a charming Indian screen;
A third interprets motions, looks, and eyes;
At ev'ry word a reputation dies.
Snuff, or the fan, supply each pause of chat,
With singing, laughing, ogling, and all that.

ALEXANDER POPE (1688-1744)
The Rape of the Lock

RANELAGH AND VAUXHALL

(*The opinions of Miss Lydia Melford*)

The cities of London and Westminster are spread out
into an incredible extent. The streets, squares, rows,
lanes, and alleys, are innumerable. Palaces, public
buildings, and churches rise in every quarter; and,
among these last, St. Paul's appears with the most
astonishing pre-eminence. They say it is not so large as
St. Peter's at Rome; but, for my own part, I can have no
idea of any earthly temple more grand and magnificent.

But even these superb objects are not striking as the
crowds of people that swarm in the streets. I at first
imagined that some great assembly was just dismissed,
and wanted to stand aside till the multitude should pass;
but this human tide continues to flow, without inter-
ruption or abatement, from morn till night. Then there
is such an infinity of gay equipages, coaches, chariots,
chaises, and other carriages, continually rolling and
shifting before your eyes, that one's head grows giddy
looking at them; and the imagination is quite confounded with splendour and variety. Nor is the prospect

by water less grand and astonishing than that by land: you see three stupendous bridges, joining the opposite banks of a broad, deep, and rapid river; so vast, so stately, so elegant, that they seem to be the work of the giants; betwixt them, the whole surface of the Thames is covered with small vessels, barges, boats, and wherries, passing to and fro; and below the three bridges, such a prodigious forest of masts, for miles together, that you would think all the ships in the universe were here assembled. All that you read of wealth and grandeur in the Arabian Nights' Entertainment, and the Persian Tales, concerning Bagdad, Diarbekir, Damascus, Ispahan, and Samarkand, is here realized.

Ranelagh looks like the enchanted palace of a genie, adorned with the most exquisite performances of painting, carving, and gilding, enlightened with a thousand golden lamps, that emulate the noon-day sun; crowded with the great, the rich, the gay, the happy, and the fair; glittering with cloth of gold and silver, lace, embroidery, and precious stones. While these exulting sons and daughters of felicity tread this round of pleasure, or regale in different parties, and separate lodges, with fine imperial tea and other delicious refreshments, their ears are entertained with the most ravishing delights of music both instrumental and vocal. There I heard the famous Tenducci, a thing from Italy—It looks for all the world like a man, though they say it is not. The voice, to be sure, is neither man's nor woman's; but it is more melodious than either; and it warbled so divinely, that, while I listened, I really thought myself in paradise.

At nine o'clock, in a charming moonlight evening, we embarked at Ranelagh for Vauxhall, in a wherry so light and slender that we looked like so many fairies sailing in a nut-shell. My uncle, being apprehensive of catching cold upon the water, went round in the coach, and my aunt would have accompanied him, but he would not suffer me to go by water if she went by land; and there-

fore she favoured us with her company, as she perceived
I had a curiosity to make this agreeable voyage—After
all, the vessel was sufficiently loaded; for, besides the
waterman, there was my brother Jerry, and a friend of
his, one Mr. Barton, a country gentleman, of a good
fortune, who had dined at our house—The pleasure of
this little excursion was, however, damped by my being
sadly frighted at our landing; where there was a terrible
confusion of wherries, and a crowd of people bawling,
and swearing, and quarrelling; nay, a parcel of ugly-
looking fellows came running into the water, and laid
hold of our boat with great violence, to pull it a-shore;
nor would they quit their hold till my brother struck
one of them over the head with his cane.

But this flutter was fully recompensed by the pleasures
of Vauxhall; which I no sooner entered, than I was
dazzled and confounded with the variety of beauties
that rushed all at once upon my eye. Image to yourself
my dear Letty, a spacious garden, part laid out in delightful walks, bounded with high hedges and trees, and
paved with gravel; part exhibiting a wonderful assemblage of the most picturesque and striking objects,
pavilions, lodges, groves, grottoes, lawns, temples, and
cascades; porticos, colonades, and rotundos; adorned
with pillars, statues, and paintings; the whole illuminated with an infinite number of lamps, disposed in
different figures of suns, stars, and constellations; the
place crowded with the gayest company, ranging
through those blissful shades, or supping in different
lodges on cold collations, enlivened with mirth, freedom,
and good humour, and animated by an excellent band of
music. Among the vocal performers I had the happiness
to hear the celebrated Mrs. ———, whose voice was loud
and so shrill, that it made my head ake through excess of
pleasure.

TOBIAS SMOLLETT (1721-1771)
Humphry Clinker

(The views of Lydia Melford's uncle, Matthew Bramble, a testy country-lover and hypochondriac, were by no means the same.)

The diversions of the times are not illsuited to the genius of this incongruous monster, called the public. Give it noise, confusion, glare, and glitter; it has no idea of elegance and propriety—What are the amusements of Ranelagh? One half of the company are following at the other's tails, in an eternal circle; like so many blind asses in an olive-mill, where they can neither discourse, distinguish, nor be distinguished; while the other half are drinking hot water, under the denomination of tea, till nine or ten o'clock at night, to keep them awake for the rest of the evening. As for the orchestra, the vocal music especially, it is well for the performers that they cannot be heard distinctly.

Vauxhall is a composition of baubles, overcharged with paltry ornaments, ill conceived, and poorly executed; without any unity of design, or propriety of disposition. It is an unnatural assembly of objects, fantastically illuminated in broken masses; seemingly contrived to dazzle the eyes and divert the imagination of the vulgar —Here a wooden lion, there a stone statue; in one place, a range of things like coffeehouse boxes, covered a-top; in another, a parcel of ale-house benches; in a third, a puppet-show representation of a tin cascade; in a fourth, a gloomy cave of a circular form, like a sepulchral vault half lighted; in a fifth, a scanty flip of grass-plat, that would not afford pasture sufficient for an ass's colt. The walks, which nature seems to have intended for solitude, shade, and silence, are filled with crowds of noisy people, sucking up the nocturnal rheums of an aguish climate; and through these gay scenes, a few lamps glimmer like so many farthing candles.

When I see a number of well dressed people, of both sexes, sitting on the covered benches, exposed to the eyes of the mob; and, which is worse, to the cold, raw, night-air, devouring sliced beef, and swilling port, and punch, and cyder, I can't help compassionating their temerity; while I despise their want of taste and decorum; but, when they course along those damp and gloomy walks, or crowd together upon the wet gravel, without any other cover than the cope of Heaven, listening to a song, which one half of them cannot possibly hear, how can I help supposing they are actually possessed by a spirit, more absurd and pernicious than anything we meet with in the precincts of Bedlam? In all probability, the proprietors of this, and other public gardens of inferior note, in the skirts of the metropolis, are, in some shape, connected with the faculty of physic, and the company of undertakers; for, considering that eagerness in the pursuit of what is called pleasure, which now predominates through every rank and denomination of life, I am persuaded that more gouts, rheumatisms, catarrhs, and consumptions are caught in these nocturnal pastimes, *sub deo*, than from all the risques and accidents to which a life of toil and danger is exposed.

TOBIAS SMOLLETT (1721-1771)
Humphry Clinker

ROTTEN ROW

There's a tempting bit of greenery—of *rus in urbe*
     scenery—
That's haunted by the London " upper ten ";
Where, by exercise on horseback, an equestrian may force
     back
Little fits of *tedium vitae* now and then.

Oh! the times that I have been there, and the types that I
    have seen there
Of that gorgeous Cockney animal, the " swell ";
And the scores of pretty riders (both patricians and out-
    siders)
Are considerably more than I can tell.

When first the warmer weather brought these people all
    together,
And the crowds began to thicken through the Row,
I reclined against the railing on a sunny day, inhaling
All the spirits that the breezes could bestow.

And the riders and the walkers and the thinkers and the
    talkers
Left me lonely in the thickest of the throng,
Not a touch upon my shoulder—not a nod from one be-
    holder—
As the stream of Art and Nature went along.

But I brought away one image, from that fashionable
    scrimmage,
Of a figure and a face—ah, such a face!
Love has photograph'd the features of that loveliest of
    creatures
On my memory, as Love alone can trace.

Did I hate the little dandy in the whiskers (they were
    sandy),
Whose absurd salute was honour'd by a smile?
Did I marvel at his rudeness in presuming on her good-
    ness,
When she evidently loathed him all the while?

Oh the hours that I have wasted, the regrets that I have
    tasted,
Since the day (it seems a century ago)
When my heart was won instanter by a lady in a canter,
On a certain sunny day in Rotten Row!

HENRY S. LEIGH (1837-1883)
Carols of Cockayne, 1874

DAMES AND DAMASKS

Where Kensington high o'er the neighb'ring lands
'Midst greens and sweets, a Regal fabrick, stands,
And sees each spring, luxuriant in her bowers,
A snow of blossoms, and a wilde of flowers,
The Dames of Britain oft in crowds repair
To gravel walks, and unpolluted air.
Here, while the Town in damps and darkness lies,
They breathe in sun-shine, and see azure skies;
Each walk, with robes of various dyes bespread,
Seems from afar a moving Tulip-bed,
Where rich Brocades and glossy Damasks glow,
And Chints, the rival of the show'ry Bow.

THOMAS TICKELL (1686-1740)
Kensington Gardens

Tickell's "Regal Fabrick" is the essentially domestic Palace of
Kensington, whose country-house aspect and mellow brick-work,
facing Kensington Gardens and Hyde Park, are well seen on a sunny
autumn or winter afternoon as well as amid the "snow of blossoms."
It was built for William III as an escape, since he was asthmatic, from
the river-mists of Whitehall, and much used, with its gardens expanded
by Queen Anne. Its height of glory came when Queen Caroline of
Anspach, consort of George II, summoned the wits and beauties to her
parties and parades. The "moving Tulip-bed" of human elegance
swayed amid these flowers for which the gardens are still famous.
The Orangery and some of the gardens are open to the public. So are
many rooms of the old Palace, including Queen Victoria's nursery and
the room in which she received the news of her succession. The
London Museum is housed there and brings many phases of London
history to the eye.

IN KENSINGTON GARDENS

In this lone, open glade I lie,
Screen'd by deep boughs on either hand;
And at its end, to stay the eye,
Those black-crown'd, red-boled pine-trees stand!

Birds here make song, each bird has his,
Across the girdling city's hum.
How green under the boughs it is!
How thick the tremulous sheep-cries come!

Sometimes a child will cross the glade
To take his nurse his broken toy;
Sometimes a thrush flit overhead
Deep in her unknown day's employ.

Here at my feet what wonders pass,
What endless, active life is here!
What blowing daisies, fragrant grass!
An air-stirr'd forest, fresh and clear.

Scarce fresher is the mountain-sod
Where the tired angler lies, stretch'd out,
And, eased of basket and of rod,
Counts his day's spoil, the spotted trout.

In the huge world, which roars hard by,
Be others happy if they can!
But in my helpless cradle I
Was breathed on by the rural Pan.

I, on men's impious uproar hurl'd,
Think often, as I hear them rave,
That peace has left the upper world
And now keeps only in the grave.

Yet here is peace for ever new!
When I who watch them am away,
Still all things in this glade go through
The changes of their quiet day.

Then to their happy rest they pass!
The flowers upclose, the birds are fed,
The night comes down upon the grass,
The child sleeps warmly in his bed.

Calm soul of all things! make it mine
To feel, amid the city's jar,
That there abides a peace of thine,
Man did not make, and cannot mar.

The will to neither strive nor cry,
The power to feel with others give!
Calm, calm me more! nor let me die
Before I have begun to live.

MATTHEW ARNOLD (1828-1888)
Poems

FROLICS ON THE LAWN

Ye belles, and ye flirts, and ye pert little things,
　　Who trip in this frolicksome round,
Pray tell me from whence this impertinence springs,
　　The sexes at once to confound?
What means the cock'd hat, and the masculine air,
　　With each motion design'd to perplex?
Bright eyes were intended to languish, not stare,
　　And softness the test of your sex.

The girl, who on beauty depends for support,
　　May call every art to her aid;
The bosom display'd, and the petticoat short,
　　Are samples she gives of her trade.

TO MOVE OR NOT TO MOVE?

As the London County Council gradually rebuilds the East End, public inquiries are held to find the views of those who may be displaced. Amid the dingy old housing of Planet Street, E. family groups discuss their problem. Banting seems unpopular, whatever the views on housing.

SWANS AT LOW TIDE

The fact that the Thames is tidal up to Teddington creates constant variation of the river-side scene. Low-tide is feeding-time for many birds. The swans have been Londoners for centuries and a theatre next door to Shakespeare's Globe was named The Swan in their honour.

SURVEY OF GREENWICH

At Greenwich was the Palace of Placentia, birth-place of Henry VIII and Elizabeth I. Inigo Jones built a home there for Anne of Denmark, and Charles II began a new palace. The magnificent buildings now include the Maritime Museum, a Naval School and the Painted Hall.

But you, on whom fortune indulgently smiles,
  And whom pride has preserv'd from the snare,
Should slily attack us with coyness, and wiles,
  Not with open and insolent war.

The Venus, whose statue delights all mankind,
  Shrinks modestly back from the view,
And kindly should seem by the artist design'd
  To serve as a model for you.
Then learn, with her beauty, to copy her air,
  Nor venture too much to reveal:
Our fancies will paint what you cover with care,
  And double each charm you conceal.

The blushes of Morn, and the mildness of May,
  Are charms which no art can procure:
O be but yourselves, and our homage we pay,
  And your empire is solid and sure.
But if, Amazon-like, you attack your gallants,
  And put us in fear of our lives,
You may do very well for sisters and aunts,
  But, believe me, you'll never be wives.

WILLIAM WHITEHEAD (1715-1785)
A Song for Ranelagh Gardens

This "warning to wantons" is the work of a Poet Laureate, a Cambridge tutor, and a friend of David Garrick. The Laureates of the Eighteenth Century, Nahum Tate, Nicholas Rowe, Laurence Eusden, Colley Cibber, William Whitehead, Thomas Warton, and Henry James Pye, were far from the summits of English poetry. After these men of the foot-hills, the heights were approached by the appointment of Southey in 1813 and reached when Wordsworth and Tennyson succeeded him.

OUT INTO ESSEX

" The vagrant visitor erstwhile,"
  My colour-plate books says to me,
" Could wend by hedgerow-side and stile,
From Benfleet down to Leigh-on-sea."

And as I turn the colour-plates
  Edwardian Essex opens wide,
Mirrored in ponds and seen through gates,
  Sweet uneventful countryside.

Like streams the little by-roads run
  Through oats and barley round a hill
To where blue willows catch the sun
  By some white weather-boarded mill.

" A Summer Idyll Matching Tye "
  " At Havering-atte-Bower, the Stocks "
And cobbled pathways lead the eye
  To cottage doors and hollyhocks.

Far Essex,—fifty miles away
  The level wastes of sucking mud
Where distant barges high with hay
  Come sailing in upon the flood.

Near Essex of the River Lea
  And anglers out with hook and worm
And Epping Forest glades where we
  Had beanfeasts with my father's firm.

At huge and convoluted pubs
  They used to set us down from brakes
In that half-land of football clubs
  Which London near the Forest makes.

The deepest Essex few explore
　　Where steepest thatch is sunk in flowers
And out of elm and sycamore
　　Rise flinty fifteenth-century towers.

I see the little branch line go
　　By white farms roofed in red and brown,
The old Great Eastern winding slow
　　To some forgotten country town.

Now harrow chokes the railway track,
　　Brambles obliterate the stile,
No motor coach can take me back
　　To that Edwardian " erstwhile."

JOHN BETJEMAN (1906-　　)
Collected Poems

BOATS ON THE POND

The sailing of what a contemptuous person might call "children's
boats" by middle-aged and even elderly men is one of London's
week-end spectacles. Norman Collins here presents the scene that can
be viewed on any fine Sunday morning on the pond below Highgate
Hill especially favoured by such devotees of the sport as his Mr.
Privett with his treasured new vessel, *Dianthe*.

There is no place in the world like the Highgate Ponds.
Especially early on a Sunday morning. There may be
other places that are more central. And more fashionable. Like the Round Pond in Kensington Gardens, for
instance. But fashion never had any connection with
serious yachting. And centralness is exactly what isn't
wanted. There is no real feeling of escape, of being
away from it all, with just the wind in your face and the
splash and ripple of water coming up at you, if you can
hear the sound of motor horns from all quarters and see
the red sides of the buses as they go trundling along
to Knightsbridge.

Up at Highgate, there is nothing but green Nature.
Great park-land trees. And rolling meadows. And the
placid, duck-bearing surface of the lake. Standing on
the little wooden jetty there is not a house to be seen.
Not one. Not even in the misty distance. Just reed-beds
and osiers. And willow-herb. And the massive forest
skyline of Ken Wood where the whole dangling necklace
of ponds begins in a dark, ferny grotto. Admittedly, by
turning round you can see the top stages of the L.C.C.
diving-board over in the bathing-pool across the path.
That belongs to a lower order of things altogether. And
on a fine day it can become quite unpleasantly crowded.
But you can't expect everything. Even the farthest of
the ponds, the fenced-in one, with its coot and moor-
hens, its dragon-flies and its water-rats, is only five miles
from the City. And at any time up to about nine-thirty
you've got the whole thing entirely to yourself. It's like
being a great landowner. But without the threat of
death duties, of course.

Mr. Privett was the first person up there. At least he
thought he was until a tall, sad-looking man with a
large, damp dog passed him disconsolately homeward
bound already. Anyhow, the pond was all his. It was
like a one-man regatta. And it nearly had its incident.
The first racing fatality of the season. Because the
Dianthe was longer than Mr. Privett had realised. And
heavier. A good fourteen ounces more of her than there
had been of *Daisy II.* Also, the keel was entirely different.
It was a scooped-out, backward-facing, C-shaped affair
like modern sculpture. The bit that Mr. Privett tried to
get hold of wasn't there. When he grabbed, he missed.
And, when he missed, he went forward with his left leg
in the water right up to his thigh. The little lozenge
with the word " Dunlop " on the top of his wader was
completely covered.

But he clambered back on to the jetty all right. Heaved
himself up with the thick bamboo rod with the rudder

ferrule on the end. And after that he was extra careful.
For a model yachtsman to fall in is to risk being made a
laughing stock. He had seen it happen. And he knew.
It wasn't easy to be careful, however. He was too excited.
Trembling all over, as he finally lowered the *Dianthe*
into her own native element. And not only excited.
Slow as well. He had to keep on stepping-back to admire.
First, stepping back. Then leaning forward to stroke.
Fondle. Caress. He might have been a bridegroom.

But science, cold and analytical, has a way of cutting
across life's rapture. When Mr. Privett did finally push
the *Dianthe* off from the jetty—and it was the merest
nudge, a request rather than an order—he saw at once
that she wasn't sailing properly. Instead of sliding art-
fully, cheek-by-cheek alongside the wind, she turned
into it, fighting. She shuddered. Her sails flapped madly.
She shipped water. For a moment the *Dianthe* had ceased
to be beautiful.

It was nothing serious, however. No basic fault on the
drawing-board. Nothing that Mr. Privett himself
couldn't put right in a jiffy. And, in a way, he loved the
Dianthe all the more because of it. It showed that she
had her secrets. Temperament. A streak of over-
comable obstinacy somewhere. And he alone understood
her. Give her to any other man, no matter how experienced, and she would make the same lamentable
exhibition of herself.

By ten o'clock, the *Dianthe* had made her measure of
the pond. Running with the wind. And against it. She
was big. Unbelievably big. A good head taller than Mr.
Privett himself. She towered. And, now that she was
tamed, disciplined, she was unbelievably beautiful
again. She became one with the water. Temporarily
dividing, rather than cutting through it. As Mr. Privett
hurried along the bank to her, she might have been a
huge, white bird, a swan straight out of legend, that he
was standing there so romantically to meet.

But romantic or not, he was sweating. After all, he had run three times round the pond already. Before he left home Mrs. Privett had reminded him about his thick undervest. The woollen one. And he had not disobeyed. In consequence, he might have been on fire underneath his flannel shirt, his reefer-jacket and his raincoat. He could feel ants crawling all over him. There was nothing for it but to take a breather. After he had swabbed the *Dianthe* out, even using his handkerchief to get up the last tiny droplets, he sat there on the jetty, his collar undone and the *Dianthe* on dry dock beside him, an entirely happy man. He basked.

By eleven o'clock there was still no sign of Mr. Bloot. But the jetty had become populated by now. The members of the N.L.M.Y.R.A. were there in force. All five of them. And all wearing the little flag and anchor badge that matched Mr. Privett's own. As a reunion it could not have been more cordial. There were wet handshakes all round. The North London Model Yacht Racing Association was a body of nice steady men. They were genuinely pleased to see Mr. Privett. Most sailing yacht owners are somewhere on the other side of middle age. Distinctly elderly some of them. And prolonged absence from the jetty may mean anything. Even the worst.

Also, they were openly eager to see the *Dianthe*. They crouched round her on their haunches, gum boots creaking, like a group of elderly, heavily-breathing infants. At one point Mr. Privett got elbowed completely out of it. But he didn't care. There is nothing in life more profoundly satisfying than to be envied for one's possessions.

And it was only natural that the *Dianthe* should cause a bit of a stir. She was a stranger to these parts. A complete stranger. It was from somewhere up north by Bridlington that Mr. Lumley had bought her. All her previous sailing had been under steely grey skies, with the threat of sudden squalls and a hint of ice in the rigging. This morning's was her first voyage in the balmy, southern lagoons of Highgate. Blue sky. A gentle breeze. Barometer high. Temperature in the upper sixties. It might have been angel-fish and coral gardens rather than sheer London clay over which she was sailing.

Not that the water was without its dangers. Every five minutes or so a new menace arrived. And not merely the litter of small craft that children with parents kept bringing. There were unpleasant, mechanical looking men with bottles of methylated spirit and petrol, bent over motor boats. Miniature two-stroke engines that roared and crackled like machine-guns and then spat themselves out in fury somewhere in the mid-channel. Hydroplanes with whirling aeroplane propellers that went bouncing along the surface like demented tea trays. Scale models of gunboats with bows like an ice-breaker's, churning up the surface, ready and waiting to ram anything with sails.

NORMAN COLLINS (1907-)
Bond Street Story

Shops

THE GAY APPRENTICE

There was a prentice living in our town
Worked in the victualling trade, and he was brown,
Brown as a berry; spruce and short he stood,
As gallant as a goldfinch in the wood.
Black were his locks and combed with fetching skill;
He danced so merrily, with such a will,
That he was known as revelling Peterkin.
He was as full of love, as full of sin
As hives are full of honey, and as sweet.
Lucky the wench that Peter chanced to meet.
At every wedding he would sing and hop

And he preferred the tavern to the shop.
  Whenever any pageant or procession
Came down Cheapside, goodbye to his profession!
He'd leap out of the shop to see the sight
And join the dance and not come back that night.
He gathered round him many of his sort
And made a gang for dancing, song and sport.
They used to make appointments where to meet
For playing dice in such and such a street,
And no apprentice had a touch so nice
As Peter when it came to casting dice.
Yet he was free with money and persisted
In being reckless rather than close-fisted.
Of this his master soon became aware;
Many a time he found the till was bare,
For when apprentices are caught in whirls
Of dancing-parties, dice, and easy girls,

They cost their master's shop a pretty penny;
Little the minstrelsy for him, if any.
Riot and theft can interchange and are
Convertible by fiddle and guitar.
Revels and honesty among the poor
Are pretty soon at strife, you may be sure.

This jolly prentice, doing little good,
Stayed with his master through his prenticehood
Though scolded night and morning without fail
And often led with minstrelsy to jail.

But in the end his master, taking thought
While casting up what he had sold and bought,
Hit on a proverb as he sat and pored:
" Throw out a rotten apple from the hoard
Or it will rot the others," said the tag.
So with a squandering servant; let him brag
And he'll corrupt all servants in the place.
Far better to dismiss him in disgrace.

His master, then, gave Peterkin the sack
With curses and forbade him to come back,
And so this jolly prentice left his shop.
Now let him revel all the night, or stop.

GEOFFREY CHAUCER (1345-1400)
The Canterbury Tales (*The Cook's Tale*)
translated by NEVILL COGHILL

JACOBEAN SHOPS

There flourished in the city of London an ingenious but
whimsical and self-opinioned mechanic, much devoted
to abstract studies, David Ramsay by name, who, whether
recommended by his great skill in his profession, as the
courtiers alleged, or, as was murmured among his
neighbours, by his birthplace, in the good town of
Dalkeith, near Edinburgh, held in James's household the
post of maker of watches and horologes to his Majesty.

He scorned not, however, to keep open shop within Temple Bar, a few yards to the eastward of Saint Dunstan's Church.

The shop of a London tradesman at that time, as it may be supposed, was something very different from those we now see in the same locality. The goods were exposed to sale in cases, only defended from the weather by a covering of canvas, and the whole resembled the stalls and booths now erected for the temporary accommodation of dealers at a country fair, rather than the established emporium of a respectable citizen. But most of the shopkeepers of note, and David Ramsay amongst others, had their booth connected with a small apartment which opened backward from it, and bore the same resemblance to the front shop that Robinson Crusoe's cavern did to the tent which he erected before it. To this Master Ramsay was often accustomed to retreat to the labour of his abstruse calculations; for he aimed at improvement and discoveries in his own art, and sometimes pushed his researches, like Napier and other mathematicians of the period, into abstract science. When thus engaged, he left the outer posts of his commercial establishment to be maintained by two stout-bodied and strong-voiced apprentices, who kept up the cry of "What d'ye lack? what d'ye lack?" accompanied with the appropriate recommendations of the articles in which they dealt. This direct and personal application for custom to those who chanced to pass by is now, we believe, limited to Monmouth Street (if it still exists even in that repository of ancient garments), under the guardianship of the scattered remnant of Israel. But at the time we are speaking of, it was practised alike by Jew and Gentile, and served, instead of all our present newspaper puffs and advertisements, to solicit the attention of the public in general, and of friends in particular, to the unrivalled excellence of the goods, which they offered to sale upon such easy terms that it might fairly appear that the venders had rather a view to the general service of the public than to their own particular advantage.

The verbal proclaimers of the excellence of their commodities had this advantage over those who, in the present day, use the public papers for the same purpose, that they could in many cases adapt their address to the peculiar appearance and apparent taste of the passengers. This direct and personal mode of invitation to customers became, however, a dangerous temptation to the young wags who were employed in the task of solicitation during the absence of the principal person interested in the traffic; and, confiding in their numbers and civic union, the 'prentices of London were often seduced into taking liberties with the passengers, and exercising their wit at the expense of those whom they had no hopes of converting into customers by their eloquence. If this were resented by any act of violence, the inmates of each shop were ready to pour forth in succour; and, in the words of an old song which Dr. Johnson was used to hum,—

> " Up then rose the 'prentices all,
>   Living in London, both proper and tall."

Desperate riots often arose on such occasions, especially when the Templars, or other youths connected with the aristocracy, were insulted, or conceived themselves to be so. Upon such occasions bare steel was frequently opposed to the clubs of the citizens, and death sometimes ensued on both sides. The tardy and inefficient police of the time had no other resource than by the alderman of the ward calling out the householders, and putting a stop to the strife by overpowering numbers, as the Capulets and Montagues are separated upon the stage.

SIR WALTER SCOTT (1771-1832)
The Fortunes of Nigel

WINDOW-SHOPPING

The next step is to the pastry-cook's, where the plain bun is still the pleasantest thing in our eyes, from its respectability in those of childhood. The pastry, less patronised by judicious mothers, is only so much elegant indigestion; yet it is not easy to forget the pleasure of nibbling away the crust all round a raspberry or currant tart, in order to enjoy the three or four delicious semicircular bites at the fruity plentitude remaining. There is a custard with a wall of paste round it, which provokes a siege of this kind; and the cheese-cake has its amenities of approach. The acid flavour is a relief to the mawkishness of the biffin or pressed baked apple, and an addition to the glib and quivering lightness of the jelly. Twelfthcake, which, when cut, looks like the side of a rich pit of earth covered with snow, is pleasant from warmer associations.

Confectionery does not seem in the same request as of old. Its paint has hurt its reputation. Yet the schoolboy has still much to say for its humbler suavities, such as elecampane, hardbake, bull's-eyes, comfits, the rocky crystals of sugar-candy, the smooth twist of barley-sugar, which looks like a petrified stream of tea, and the melting powderiness of peppermint. There used to be a mystery called mimpins, which, as Dr. Johnson would say, made a pretty sweet-meat. Kisses are very amiable and allegorical. Eight or ten of them, judiciously wrapped up in pieces of letter-paper, have saved many a loving heart the trouble of a less eloquent billet-doux. Candid citron we look upon to be the very acme and atticism of confectionery grace. Preserves are too much of a good thing, with the exception of the jams that retain their fruit-skins. " *Jam satis.*" They qualify the cloying. Yet marmalade must not be passed over in these

times, when it has been raised to the dignity of the peer-
age. There is a Duke of Marmalade in Hayti, and a
Count of Lemonade—so called, we presume, from places
in which those eminent relishes are manufactured. We
have not yet heard of a Lord Viscount Jam.

* * *

We have unaccountably omitted two excellent shops—
the fruiterer's and the sculptor's. There is great beauty,
as well as other agreeableness, in a well-disposed fruiterer's window. Here are the round piled-up oranges,
deepening almost into red, and heavy with juice; the
apple, with its brown red cheek, as if it had slept in the
sun; the pear, swelling downwards, and provocative of
a huge bite in the side; thronging grapes, like so many
tight little bags of wine; the peach, whose handsome
leathern coat strips off so finely; the pearly or ruby-like
currants, heaped in light, long baskets; the red little
mouthfuls of strawberries, ditto; the larger purple ones
of plums; cherries, whose old comparison with lips is
better than anything new; mulberries, dark and rich
with juice, fit to grow over what Homer calls the deep
black-watered fountains; the swelling pomp of melons;
the rough, inexorable-looking cocoa-nut, milky at heart;
the elaborate elegance of walnuts; the quaint cashoo-
nut; almonds, figs, raisins, tamarinds, green leaves: in
short,

" Whatever Earth, all-bearing mother, yields
    In Indian East or West, or middle shore
    In Pontus or the Punic coast, or where
    Alcinous reign'd; fruit of all kinds, in coat
    Rough, or smooth rind, or bearded husk, or shell."
                                                MILTON

There is something of more refined service in waiting
upon a lady in a fruit-shop than in a pastry-cook's. The
eating of tarts, as Sir Walter Scott handsomely saith in
his " Life of Dryden " (who used to enjoy them, it seems,
in company with " Madam Reeves "), is " no inelegant
pleasure "; but there is something still more graceful
and suitable in the choosing of the natural fruit, with its
rosy lips and red cheeks. A white hand looks better on
a basket of plums than in the doubtful touching of
syrupy and sophisticated pastry.

LEIGH HUNT (1784-1859)
Essays

DAYS AND SEASONS

Experienc'd men, inur'd to city ways,
Need not the Calendar to count their days.
When through the town with slow and solemn air,
Led by the nostril, walks the muzzled bear;
Behind him moves majestically dull,
The pride of Hockley-hole, the surly bull;
Learn hence the periods of the week to name,
Mondays and Thursdays are the days of game.

When fishy stalls with double store are laid;
The golden-belly'd carp, the broad-finn'd maid,
Red-speckled trouts, the salmon's silver joul,
The joynted lobster, and unscaly soale,
The luscious 'scallops, to allure the tastes
Of rigid zealots to delicious fasts;
Wednesdays and Fridays you'll observe from hence,
Days, when our sires were doom'd to abstinence.

When dirty waters from balconies drop,
And dex'trous damsels twirle the sprinkling mop,
And cleanse the spatter'd sash, and scrub the stairs;
Know Saturday's conclusive morn appears.

Successive crys the seasons' change declare,
And mark the monthly progress of the year.

Hark, how the streets with treble voices ring,
To sell the bounteous product of the spring!
Sweet-smelling flow'rs, and elder's early bud,
With nettle's tender shoots, to cleanse the blood:
And when June's thunder cools the sultry skies,
Ev'n Sundays are prophan'd by mackrell cries.

Wallnuts the fruit'rer's hand, in autumn, stain,
Blue plumbs and juicy pears augment his gain;
Next oranges the longing boys entice,
To trust their copper fortunes to the dice.

When rosemary, and bays, the Poet's crown,
Are bawl'd, in frequent cries, through all the town,
Then judge the festival of Christmas near,
Christmas, the joyous period of the year.
Now with bright holly all your temples strow,
With lawrel green, and sacred mistletoe.
Now, heav'n-born Charity, thy blessings shed;
Bid meagre Want uprear her sickly head:
Bid shiv'ring limbs be warm; let plenty's bowle
In humble roofs make glad the needy soul.
See, see, the heav'n-born maid her blessings shed;
Lo! meagre Want uprears her sickly head;
Cloath'd are the naked, and the needy glad,
While selfish Avarice alone is sad.

JOHN GAY (1685-1732)
Trivia: or the Art of Walking the Streets of London

JANE AUSTEN, SHOPPING, GOING TO DENTIST, AND SEEING PLAYS

Oh, dear me! When shall I ever have done? We did go to Layton and Shear's before breakfast. Very pretty English poplins at 4s. 3d.; Irish ditto at 6s.; more pretty, certainly—beautiful.

Fanny and the two girls are gone to take places for to-night at Covent Garden; *Clandestine Marriage* and *Midas*.

The latter will be a fine show for L. and M. They revelled last night in *Don Juan*, whom we left in Hell at half-past eleven. We had Scaramouch and a ghost, and were delighted. I speak of *them*; *my* delight was very tranquill and the rest of us were sober-minded. *Don Juan* was the last of three musical things. *Five Hours at Brighton*, in three acts—of which one was over before we arrived, none the worse—and the *Beehive*, rather less flat and trumpery.

Four o'clock.—We are just come back from doing Mr. Tickars, Miss Hare, and Mr. Spence. Mr. Hall is here, and, while Fanny is under his hands, I will try to write a little more.

Miss Hare had some pretty caps, and is to make me one like one of them, only white satin instead of blue. It will be white satin and lace, and a little white flower perking out of the left ear, like Harriot Byron's feather. I have allowed her to go as far as £1 16s. My gown is to be trimmed everywhere with white ribbon plaited on somehow or other. She says it will look well. I am not sanguine. They trim with white very much.

I learnt from Mrs. Tickars' young lady, to my high amusement, that the stays now are not made to force the bosom up at all; that was a very unbecoming, unnatural fashion. I was really glad to hear that they are not to be so much off the shoulders as they were.

Going to Mr. Spence's was a sad business and cost us many tears; unluckily we were obliged to go a second time before he could do more than just look. We went first at half-past twelve and afterwards at three; papa with us each time; and, alas! we are to go again tomorrow.

Lizzy is not finished yet. There have been no teeth taken out, however, nor will be, I believe, but he finds *hers* in a very bad state, and seems to think particularly ill of their durableness. They have been all cleaned, *hers* filed, and are to be filed again. There is a very sad hole between two of her front teeth.

Thursday morning, half-past seven.—Up and dressed and downstairs in order to finish my letter in time for the parcel. At eight I have an appointment with Madame B., who wants to show me something downstairs. At nine we are to set off for Grafton House, and get that over before breakfast. Edward is so kind as to walk there with us. We are to be at Mr. Spence's again at 11.5; from that time shall be driving about I suppose till four o'clock at least. We are, if possible, to call on Mrs. Tilson.

Mr. Hall was very punctual yesterday, and curled me out at a great rate. I thought its look hideous, and longed for a snug cap instead, but my companions silenced me by their admiration. I had only a bit of velvet round my head. I did not catch cold, however. The weather is all in my favour. I have no pain in my face since I left you.

We had very good places in the box next the stage-box, front and second row; the three old ones behind of course. I was particularly disappointed at seeing nothing of Mr. Crabbe. I felt sure of him when I saw that the boxes were fitted up with crimson velvet. The new Mr. Terry was Lord Ogleby, and Henry thinks he may do; but there was no acting more than moderate, and I was as much amused by the remembrances connected with *Midas* as with any part of it. The girls were very much delighted, but still prefer *Don Juan*; and I must say that I have seen nobody on the stage who has been a more interesting character than that compound of cruelty and lust.

I long to have you hear Mr. H.'s opinion of *P and P.*[1] His admiring my Elizabeth so much is particularly welcome to me.

Instead of saving my superfluous wealth for you to spend, I am going to treat myself with spending it my-

[1] Pride and Prejudice

self. I hope, at least, that I shall find some poplin at Layton and Shear's that will tempt me to buy it. If I do, it shall be sent to Chawton, as half will be for you; for I depend upon your being so kind as to accept it, being the main point. It will be a great pleasure to me. Don't say a word. I only wish you could choose too. I shall send twenty yards.

(Henrietta Street, W.C. Sept. 15, 1813. 8.30 a.m.)

JANE AUSTEN (1775-1817)
Letters

AT MRS. TINCKHAM'S

In the main streets of central London the great stores constantly expand their premises and increase their turn-over: in the suburban High Streets the "multiples" or "chain stores" thrive and increase. Yet the small shop-keeper seems to be indestructible. In the little streets that lead into the High Street he or she (or often both) maintains in cramped but well-stocked premises a service of general provision such as one might expect to find in a village. Even in Mayfair itself these village-shops remain. They are centres of gossip and conversation where the purchaser enjoys an atmosphere entirely different from that of a chain store. The owner's personality is one of the assets of the business.

In the middle of London, especially in part of the area west of Tottenham Court Road, a district with a Bohemian reputation and a shabby, crumbling look, a district so central that one would expect high site values and busy exploitation of those positions, there are still many "undeveloped" streets containing small shops whose continuance may puzzle the passer-by since there is no sign of abundant custom. Only an occasional individual drifts in and out. The articles for sale are miscellaneous and sometimes a little mysterious. Having often passed by this kind of shop with curiosity I was the more amused and impressed by the description of one of them and of its proprietress which I met in a novel by Iris Murdoch.

Mrs. Tinckham keeps a newspaper shop in the neighbourhood of Charlotte Street. It's a dusty, dirty, nasty-

looking corner shop, with a cheap advertisement board
outside it, and it sells papers in various languages, and
women's magazines, and Westerns and Science fiction
and Amazing Stories. At least these articles are displayed for sale in chaotic piles, though I have never seen
anyone buy anything in Mrs. Tinckham's shop except
ice cream, which is also for sale, and the *Evening News*.
Most of the literature lies there year after year, fading in
the sun, and is only disturbed when Mrs. Tinckham
herself has a fit of reading, which she does from time to
time, and picks out some Western, yellow with age, only
to declare half-way through that she's read it before but
had quite forgotten. She must by now have read the
whole of her stock, which is limited and slow to increase.
I've seen her sometimes looking at French newspapers,
though she professes not to know French, but perhaps
she is just looking at the pictures. Besides the ice-cream
container there is a little iron table and two chairs, and
on a shelf above there are red and green non-alcoholic
drinks in bottles. Here I have spent many peaceful
hours.

Another peculiarity of Mrs. Tinckham's shop is that it
is full of cats. An ever-increasing family of tabbies,
sprung from one enormous matriarch, sit about upon the
counter and on the empty shelves, somnolent and con-
templative, their amber eyes narrowed and winking in
the sun, a reluctant slit of liquid in an expanse of hot fur.
When I come in, one often leaps down and on to my knee,
where it sits for a while in a sedate objective way, before
slinking into the street and along by the shop fronts.
But I have never met one of these animals farther than
ten yards away from the shop. In the midst sits Mrs.
Tinckham herself, smoking a cigarette. She is the only
person I know who is literally a chain-smoker. She
lights each one from the butt of the last; how she
lights the first one of the day remains to me a mystery,
for she never seems to have any matches in the house

when I ask her for one. I once arrived to find her in
great distress because her current cigarette had fallen
into a cup of coffee and she had no fire to light another.
Perhaps she smokes all night, or perhaps there is an un-
dying cigarette which burns eternally in her bedroom.
An enamel basin at her feet is filled, usually to over-
flowing, with cigarette ends; and beside her on the
counter is a little wireless which is always on, very
softly and inaudibly, so that a sort of murmurous music
accompanies Mrs. Tinckham as she sits, wreathed in
cigarette smoke, among the cats.

I came in and sat down as usual at the iron table, and
lifted a cat from the nearest shelf on to my knee. Like a
machine set in motion it began to purr. I gave Mrs.
Tinckham my first spontaneous smile of the day. She is
what Finn calls a funny old specimen, but she has been
very kind to me, and I never forget kindness.

" Well, now, back again," said Mrs. Tinckham, laying
aside Amazing Stories, and she turned the wireless down
a bit more until it was just a mumble in the background.

" Yes, unfortunately," I said. " Mrs. Tinck, what about
a glass of something? "

For a long time I have kept a stock of whisky with
Mrs. Tinckham in case I ever need a medicinal drink, in
quiet surroundings, in central London, out of hours.
By now they were open, but I needed the soothing peace
of Mrs. Tinckham's shop, with the purring cat and the
whispering wireless and Mrs. Tinckham like an earth
goddess surrounded by incense. When I first devised this
plan I used to mark the bottle after every drink, but this
was before I knew Mrs. Tinckham well. She is equal to
a law of nature in respect of her reliability. She can keep
counsel too. I once overheard one of her odder-looking
clients, who had been trying to pump her about something, shout out, " You are pathologically discreet! "
and this is how she is.

I suspect indeed that this is the secret of Mrs. Tinck-

ham's success. Her shop serves as what is known as an
"accommodation address," and is a rendezvous for
people who like to be very secretive about their affairs.
I sometimes wonder how much Mrs. Tinckham knows
about the business of her customers. When I am away
from her I feel sure that she cannot be so naïve as not to
have some sort of appreciation of what is going on under
her nose. When I am with her, she looks so plump and
vague, and blinks in a way so much like one of her cats,
that I am filled with doubt. There are moments when,
out of the corner of my eye, I seem to see a look of acute
intelligence upon her face; but however fast I turn
about I can never surprise any expression there except
one of beaming and motherly solicitude and more or
less vacant concern. Whatever may be the truth, one
thing is certain, that no one will ever know it. The
police have long ago given up questioning Mrs. Tinckham. It was time lost. However much or little she
knows, she has never in my experience, displayed either
for profit or for effect any detailed acquaintance with the
little world that circulates round her shop. A woman who
does not talk is a jewel in velvet. I am devoted to Mrs.
Tinckham.

IRIS MURDOCH (1919-   )
Under the Net

Riverside

RIVERSIDE WEDDING

Calm was the day, and through the trembling air
Sweet-breathing Zephyrus did softly play—
A gentle spirit, that lightly did delay
Hot Titan's beams, which then did glisten fair
When I, (whom sullen care,
Through discontent of my long fruitless stay
In princes' court, and expectation vain
Of idle hopes, which still do fly away
Like empty shadows, did afflict my brain)
Walk'd forth to ease my pain
Along the shore of silver-streaming Thames;
Whose rutty bank, the which his river hems,
Was painted all with variable flowers,
And all the meads adorn'd with dainty gems
Fit to deck maidens' bowers,
And crown their paramours
Against the bridal day, which is not long:
   Sweet Thames! run softly, till I end my song.

There in a meadow by the river's side
A flock of nymphs I chanced to espy,
All lovely daughters of the flood thereby,
With goodly greenish locks all loose untied
As each had been a bride;
And each one had a little wicker basket
Made of fine twigs, entrailed curiously.
In which they gather'd flowers to fill their flasket
And with fine fingers cropt full feateously
The tender stalks on high.

Of every sort which in that meadow grew
They gather'd some; the violet, pallid blue,
The little daisy that at evening closes,
The virgin lily and the primrose true,
With store of vermeil roses,
To deck their bridegrooms' posies
Against the bridal day, which was not long;
    Sweet Thames! run softly, till I end my song.

   * * *

At length they all to merry London came,
To merry London, my most kindly nurse,
That to me gave this life's first native source,
Though from another place I take my name,
An house of ancient fame:
There when they came whereas those bricky towers
The which on Thames' broad aged back do ride,
Where now the studious lawyers have their bowers,
There whilome wont the Templar-knights to bide,
Till they decay'd through pride;
Next whereunto there stands a stately place,
Where oft I gainéd gifts and goodly grace
Of that great lord, which therein wont to dwell,
Whose want too well now feels my friendless case;
But ah! here fits not well
Old woes, but joys to tell
Against the bridal day, which is not long:
    Sweet Thames! run softly, till I end my song.

Yet therein now doth lodge a noble peer,
Great England's glory and the world's wide wonder,
Whose dreadful name late through all Spain did thunder,
And Hercules' two pillars standing near
Did make to quake and fear:
Fair branch of honour, flower of chivalry!
That fillest England with thy triumphs' fame

Joy have thou of thy noble victory,
And endless happiness of thine own name
That promiseth the same;
That through thy prowess and victorious arms
Thy country may be freed from foreign harms,
And great Elisa's glorious name may ring
Through all the world, fill'd with thy wide alarms,
Which some brave Muse may sing
To ages following:
Upon the bridal day, which is not long:
   Sweet Thames! run softly, till I end my song.

From those high towers this noble lord issuing
Like radiant Hesper, when his golden hair
In th'ocean billows he hath bathéd fair,
Descended to the river's open viewing
With a great train ensuing.
Above the rest were goodly to be seen
Two gentle knights of lovely face and feature,
Beseeming well the bower of any queen,
With gifts of wit and ornament of nature,
Fit for so goodly stature,
That like the twins of Jove they seem'd in sight
Which deck the baldric of the Heavens bright;
They two, forth pacing to the river's side,
Received those two fair brides, their love's delight;
Which, at th' appointed tide,
Each one did make his bride
Against their bridal day, which is not long:
   Sweet Thames! run softly, till I end my song.

EDMUND SPENSER (1553-1598)
Prothalamion

The Tudor lord with the riverside mansion was the Earl of Worcester.
There was a double marriage of his two daughters the Ladies Elizabeth
and Catherine Somerset to " the two worthy gentlemen. Mr. Henry
Gilford and Mr. William Peter." They are "esquires" in the sub-
title of this "Spousal Verse," in which they later become "gentle
knights."

RIVERSIDE LONDON, 1599

In 1599 England was visited by a Swiss citizen, Thomas Platter, of Basle, who has left a valuable record of his experiences in the streets, palaces, shops, and theatres.

London is the capital of England and so superior to other English towns that London is not said to be in England, but rather England to be in London, for England's most resplendent objects may be seen in and around London; so that he who sightsees London and the royal courts in its immediate vicinity may assert without impertinence that he is properly acquainted with England. The town is called in Latin Londinium, in French Londres, by the ancients Trinovantum, and is situated on the river Thames (Tamesis) sixty Italian miles or 60,000 paces from the sea, which ebbs and flows as far as London and yet further, as may be observed every six hours from the banks and from the bridge. For which reason ocean-craft are accustomed to run in here in great numbers as into a safe harbour, and I myself beheld one large galley next the other the whole city's length from St. Catherine's suburb to the bridge, some hundred vessels in all, nor did I ever behold so many large ships in one port in all my life.

This river, the foremost in all England because of the city of London, does not swell or gain in size, no matter how long it may rain, which is a remarkable thing; and in all parts of this river swans in great numbers may be seen at all times, and it is forbidden to catch them, since they serve as down stuffing to her Majesty.

And while a very fine long bridge is built across this stream, it is more customary to cross the water or travel up and down the town as at Lyons and elsewhere by attractive pleasure craft, for a number of tiny streets lead to the Thames from both ends of the town; the boatmen wait there in great crowds, each one eager to be first to catch one, for all are free to choose the ship they find most attractive and pleasing, while every boatman has the privilege on arrival of placing his ship to best advantage for people to step into.

The wherries are charmingly upholstered and embroidered cushions laid across the seats, very comfortable to sit on or lean against, and generally speaking the benches only seat two people next to one another; many of them are covered in, particularly in rainy weather or fierce sunshine. They are extremely pleasant to travel in and carry one or a couple of boatmen. I took a ferry across the river to a boathouse where the Thames runs in, and there I saw the queen's barge, quite closed up and very prettily designed with gangways, and beside it in this same boathouse there stood another ship in which the oarsmen had to sit to steer the queen's barge in and out, and so that it might glide more smoothly it was lashed on to this steerage boat, for none was allowed to row in it.

Much salmon and sturgeon are caught with lines in this river.

The bridge across the river is of squared stone, very long and with twenty arches, and on it are built very splendid, finely constructed dwelling houses of prosperous merchants. This makes the appearance of a very fine street.

At the top of one tower almost in the centre of the bridge, were stuck on tall stakes more than thirty skulls of noble men who had been executed and beheaded for treason and for other reasons. And their descendants are accustomed to boast of this, themselves even pointing out to one their ancestors' heads on this same bridge, believing that they will be esteemed the more because their antecedents were of such high descent that they could even covet the crown, but being too weak to attain it were executed for rebels; thus they make an honour for themselves of what was set up to be a disgrace and an example.

Just as only recently here in Basel, the young earl of Suffolk, grandson to the duke of Norfolk, in order to raise the honour of his family, showed that he was so well connected that his forefathers' heads too were on the tower of London Bridge for having coveted the English crown, and so were executed. On this same bridge are as aforesaid many tall handsome merchant dwellings and expensive shops, where all manner of wares are for sale, resembling a long street.

THOMAS PLATTER
Travels in England, 1599
translated and edited by
CLARE WILLIAMS

THE FROZEN THAMES

January 24, 1684. The frost continuing more and more severe, the Thames before London was still planted with boothes in formal streets, all sorts of trades and shops furnish'd and full of commodities, even to a printing presse, where the people and ladyes tooke a fancy to have their own names printed, and the day and yeare set down when printed on the Thames; this humour tooke so universally, that 'twas estimated the printer gain'd £5 a day, for printing a line onely, at sixpence a name, besides what he got by ballads, etc. Coaches plied from Westminster to the Temple, and from several other staires to and fro, as in the streetes, sleds, sliding with skeetes, a bull-baiting, horse and coach races, puppet plays and interludes, cookes, tipling, and other lewd places, so that it seem'd to be a bacchanalian triumph, or carnival on the water, whilst it was a severe judgment on the land, the trees not onely splitting as if by lightning-struck, but men and cattle perishing in divers places, and the very seas so lock'd up with ice, that no vessells could stir out or come in. The fowles, fish, and birds, and all our exotic plants and greenes universally perishing.

Many parkes of deer were destroied, and all sorts of fuell so deare that there were greate contributions to preserve the poore alive. Nor was this severe weather much lesse intense in most parts of Europe, even as far as Spaine and the most Southern tracts. London, by reason of the excessive coldness of the aire hindering the ascent of the smoke, was so fill'd with the fuliginous steame of the seacoale, that hardly could one see crosse the streets, and this filling the lungs with its grosse particles, exceedingly obstructed the breast, so as one could scarcely breathe. Here was no water to be had from the pipes and engines, nor could the brewers and divers other tradesmen worke, and every moment was full of disastrous accidents.

JOHN EVELYN (1620-1706)
Diary

THAMES, LONDON'S LINK WITH THE WORLD

My eye descending from the Hill, surveys
Where Thames amongst the wanton valleys strays.
Thames, the most loved of all the Ocean's sons,
By his old sire to his embrace runs,
Hastening to pay his tribute to the sea,
Like mortal life to meet Eternity.
Though with those streams he no resemblance hold,
Whose foam is amber and their gravel gold;
His genuine and less guilty wealth t' explore,
Search not his bottom, but survey his shore;
O'er which he kindly spreads his spacious wing
And hatches plenty for th' ensuing spring.

Nor then destroys it with too fond a stay,
Like mothers which their infants overlay.
Nor with a sudden and impetuous wave,
Like profuse kings, resumes the wealth he gave.
No unexpected inundations spoil
The mower's hopes nor mock the ploughman's toil,
But God-like his unwearied bounty flows,
First loves to do, then loves the good he does.
Nor are his blessings to his banks confined,
But free and common as the sea or wind;
When he to boast or to disperse his stores
Full of the tributes of his grateful shores,
Visits the world, and in his flying towers
Brings home to us, and makes both Indies ours;
Finds wealth where 'tis, bestows it where it wants,
Cities in deserts, woods in cities plants.
So that to us no thing, no place is strange,
While his fair bosom is the world's exchange.
Oh, could I flow like thee, and make thy stream
My great example, as it is my theme!
Though deep, yet clear, though gentle, yet not dull,
Strong without rage, without o'er-flowing full.

SIR JOHN DENHAM (1615-1669)
Cooper's Hill

THE EXILE'S TEARS FOR THE THAMES

I send, I send here my supremest kiss
To thee, my silver-footed Thamasis.
No more shall I reiterate thy Strand,
Whereon so many Stately Structures stand:
Nor in the summer's sweeter evenings go
To bath in thee (as thousand others doe),
No more shall I along thy christall glide,
In Barge (with boughes and rushes beautifi'd)

With soft-smooth Virgins (for our chaste disport)
To Richmond, Kingstone, and to Hampton-Court:
Never againe shall I with Finnie-Ore
Put from, or draw unto the faithful shore:
And Landing here, or safely Landing there,
Make way to my Beloved Westminster:
Or to the Golden-cheap-side, where the earth
Of Julia Herrick gave to me my Birth.
May all clean Nimphs and curious water Dames,
With Swan-like-state flote up and down thy streams:
No drought upon thy wanton waters fall
To make them Leane, and languishing at all.
No ruffling winds come hither to discease
Thy pure, and Silver-wristed Naides.
Keep up your state, ye streams; and as ye spring,
Never make sick your Banks by surfeiting.
Grow young with Tydes, and though I see ye never,
Receive this vow, so fare-ye-well for ever.

ROBERT HERRICK (1591-1674)
Hesperides

CHELSEA IN 1834

With the House we are all highly pleased, and, I think, the better, the longer we know it hitherto. I know not if you ever were at Chelsea, especially at Old Chelsea, of which this is a portion. It stretches from Battersea Bridge (a queer wooden structure, where they charge you a half-penny) along the bank of the River, Westward a little way; and Eastward (which is our side) some quarter of a mile, forming a " Cheyne Walk " (pronounced Chainie walk) of really grand old brick mansions, dating perhaps from Charles II's time (" Don Saltero's Coffeehouse " of the Tatler is still fresh and brisk among them), with flagged pavement; carriage way between two rows of stubborn looking high old pollarded trees; and then the River with its varied small craft, fast moving or safe-moored, and the wholesome smell (among the breezes) of sea tar. Cheyne Row (or Great Cheyne Row, when we wish to be grand) runs up at right angles from this, has some twenty Houses of the same fashion; Upper Cheyne Row (where Hunt lives) turning again at right angles, some stone-cast from this door.

Frontwards we have the outlook I have described already (or if we shove out our heads, the River is disclosed some hundred paces to the left); backwards, from the ground floor, our own gardenkin (which I with new garden tools am actively re-trimming every morning), and, from all other floors, nothing but leafy clumps, and green fields, and red high-peaked roofs glimmering through them: a most clear, pleasant prospect, in these fresh westerly airs! Of London nothing visible but Westminster Abbey and the topmost dome of St. Paul's; other faint ghosts of spires (one other at least) disclose themselves, as the smoke-clouds shift; but I have not yet made out what they are. At night we are pure and silent, almost as at Puttock; and the gas-light shimmer of the great Babylon hangs stretched from side to side of our horizon. To Buckingham Gate it is thirty-two minutes of my walking (Allan Cunningham's door about half-way); nearly the very same to Hyde-Park Corner, to which latter point we have omnibuses every quarter of an hour (they say) that carry you to the Whitehorse Cellar, or even to Coventry Street for sixpence; calling for you at the very threshold. Nothing was ever so discrepant in my experience as the Craigenputtock-silence of this House, and then the world-hubbub of London and its people into which a few minutes brings you: I feel as if a day spent between the two must be the epitome of a month . . .

The rent is £35; which really seems £10 cheaper than such a House could be had for in Dumfries or Annan.

The secret is our old friend, " Gigmanity "[1]: Chelsea is
unfashionable; it is also reported unhealthy. The former
quality we rather like (for our neighbours still are all
polite-living people); the latter we do not in the faintest
degree believe in, remembering that Chelsea was once
considered the " London Montpelier," and knowing that
in these matters now as formerly the Cockneys " know
nothing," only rush in masses blindly and sheep-wise.
Our worst fault is the want of a good free rustic walk,
like Kensington Gardens, which are above a mile off:
however, we have the " College " or Hospital grounds,
with their withered old pensioners; we have open
carriage ways, and lanes, and really a very pretty route
to Piccadilly (different from the omnibus route) through
the New Grosvenor edifices, Eaton Square, Belgrave
Place, etc. I have also walked to Westminster Hall by
Vauxhall, Bridge-End, Millbank, etc.; but the road is
squalid, confused, dusty and detestable, and happily need
not be returned to. To conclude, we are here on literary
classical ground, as Hunt is continually ready to declare
and unfold: not a stone-cast from this House Smollett
wrote his Count Fathom (the house is ruined and we
happily do not see it); hardly a stone-cast off, old More
entertained Erasmus: to say nothing of Bolingbroke
St. John, of Paradise Row and the Count de Grammont,
for in truth we care almost nothing for them.

THOMAS CARLYLE (1795-1881)
Letter to His Brother

THE RATCATCHER'S DAUGHTER

Not long ago in Vestminstier,
   There liv'd a ratcatcher's daughter—
But she didn't quite live in Vestminstier
   'Cause she lived t'other side of the water;

[1] Gigman, " One who keeps a gig," used by Carlyle for one whose
respectability is measured by keeping a gig: a " Philistine "

REGENT'S PARK

Regent's Park, with Primrose Hill and the Zoo, covers 472 acres and is a priceless asset to Central London. Laid out by John Nash for the Prince Regent in 1812 it offers a superb array of flowers from spring to autumn and its islanded lake gives sailing and rowing in summer.

TRUNK CALL AT THE ZOO

The Zoological Gardens in Regent's Park were laid out by Decimus Burton and first opened to the public in 1828, since when the premises have been continually expanded and improved. The picture shows Diksie, an African elephant, beloved of children.

ROYAL ALBERT DOCKS

The Royal Albert Docks were opened in 1880. With the Victoria Docks
opened in 1885 a stretch of marshland extending for nearly three miles
was turned into the busy region of West Ham and Canning Town where
ships of great size can be berthed.

Her father caught rats, and she sold sprats,
  All round and about that quarter;
And the gentlefolks all took off their hats
  To the putty little ratcatcher's daughter.

She vore no 'at upon 'er 'ead,
  Nor cap nor dandy bonnet—
The 'air of 'er 'ead all 'ung down 'er back,
  Like a bunch of carrots upon it;
Ven she cried ' Sprats! ' in Vestminstier,
  She had a sweet loud voice, sir,
You could hear her all down Parliament Street,
  As far as Charing Cross, sir.

Now rich and poor, both far and near,
  In matrimony sought her;
But at friends and foes she turn'd up her nose,
  Did the putty little ratcatcher's daughter.
For there was a man, sold lily-vite sand,
  In Cupid's net had caught her;
And right over head and ears in love
  Vent the putty little ratcatcher's daughter.

Now ' Lily-vite sand ' so ran in 'er 'ead
  As she went along the Strand, oh!
She forgot as she'd got sprats on 'er 'ead,
  And cried ' D'ye vant any lily-vite sand, oh! '
The folks amazed, all thought her crazed,
  As she went along the Strand, oh!
To see a gal with sprats on 'er 'ead
  Cry ' D'ye vant any lily-vite sand, oh! '

Now ' Ratcatcher's daughter ' so ran in his head
  He couldn't tell vat he was arter,
So, instead of crying, ' D'ye vant any sand! '
  He cried, ' D'ye vant any ratcatcher's darter? '

7

His donkey cock'd his ears and laughed,
   And couldn't think vat he was arter,
Ven he heard his lily-vite sandman cry,
   ' D'ye vant any ratcatcher's darter?'

They both agreed to married be
   Upon next Easter Sunday,
But ratcatcher's daughter she had a dream
   That she wouldn't be alive on Monday;—
She vent vunce more to buy some sprats,
   And she tumbled into the vater,
And down to the bottom, all kiver'd up with mud,
   Vent the putty little ratcatcher's daughter.

Ven Lily-vite sand 'e 'eard the news,
   His eyes ran down with water,
Said 'e, ' In love I'll constant prove;
   And—blow me if I'll live long arter!'
So 'e cut 'is throat with a pane of glass,
   And stabb'd 'is donkey arter!
So 'ere is an end of Lily-vite-Sand,
   Donkey, and the ratcatcher's darter.

The neighbours all, both great and small,
   They flocked unto her berrein',
And vept that a gal who'd cried out sprats,
   Should be dead as any herrein.
The Corrioner's Inquest on her sot,
   At the sign of the Jack i' the Vater,
To find what made life's sand run out
   Of the putty little ratcatcher's daughter.

The werdict was that too much vet
   This poor young woman died on;
For she made an 'ole in the Riviere Thames,
   Vot the penny steamers ride on!

Twas a haccident they all agreed,
   And nuffink like self slaughter;
So not guilty o' fell in the sea
   They brought in the ratcatcher's daughter.

ANONYMOUS (early Victorian)

MAKERS OF THE THAMES

Around his throne the sea-borne brothers stood,
Who swell with tributary urns his flood:
First the fam'd authors of his ancient name,
The winding Isis, and the fruitful Tame:
The Kennet swift, for silver eels renown'd;
The Loddon slow, with verdant alders crown'd;
Cole, whose dark streams his flow'ry islands lave;
And chalky Wey, that rolls a milky wave:
The blue transparent Vandalis appears;
The gulphy Lee his sedgy tresses rears;
And sullen Mole, that hides his diving flood;
And silent Darent, stain'd with Danish blood.

ALEXANDER POPE (1688-1744)
Windsor Forest

Vandalis, now Wandle, name-giver to Wandsworth, has long lost its
right to the kindly adjectives here bestowed on it. But the Hertford-
shire and Essex Lee has still its claim to be " gulphy " and to have a
coiffure of sedges.

PORT OF LONDON

In May 1861, Dickens made a trip with a company of friends on a
steamer from the Port of London to Southend. He was just finishing
Great Expectations and he was seeking to describe the watery and
marshy background of the attempt made at the climax of that story
to get the hunted ex-criminal Magwitch safely out of the country.
The hero, Pip, and two friends are in a rowing-boat and intending to
get picked-up by a steamer bound for Hamburg. The time of the
story is a good deal earlier than 1861 since railways are not mentioned
and the characters travel on land by coach. The book begins amid the
marshlands of the Thames Estuary and to them the tale returns.

We loitered down to the Temple stairs, and stood loitering there, as if we were not quite decided to go upon the
water at all. Of course I had taken care that the boat
should be ready and everything in order. After a little
show of indecision, which there were none to see but the
two or three amphibious creatures belonging to our
Temple stairs, we went on board and cast off; Herbert
in the bow, I steering. It was then about high-water—
half-past eight.

Our plan was this. The tide, beginning to run down
at nine, and being with us until three, we intended still
to creep on after it had turned, and row against it until
dark. We should then be well in those long reaches
below Gravesend, between Kent and Essex, where the
river is broad and solitary, where the water-side inhabitants are very few, and where lone public-houses are
scattered here and there, of which we could choose one
for a resting-place. There we meant to lie by, all night.
The steamer for Hamburg, and the steamer for Rotterdam, would start from London at about nine on Thursday morning. We should know at what time to expect
them, according to where we were, and would hail the
first; so that if by any accident we were not taken aboard,

we should have another chance. We knew the distinguishing marks of each vessel.

The relief of being at last engaged in the execution of the purpose was so great to me that I felt it difficult to realise the condition in which I had been a few hours before. The crisp air, the sunlight, the movement on the river, and the moving river itself—the roar that ran with us, seeming to sympathise with us, animate us, and encourage us on—freshened me with new hope. I felt mortified to be of so little use in the boat; but there were few better oarsmen than my two friends, and they rowed with a steady stroke that was to last all day.

At that time, the steam-traffic on the Thames was far below its present extent, and watermen's boats were far more numerous. Of barges, sailing colliers, and coasting-traders, there were perhaps as many as now; but of steamships, great and small, not a tithe or a twentieth part so many. Early as it was, there were plenty of scullers going here and there that morning, and plenty of barges dropping down with the tide; the navigation of the river between bridges, in an open boat, was a much easier and commoner matter in those days than it is in these; and we went ahead among many skiffs and wherries, briskly.

Old London Bridge was soon passed, and Old Billingsgate market with its oyster-boats and Dutchmen, and the White Tower and Traitors' Gate, and we were in among the tiers of shipping. Here were the Leith, Aberdeen, and Glasgow steamers, loading and unloading goods, and looking immensely high out of the water as we passed alongside; here were colliers by the score and score, with the coal-whippers plunging off stages on deck, as counter-weights to measures of coal swinging up, which were then rattled over the side into barges; here, at her moorings, was tomorrow's steamer for Rotterdam, of which we took good notice; and here tomorrow's for Hamburg, under whose bowsprit we crossed. And now I, sitting in the stern, could see with a faster beating heart, Mill Pond Bank and Mill Pond stairs.

" Is he there? " said Herbert.

" Not yet."

" Right! He was not to come down till he saw us. Can you see his signal? "

" Not well from here; but I think I see it.—Now, I see him! Pull both. Easy, Herbert. Oars! "

We touched the stairs lightly for a single moment, and he was on board and we were off again. He had a boat-cloak with him, and a black canvas bag, and he looked as like a river-pilot as my heart could have wished.

" Dear boy! " he said, putting his arm on my shoulder as he took his seat. " Faithful dear boy, well done. Thankye, thankye! "

Again among the tiers of shipping, in and out, avoiding rusty chain-cables, frayed hempen hawsers and bobbing buoys, sinking for the moment floating broken baskets, scattering floating chips of wood and shaving, cleaving floating scum of coal, in and out, under the figure-head of the John of Sunderland making a speech to the winds (as is done by many Johns), and the Betsy of Yarmouth with a firm formality of bosom and her knobby eyes staring two inches out of her head, in and out, hammers going in ship-builders' yards, saws going at timber, clashing engines going at things unknown, pumps going in leaky ships, capstans going, ships going out to sea, and unintelligible sea-creatures roaring curses over the bulwarks at respondent lightermen, in and out—out at last upon the clearer river, where the ships' boys might take their fenders in, no longer fishing in troubled waters with them over the side, and where the festooned sails might fly out to the wind.

At the Stairs where we had taken him aboard, and ever since, I had looked warily for any token of our being suspected. I had seen none. We certainly had not been, and at that time as certainly we were not either attended or followed by any boat. If we had been waited on by any boat, I should have run in to shore, and have obliged her to go on, or to make her purpose evident. But we held our own, without any appearance of molestation.

The air felt cold upon the river, but it was a bright day, and the sunshine was very cheering. The tide ran strong, I took care to lose none of it, and our steady stroke carried us on thoroughly well. By imperceptible degrees, as the tide ran out, we lost more and more of the nearer woods and hills, and dropped lower and lower between the muddy banks, but the tide was yet with us when we were off Gravesend. As our charge was wrapped in his cloak, I purposely passed within a boat or two's length of the floating Custom House, and so out to catch the stream, alongside of two emigrant ships, and under the bows of a large transport with troops on the forecastle looking down at us. And soon the tide began to slacken, and the craft lying at anchor to swing and presently they had all swung round, and the ships that were taking advantage of the new tide to get up to the Pool, began to crowd upon us in a fleet, and we kept under the shore, as much out of the strength of the tide now as we could, standing carefully off from low shallows and mud-banks.

Our oarsmen were so fresh, by dint of having occasion-ally let her drive with the tide for a minute or two, that a quarter of an hour's rest proved full as much as they wanted. We got ashore among some slippery stones while we ate and drank what we had with us, and looked about. It was like my own marsh country, flat and monotonous, and with a dim horizon; while the winding river turned and turned, and the great floating buoys upon it turned and turned, and everything else seemed stranded and still. For, now, the last of the fleet of ships was round the last low point we had headed; and the last green

barge, straw-laden, with a brown sail, had followed; and
some ballast-lighters, shaped like a child's first rude
imitation of a boat, lay low in the mud; and a little
squat shoal-lighthouse on open piles, stood crippled in
the mud on stilts and crutches; and slimy stakes stuck
out of the mud, and slimy stones stuck out of the mud,
and red landmarks and tidemarks stuck out of the mud,
and an old landing-stage and an old roofless building
slipped into the mud, and all about us was stagnation
and mud.

We pushed off again, and made what way we could. It
was much harder work now, but Herbert and Startop
persevered, and rowed, and rowed, and rowed, until the
sun went down. By that time the river had lifted us a
little, so that we could see above the bank. There was the
red sun, on the low level of the shore, in a purple haze,
fast deepening into black; and there was the solitary
flat marsh; and far away there were the rising grounds,
between which and us there seemed to be no life save
here and there in the foreground a melancholy gull.

CHARLES DICKENS (1812-1870)
Great Expectations

GREENWICH FOR WHITEBAIT

The habit of going down the river to eat whitebait at Greenwich was
much favoured in Victorian times by all classes of society, including
the highest Ministers of State. The inns mentioned by Thackeray
were long famous for their excellent provision of this "fish fry"
dear to Londoners.

The lusty salmon flaps in other waters: by the fair tree-
clad banks of Lismore, by the hospitable margin of
Ballynahinch, by the beauteous shores of Wye, and on
the sandy flats of Scheveningen, I have eaten and loved
him. I do not generally eat him at Greenwich. Not that
he is not good. But he is not good in such a place. It is
like Mrs. Siddons dancing a hornpipe, or a chapter of

Burke in a novel—the salmon is too vast for Greenwich.

I would say the same, and more, regarding turtle. It has no business in such a feast as that fresh and simple one provided at the " Trafalgar " or the " Old Ship." It is indecorous somehow to serve it in that company. A fine large lively turtle and a poor little whitebait by his side! Ah, it is wrong to place them by each other.

At last we come to the bait. The twelve dishes of preparatory fish are removed, the Indian sauced salmon has been attacked in spite of our prohibition, the stewed eels have been mauled, and the flounder soup-tureen is empty. All those receptacles of pleasure are removed— eyes turned eagerly to the door, and enter

Mr. Derbyshire (with a silver dish of whitebait).

John (brown bread and butter).

Samuel (lemons and cayenne).

Frederick (a dish of whitebait).

Gustavus (brown bread and butter).

Adolphus (whitebait).

A waiter with a napkin, which he flaps about the room in an easy, dégagé manner.

" There's plenty more to follow, sir," says Mr. D., whisking off the cover. Frederick and Adolphus pass rapidly round with their dishes; John and Gustavus place their refreshments on the table; and Samuel obsequiously insinuates the condiments under his charge.

Ah! he must have had a fine mind who first invented brown bread and butter with whitebait! That man was a kind, modest, gentle benefactor to his kind. We don't recognize sufficiently the merits of those men who leave us such quiet benefactions. A statue ought to be put up to the philosopher who joined together this charming couple. Who was it? Perhaps it was done by the astronomer at Greenwich, who observed it when seeking for some other discovery. If it were the astronomer—why, the next time we go to Greenwich we will go into the

Park, and ascend the hill, and pay our respects to the Observatory.

That, by the way, is another peculiarity about Greenwich. People leave town, and say they will walk in the Park before dinner. But we never do. We may suppose there is a park from seeing trees, but we have never entered it. We walk wistfully up and down on the terrace before the hospital, looking at the clock a great many times; at the brown old seamen basking in the sun; at the craft on the river; at the nursery-maids mayhap, and the gambols of the shrill-voiced Jacks-ashore on the beach. But the truth is, one's thinking of something else all the time. Of the bait! Remark how silent fellows are on steamboats going down to Greenwich. They won't acknowledge it, but they are thinking of what I tell you.

Whitebait, then, is only a little means for acquiring a great deal of pleasure. Somehow, it is always allied with sunshine; it is always accompanied by jolly friends and good-humour. You rush after that little fish, and leave the cares of London behind you—the row and struggle, the foggy darkness, the slippery pavement where every man jostles you, striding on his way pre-occupied, with care written on his brow. Look out of the window: the sky is tinted with a thousand glorious hues—the ships pass silent over the blue glittering waters—there is no object within sight that is not calm, and happy, and beautiful. Yes! turn your head a little, and there lie the towers of London in the dim smoky sunset. There lie Care, Labour, Tomorrow. Friends, let us have another glass of claret, and thank our luck that we have still today.

About the frequenters of Greenwich and the various classes of ichthyophagi,[1] many volumes may be written.

[1] Fish-eaters

All classes of English Christians, with the exception of her Majesty and Prince Albert (and the more is the pity that their exalted rank deprives them of an amusement so charming!), frequent the hospitable taverns, the most celebrated gormandizer and the very humble. There are the annual Ministerial Saturnalia, which, whenever I am called in by her Majesty, I shall have great pleasure in describing in these pages, and in which the lowest becomes the highest for the occasion, and Taper and Tadpole take just as high rank as Lord Eskdale or Lord Monmouth. There are the private banquets in which Lord Monmouth diverts himself with his friends from the little French—but this subject has been already touched upon at much length. There are the lawyers' dinners, when Sir Frederick or Sir William is advanced to the honour of the bench or the attorney-generalship, and where much legal pleasantry is elicited. The last time I dined at the " Ship," hearing a dreadful bacchan-alian noise issuing from a private apartment, I was informed, " It's the gentlemen of ' Punch,' Sir." What would I not have given to be present at such an assemby of choice spirits. Even missionary societies and con-verters of the Quashimdoo Indians come hither for a little easy harmless pleasuring after their labours, and no doubt the whitebait slips down their reverend throats, and is relished by them as well as by the profane crowd.

*　　　*　　　*

I could continue for many more pages, but the evening grey is tingeing the river, the packet-boat bells are ringing, the sails of the ships look greyer and more ghostlike as they sweep silently by. It is time to be thinking of returning, and so let us call for the bill, and finish with a moral. My dear sir, it is this. The weather

is beautiful; the whitebait singularly fine this season.
You are sure to be happy if you go to Greenwich. Go
then; and, above all, TAKE YOUR AMIABLE LADY
WITH YOU.

W. M. THACKERAY (1811-1863)
Colburn's New Monthly Magazine, July, 1844

SEEING MISS HILARY

Seeing the bent figure of Miss Hilary
Waver about in her blue overall,
Tending, with little indeed to show for it,
Her dusty garden-plot by the London Thames;
Seeing her there, all weathers and all hours,
With knotted white determined fingers
Clip, tie, spray, and God knows what,
Or seated—this was her luxury—peering
With keen myopic eye to review
Her household troops, her still malingering flowers;

Or, Tuesday and Friday, seeing her issue orders
To the lay figure of a garden help—
An old-age pensioner, whose hob-nailed boots
Threaten alike the groundsel and the lily—
You would go your way perhaps with a pitying smile:
Poor Miss Hilary! quite eccentric,
One-idea'd, with never a thought for
Tired back or failing vision,
The stubborn remains of her strength devoted
To a task no charity could call worth while.

But could you, were it possible you could see
Clear as the teeth of her rake the fixed purpose
Summon the tender shoot from the dry seed,
Sustain, unfold the leaf and the tardy blossom,
Nor less—what edict could speak louder?—

With mute malediction
Banish the low, the anti-social weed;
And could you, clear as the bent back, see
Over the niggardly July harvest
Hope with unslack sinews contend
With rain and shine, the Powers of the Air,
While horse-manure, quick-lime and derris-powder
Are instruments of spiritual war
With snail and blackfly, grub and the thirsty sand;

Could you—oh, then look away, and you might see
What but the irrigation of a desert,
Sprouting of huts, beginning of a city,
Laws, and the spirit of a ruling people,
To-day, or wandering back if you will
To Dido and Carthage:

Then—and not, most certainly not, with pity—
Return, and here in front of you see,
Ruling a dusty ten-yard province
With hoe and watering-can and shears,
A person, an old lady to admire
And even, could you venture so far, to love,
Despite the rack of all rheumatic ill
Tough, and formidable with the mounting weight
Of eighty concentrated selfless years.

SIR GEORGE ROSTREVOR HAMILTON (1888-   )
Collected Poems and Epigrams

Streets

THE TUDOR CUT-PURSE

This trade, or rather unsufferable loitering quality, in singing of ballets and songs at the doors of such houses where plays are used, as also in open markets and other places of this city where is most resort, which is nothing else but a sly fetch to draw many together, who, listening unto a harmless ditty, afterward walk home to their houses with heavy hearts: from such as are hereof true witnesses to their cost, do I deliver this example. A subtle fellow, belike emboldened by acquaintance with the former deceit, or else, being but a beginner to practise the same, calling certain of his companions together would try whether he could attain to be master of his art or no, by taking a great many of fools with one train. But let his intent and what else beside remain to abide the censure after the matter is heard, and come to Gracious Street, where this villainous prank was performed.

A roguing mate and such another with him, were there got upon a stall singing of ballets, which belike was some pretty toy, for very many gathered about to hear it, and divers buying, as their affections served, drew to their purses and paid the singers for them. The sly mate and his fellows, who were dispersed among them that stood to hear the songs, well noted where every man that bought put up his purse again, and to such as would not buy, counterfeit warning was sundry times given by the rogue and his associate, to beware of the cutpurse, and look to their purses, which made them often feel where their purses were, either in sleeve, hose, or at girdle, to know whether they were safe or no.

Thus the crafty copesmates were acquainted with what they most desired, and as they were scattered, by shouldering, thrusting, feigning to let fall something, and other wily tricks fit for their purpose, here one lost his purse, there another had his pocket picked, and to say all in brief, at one instant, upon the complaint of one or two that saw their purses were gone, eight more in the same company found themselves in like predicament. Some angry, others sorrowful and all greatly discontented, looking about them, knew not who to suspect or challenge, in that the villains themselves that had thus beguiled them, made show that they had sustained like loss.

But one angry fellow, more impatient than all the rest, he falls upon the ballad singer, and beating him with his fists well favourably, says, if he had not listened his singing, he had not lost his purse, and therefore would not be otherwise persuaded but that they two and the cut-purses were compacted together. The rest that had lost their purses likewise and saw that so many complain together, they jump in opinion with the other fellow, and begin to tug and hail the ballad singers, when one after one, the false knaves began to shrink away with the purses. By means of some officer then being there present, the two rogues were had before a Justice, and upon his discreet examination made, it was found that they and the cut-purses were compacted together, and that by this unsuspected villainy, they had deceived many. The fine fool-taker himself, with one or two more of that company, was not long after apprehended, when I doubt not but they had their reward answerable to their deserving, for I hear of their journey westward,[1] but not of their return. Let this forewarn those that listen to singing in the streets.

ROBERT GREENE (1558-1592)
The Third Part of Connycatching

[1] To execution at Tyburn

A SMACK AT THE POLICE

These are not only the constables with the watchmen in London, but also almost through this realm, most falsely abusing the time, coming very late to the watch, sitting down in some common place of watching, wherein some falleth on sleep by the reason of labour or much drinking before, or else nature requireth rest in the night. These fellows think every hour a thousand until they go home, home, home, every man to bed. Good night, good night! God save the Queen! sayeth the constables, farewell, neighbours.

Eftsoons after their departing creepeth forth the wild rogue and his fellows, having two or three other harlots for their turn, with picklocks, handsaws, long hooks, ladders, etc., to break into houses, rob, murder, steal, and do all mischief in the houses of true men, utterly undoing honest people to maintain their harlots. Great hoses, lined cloaks, long daggers, and feathers, these must be paid for, etc. This cometh for want of punishment by the day, and idle watch in the night. God grant that some of the watch be not the scouts to the thieves. Yes; God grant that some men have not conspirators of thieves in their own houses, which, like Judases, deceive their masters. If this watch be not better looked unto, good wife, in every place in this realm, and all the night long searching every suspected corner, no man shall be able to keep a penny.

WILLIAM BULLEIN
A Dialogue Against the Pestilence, 1573

TRAFFIC PROBLEM, ELIZABETHAN

Then the number of cars, drays, carts, and coaches, more than hath been accustomed, the streets and lanes being straightened, must needs be dangerous, as daily experience proveth.

The coachman rides behind the horse tails, lasheth them, and looketh not behind him; the drayman sitteth and sleepeth on his dray, and letteth his horse lead him home. I know that, by the good laws and customs of this city, shodde[1] carts are forbidden to enter the same, except upon reasonable cause, as service of the prince, or such like, they be tolerated. Also that the fore horse of every carriage should be lead by hand; but these good orders are not observed. Of old time coaches were not known in this island, but chariots or whirlicotes, then so called, and they only used of princes or great estates, such as had their footmen about them; and for example to note, I read that Richard II, being threatened by the rebels of Kent, rode from the Tower of London to the Myles end, and with him his mother, because she was sick and weak, in a whirlicote, the Earls of Buckingham, Kent, Warwicke, and Oxford, Sir Thomas Percie, Sir Robert Knowles, the Mayor of London, Sir Aubrey de Vere, that bare the king's sword, with other knights and esquires attending on horseback. But in the next year, the said King Richard took to wife Anne, daughter to the King of Bohemia, that first brought hither the riding upon side-saddles; and so was the riding in whirlicoates and chariots forsaken, except at coronations and such like spectacles; but now of late years the use of coaches, brought out of Germany, is taken up, and made so common, as there is neither distinction of time nor difference of persons observed; for the world runs on wheels with many whose parents were glad to go on foot.

JOHN STOW (1525-1605)
Survey of London

[1] Carts bound with iron

Thomas Dekker also had something to say on the matter.

In every street, carts and coaches make such a thundering
as if the world ran upon wheels: at every corner, men,
women and children meet in such shoals, that posts
are set up of purpose to strengthen the houses, lest with
jostling one another they should shoulder them down.
Besides, hammers are beating in one place, tubs hooping
in another, pots clinking in a third, water-tankards
running at tilt in a fourth. Here are porters sweating
under burdens, there merchant's men bearing bags of
money. Chapmen (as if they were at leap frog) skip out
of one shop into another. Tradesmen (as if they were
dancing galliards) are lusty at legs and never stand still.
All are as busy as country attorneys at an assizes.

THOMAS DEKKER (1570?-1632)
The Seven Deadly Sins of London

DANCING OUT OF TOWN

In 1960 walking the entire length of the country became a popular
exercise: it is not, however, recorded that anybody danced from
John o' Groats to Land's End. But a long "jigging" journey from
London to Norwich was made in 1600 by William Kempe, the stage-
clown and dancer who had left the Lord Chamberlain's Men (Shakespeare's company) in 1599. He wrote his own record of it in a fanci-
ful style. Here is his beginning.

The first Monday in Lent, the close morning promising
a clear day, (attended on by Thomas Slye my tabourer,
William Bee my servant, and George Sprat, appointed
for my overseer, that I should take no other ease but my
prescribed order) myself, that's I, otherwise called
Cavaliero Kemp, headmaster of morrice-dancers, high
headborough of heighs, and only tricker of your trill-
lills and best bell-shangles between Sion and Mount
Surrey, began frolicly to foot it from the right honour-

able the Lord Mayor's of London towards the right worshipful (and truly bountiful) Master Mayor's of Norwich.

My setting forward was somewhat before seven in the morning; my tabourer struck up merrily; and as fast as kind peoples thronging together would give me leave, through London I leapt. By the way many good old people, and divers others of younger years, of mere kindness gave me bowed sixpences and groats blessing me with their hearty prayers and God-speeds.

Being past Whitechapel, and having left fair London with all that northeast suburb beforenamed, multitudes of Londoners left not me: but either to keep a custom which many hold, that Mile End is no walk without a recreation at Stratford Bow with cream and cakes, or else for love they bear toward me, or perhaps to make themselves merry if I should chance (as many thought) to give over my morrice within a mile of Mile End; however, many a thousand brought me to Bow; where I rested a while from dancing, but had small rest with those that would have urged me to drinking. But, I warrant you, Will Kemp was wise enough; to their full cups, kind thanks was my return, with gentlemanlike protestations, as " Truly, sir, I dare not," " It stands not with the congruity of my health." Congruity, said I? how came that strange language in my mouth? I think scarcely that it is any Christian word, and yet it may be a good word for aught I know, though I never made it, nor do very well understand it; yet I am sure I have bought it at the word-monger's at as dear a rate as I could have had a whole 100 of bavins at the wood-mongers'. Farewell, congruity, for I mean now to be more concise, and stand upon evener bases; but I must neither stand nor sit, the tabourer strikes alarum. Tickle it, good Tom, I'll follow thee. Farewell, Bow; have over the bridge, where I heard say honest conscience was once drowned: it's pity if it were so; but that's no matter belonging to our morrice, let's now along to Stratford Langton.

Many good fellows being there met, and knowing how well I loved the sport, had prepared a bear-baiting; but so unreasonable were the multitudes of people, that I could only hear the bear roar and the dogs howl; therefore forward I went with my hey-de-gays to Ilford, where I again rested, and was by the people of the town and country thereabouts very well welcomed, being offered carouses in the great spoon, one whole draught being able at that time to have drawn my little wit dry; but being afraid of the old proverb (He had need of a long spoon that eats with the devil), I soberly gave my boon companions the slip.

From Ilford, by moonshine, I set forward, dancing within a quarter of a mile of Romford; where, in the highway, two strong jades (having belike some great quarrel to me unknown) were beating and biting either of other; and such through God's help was my good hap, that I escaped their hooves, both being raised with their forefeet over my head, like two smiths over an anvil.

There being the end of my first day's morrice, a kind gentleman of London alighting from his horse, would have no nay but I should leap into his saddle. To be plain with ye, I was not proud, but kindly took his kindly offer, chiefly thereto urged by my weariness; so I rid to my inn at Romford.

In that town, to give rest to my well-laboured limbs, I continued two days, being much beholding to the townsmen for their love, but more to the Londoners that came hourly thither in great numbers to visit me, offering much more kindness than I was willing to accept.

WILLIAM KEMPE
Nine Days' Wonder, 1600

REBELS IN THE STREET

SCENE VII

London. Smithfield

Alarums. Matthew Gough is slain, and all the rest. Then enter Jack Cade, with his company.

JACK CADE: So, sirs:—now go some and pull down the Savoy; others to the Inns of court; down with them all.

DICK: I have a suit unto your lordship.

JACK CADE: Be it a lordship, thou shalt have it for that word.

DICK: Only, that the laws of England may come out of your mouth.

JOHN HOLLAND (*aside*): Mass, 'twill be sore law, then; for he was thrust in the mouth with a spear, and 'tis not whole yet.

SMITH (*aside*): Nay, John, it will be stinking law; for his breath stinks with eating toasted cheese.

JACK CADE: I have thought upon it, it shall be so. Away, burn all the records of the realm: my mouth shall be the parliament of England.

JOHN HOLLAND (*aside*): Then we are like to have biting statutes, unless his teeth be pull'd out.

JACK CADE: And henceforward all things shall be in common.

Enter a MESSENGER.

MESSENGER: My lord, a prize, a prize! here's the Lord Say, which sold the towns in France; he that made us pay one-and-twenty fifteens, and one shilling to the pound, the last subsidy.

Enter GEORGE BEVIS, *with the* LORD SAY.

JACK CADE: Well, he shall be beheaded for it ten times.
—Ah, thou say, thou serge, nay, thou buckram lord!
now art thou within point-blank of our jurisdiction
regal. What canst thou answer to my majesty for giving
up of Normandy unto Monsieur Basimecu, the dauphin
of France? Be it known unto thee by these presence, even
the presence of Lord Mortimer, that I am the besom
that must sweep the court clean of such filth as thou art.
Thou hast most traitorously corrupted the youth of the
realm in erecting a grammar-school: and whereas,
before, our forefathers had no other books but the score
and the tally, thou hast caused printing to be used; and,
contrary to the king, his crown, and dignity, thou hast
built a paper-mill. It will be proved to thy face that thou
hast men about thee that usually talk of a noun and a
verb, and such abominable words as no Christian ear can
endure to hear. Thou has appointed justices of peace, to
call poor men before them about matters they were not
able to answer. Moreover, thou hast put them in prison;
and because they could not read, thou hast hang'd them;
when, indeed, only for that cause they have been most
worthy to live.

WILLIAM SHAKESPEARE (1564-1616)
Henry VI, Part II

Jack Cade led a revolt among the men of Kent and Sussex against
high taxation and general mis-rule. Assisted by London malcontents,
he and his followers managed to cross London Bridge: but they were
driven back, and Cade was killed at Heathfield in 1450.

FAIR BUT RISKY

O bear me to the Paths of fair Pell-Mell,
Safe are thy Pavements, grateful is thy Smell!
At distance, rolls along the gilded Coach,
Nor sturdy Carmen on thy Walks encroach;
No Lets would bar thy Ways, were Chairs deny'd,
The soft Supports of Laziness and Pride;
Shops breathe Perfumes, thro' Sashes Ribbons glow,
The mutual Arms of Ladies, and the Beau.
Yet still ev'n Here, when Rains the Passage Hide,
Oft the loose Stone spirts up a muddy Tide
Beneath thy careless Foot; and from on high,
Where Masons mount the Ladder, Fragments fly;
Mortar, and crumbled Lime in Show'rs descend,
And o'er thy Head destructive Tiles impend.

JOHN GAY (1685-1732)
Trivia; or the Art of Walking the Streets of London

COACHES IN HYDE PARK

Thence Sir W. Pen and I in his coach, Tiburne way, into
the Park, where a horrid dust, and number of coaches,
without pleasure or order. That which we, and almost
all went for, was to see my Lady Newcastle; which we
could not, she being followed and crowded upon by
coaches all the way she went, that nobody could come
near her; only I could see she was in a large black
coach, adorned with silver instead of gold, and so white
curtains, and everything black and white, and herself in
her cap. But that which I did see, and wonder at with
reason, was to find Pegg Pen in a new coach, with only
her husband's pretty sister with her, both patched and
very fine, and in much the finest coach in the park, and
I think that ever I did see one or other, for neatness and

richness in gold, and every thing that is noble. My Lady
Castlemaine, the King, my Lord St. Albans, Mr. Jermyn,
have not so neat a coach, that ever I saw. And, Lord!
to have them have this, and nothing else that is corres-
pondent is to me one of the most ridiculous sights that
ever I did see, though her present dress was well enough;
but to live in the condition they do at home, and be
abroad in this coach, astonishes me. When we had spent
half an hour in the Park, we went out again, weary of the
dust, and despairing of seeing my Lady Newcastle; and
to St. James's. But we staying by the way to drink, she
got home a little before us: so we lost our labours and
then home.

SAMUEL PEPYS (1633-1703)
Diary

Of the Duchess of Newcastle Pepys had previously written " The whole
story of this lady is a romance and all she does is romantic. So many
people come to see her as if it were the Queen of Sheba."

THE LORD MAYOR'S SHOW DERIDED

When the morning came that my Lord Mayor and his
attendants were to take their amphibious journey to
Westminster Hall, where his Lordship, according to the
custom of his ancestors, was by a kiss of calves'-leather,
to make a fair promise to Her Majesty, I equipped my
carcase in order to bear with little damage the hustles
and affronts of the unmannerly mob, of whose wild
pastimes and unlucky attacks I had not a little apprehension. And when my friend and I had thus carefully
sheltered ourselves, under our ancient drabdeberries,
against their dirty assaults, we ventured to move towards Cheapside, where I thought the triumphs would
be most visible, and the rabble most rude, looking upon

the mad frolics and whimsies of the latter to be altogether as diverting (provided a man takes care of the danger) as the solemn grandeur and the gravity of the former.

When I came to the end of Blow Bladder Street, I saw such a crowd before my eyes, that I could scarce forbear thinking the very stones of the street, by the harmony of their drums and trumpets, were metamorphosed into men, women and children. The balconies were hung with old tapestry and Turkey-work tablecloths, for the cleanly leaning out of the ladies, with whom they were chiefly filled, though the mob had soon pelted them into so dirty a condition that some of them looked as nasty as the cover cloth of a horse that had travelled from St. Margaret's to London in the midst of winter. At every volley the ladies quitted their post, and retreated into dining-rooms, as safer garrisons to defend themselves from the assaults of their mischievous enemies; some fretting at their daubed scarves; others wiping their new commodes,[1] which they had brought on purpose to honour His Lordship, each expressing anger in their looks. The windows of each house from the top to the bottom were stuffed with heads, piled one upon another like skulls in a charnel house.

Whilst my friend and I were thus staring at the spectators much more than the show, the pageants were advanced within our view, upon which such a tide of mob overflowed the place we stood in, that the women cried out for room, the children for breath, and every man, whether citizen or foreigner, strove very hard for his freedom. For my own part, I was so closely imprisoned in the multitude that I was almost squeezed as flat as a napkin in the press, so that I heartily would have joined with the rabble to have cried, " Liberty, liberty."

In this pageant was a fellow riding a cock-horse upon a lion, but without either boots or spurs, as if intended,

---

[1] Hats

by the projector, to show how the citizens ride to Epsom on a Saturday night, to bear their wives company till Monday morning.

At the base of the pedestal were seated four figures representing, according to my most rational conjecture, the four principal vices of the City, viz., Fraud, Usury, Seeming-sanctity and Hypocrisy. As soon as this was past, the industrious rabble, who hate idleness, had procured a dead cat which was handed about by the babes of grace, as an innocent diversion, every now and then being tossed into the face of some gaping booby or other.

By the time this sport had gone a little about, another pageant approached us, wherein an old fellow sat in a blue gown, dressed up like a country schoolmaster, only he was armed with a scythe instead of a birch rod, by which I understood this figure represented Time, which was designed, as I suppose, to put the City in mind how apt they are to abuse the old gentleman, and not dispose of him to such good uses as the laws of God and the laws of man require, but trifle their time away in those three vanities which were represented by the three figures under the dome, viz., Falsehood, Pride and Incontinency.

When this pageant was passed, a third pageant advanced forward, which appeared to the sight much richer than the rest.

"What think you," says my friend, "of these emblems?"

"I think," said I, "the chief figure in it represents, as I imagine, a lady of pleasure, being dressed in much costlier robes than the other female representatives, which may serve to let the City know that harlots in this wicked age wear richer apparel than honest women, and those three maids that attend her, signify the sad calamities that attend the conversation of lewd women, viz., Poverty, Shame and the Gallows."

In every interval between pageant and pageant the mob

had still a new project to put on foot. This time they had got a piece of cloth a yard or more square, which they dipped in the gutter, till they had made it fit for their purpose, then tossed it about. Expanding itself in the air, and falling on the heads of two or three at once, it made 'em look like so many bearers under a pall, every one lugging a different way to get it off his head, oftentimes falling together by the ears about plucking off their cover-slut.

By the time forty or fifty heedless spectators were made as dirty as so many scavengers, the fourth pageant was come up, which was a most stately, rich and noble chariot, made of slit deal and paste-board, and in it was sitting a woman representing, I fancy, the Whore of Babylon, drawn by two goats, signifying her lust, and upon the backs of them two figures representing Jealousy and Revenge; her attendants importing the miseries that follow her, and the kettle-drums and trumpets serve to show that wheresoe'er she comes 'tis with terror and amazement.

The rabble having changed their sport to a new scene of unluckiness, had got a bullock's horn, which they filled with drain water, and poured it down people's necks, and into their pockets, so that it ran down their legs and into their shoes, the ignorant sufferers not readily discovering from whence the wet came.

NED WARD
The London Spy, 1703

The "pageants," open wagons with *tableaux vivants* staged on them to present aspects of commerce or public service, are still part of the Lord Mayor's Show. The conduct of the spectators, as reported by Ward, has fortunately altered. It must be remembered that Ward wrote his sketches more for entertainment than as contributions to social history. He kept his eye on the ugly, squalid, and absurd rather than on the silks and graces of Queen Anne's London.

THE LOVING APPRENTICE

Of all the girls that are so smart
  There's none like pretty Sally;
She is the darling of my heart,
  And she lives in our alley.
There is no lady in the land
  Is half so sweet as Sally;
She is the darling of my heart,
  And she lives in our alley.

Her father he makes cabbage-nets
  And through the streets does cry 'em;
Her mother she sells laces long
  To such as please to buy 'em:
But sure such folks could ne'er beget
  So sweet a girl as Sally!
She is the darling of my heart,
  And she lives in our alley.

When she is by, I leave my work,
  I love her so sincerely;
My master comes like any Turk,
  And bangs me most severely—
But let him bang his bellyful,
  I'll bear it all for Sally;
She is the darling of my heart,
  And she lives in our Alley.

Of all the days that's in the week
  I dearly love but one day—
And that's the day that comes betwixt
  A Saturday and Monday;

For then I'm drest all in my best
  To walk abroad with Sally;
She is the darling of my heart,
  And she lives in our alley.

My master carries me to church,
  And often am I blamed
Because I leave him in the lurch
  As soon as text is named;
I leave the church in sermon-time
  And slink away to Sally;
She is the darling of my heart,
  And she lives in our alley.

When Christmas comes about again
  O then I shall have money;
I'll hoard it up, and box it all,
  I'll give it to my honey:
I would it were ten thousand pound,
  I'd give it all to Sally;
She is the darling of my heart,
  And she lives in our alley.

My master and the neighbours all
  Make game of me and Sally,
And, but for her, I'd better be
  A slave and row a galley;
But when my seven long years are out
  O then I'll marry Sally,—
O then we'll wed, and then we'll bed . . .
  But not in our alley!

HENRY CAREY (1693?-1743)
Sally in Our Alley

A FRUITFUL JOURNEY

It is an inexpressible pleasure to know a little of the world and to be of no character or significancy in it.

To be ever unconcerned, and ever looking on new objects with an endless curiosity, is a delight known only to those who are turned for speculation: nay, they who enjoy it must value things only as they are the objects of speculation, without drawing any worldly advantage to themselves from them, but just as they are what contribute to their amusement, or the improvement of the mind. I lay one night last week at Richmond; and being restless, not out of dissatisfaction, but a certain busy inclination one sometimes has, I rose at four in the morning, and took boat for London, with a resolution to rove by boat and coach for the next four-and-twenty hours, till the many different objects I must needs meet with should tire my imagination, and give me an inclination to a repose more profound than I was at that time capable of. I beg people's pardon for an odd humour I am guilty of, and was often that day, which is saluting any person whom I like, whether I know him or not. This is a particularity would be tolerated in me, if they considered that the greatest pleasure I know I receive at my eyes, and that I am obliged to an agreeable person for coming abroad into my view, as another is for a visit of conversation at their own houses.

The hours of the day and night are taken up in the cities of London and Westminster, by people as different from each other as those who are born in different centuries. Men of six o'clock give way to those of nine, they of nine to the generation of twelve; and they of twelve disappear, and make room for the fashionable world, who have made two o'clock the noon of the day.

When we first put off from shore, we soon fell in with a

fleet of gardeners, bound for the several market ports of London; and it was the most pleasing scene imaginable to see the cheerfulness with which those industrious people plied their way to a certain sale of their goods. The banks of each side are as well peopled, and beautified with as agreeable plantations, as any spot on the earth; but the Thames itself, loaded with the product of each shore, added very much to the landscape. It was very easy to observe by their sailing, and the countenances of the ruddy virgins, who were supercargoes, the parts of the town to which they were bound. There was an air in the purveyors for Covent Garden, who frequently converse with morning rakes, very unlike the seeming sobriety of those bound for Stocks Market.

Nothing remarkable happened in our voyage; but I landed with ten sail of apricot-boats, at Strand Bridge, after having put in at Nine Elms, and taken in melons, consigned by Mr. Cuffe, of that place, to Sarah Sewell and Company, at their stall in Covent Garden. We arrived at Strand Bridge at six of the clock, and were unloading; when the hackney-coachmen of the foregoing night took their leave of each other at the Dark-house, to go to bed before the day was too far spent. Chimney-sweepers passed by us as we made up to the market, and some raillery happened between one of the fruit-wenches and those black men about the Devil and Eve, with allusion to their several professions. I could not believe any place more entertaining than Covent Garden; where I strolled from one fruit-shop to another, with crowds of agreeable young women around me, who were purchasing fruit for their respective families. It was almost eight of the clock before I could leave that variety of objects.

SIR RICHARD STEELE (1671-1729)
The Spectator

CARRIAGE FOLK

O ye associate walkers, O my friends,
Upon your state what happiness attends!
What, though no coach to frequent visit rolls,
Nor for your shilling chairmen sling their poles;
Yet still your nerves rheumatic pains defye,
Nor lazy jaundice dulls your saffron eye,
No wasting cough discharges sounds of death,
Nor wheezing asthma heaves in vain for breath;
Nor from your restless couch is heard the groan
Of burning gout, or sedentary stone,
Let others in the jolting coach confide,
Or in the leaky boat the Thames divide;
Or, box'd within the chair, contemn the street,
And trust their safety to another's feet,
Still let me walk; for oft' the sudden gale
Ruffles the tide, and shifts the dang'rous sail.
Then shall the passenger too late deplore
The whelming billow, and the faithless oar;
The drunken chairman in the kennel spurns,
The glasses shatters, and his charge o'erturns.
Who can recount the coach's various harms,
The legs disjointed, and the broken arms?
I've seen a beau, in some ill-fated hour,
When o'er the stones choak'd kennels swell the show'r
In gilded chariot loll; he with disdain
Views spatter'd passengers all drench'd in rain;
With mud fill'd high, the rumbling cart draws near,
Now rule thy prancing steeds, lac'd charioteer!
The dust-man lashes on with spiteful rage,
His pond'rous spokes thy painted wheel engage,
Crush'd is thy pride, down falls the shrieking beau,
The slabby pavement crystal fragments strow,

BUSKERS IN LEICESTER SQUARE

People waiting in theatre queues have long been entertained by strolling players known as Buskers. These two well-known drolls with portable orchestra are taking a chance in the middle of Leicester Square against regulations—and with public sympathy—until the police appear.

COVENT GARDEN OPERA HOUSE

Covent Garden, once the Convent Garden, has been a market for fruit, flowers and vegetables since early in the seventeenth century. A theatre opened there in 1732 became the home of classic drama and later of grand opera and ballet. The present building dates from 1858.

LUNCH BREAK IN THE NEW CITY

The terrible war-time devastation in the City gave scope for radical rebuilding. In and around the new rectangular office-blocks there is space and light for the workers and external amenities too. This garden at New Change by St. Paul's is much enjoyed when the sun shines.

STREET SCENE, BETHNAL GREEN

"Grimy and dismal", says an old guidebook of the East End's Bethnal Green, long the home of the silk-weavers. But prosperity has brought a new look: the old buildings are far from gay, but nobody in this gathering of families seems grimy, dismal or under-fed.

Black floods of mire th' embroidere'd coat disgrace,
And mud enwraps the honours of his face.

If the pale walker pant with weak'ning ills,
His sickly hand is stor'd with friendly bills:
From hence he learns the seventh-born doctor's fame,
From hence he learns the cheapest tailor's name.
Shall the large mutton smoak upon your boards?
Such, Newgate's copious market best affords.
Would'st thou with mighty beef augment thy meal?
Seek Leaden-hall; St. James's sends thee veal.
Thames-street gives cheeses; Covent-garden fruits;
Moor-fields old books; and Monmouth-street old suits.
Hence may'st thou well supply the wants of life,
Support thy family, and cloath thy wife.

What walker shall his mean ambition fix
On the false lustre of a coach and six?
Let the vain virgin, lur'd by glarink show,
Sigh for the liv'ries of th' embroider'd beau.
See yon bright chariot on its braces swing,
With Flanders mares, and on an arched spring;
That wretch, to gain an equipage and place,
Betray'd his sister to a lewd embrace.
This coach, that with the blazon'd 'scutcheon glows,
Vain of his unknown race, the coxcomb shows.
Here the brib'd lawyer, sunk in velvet, sleeps;
The starving orphan, as he passes, weeps;
There flames a fool, begirt with tinsell'd slaves,
Who wastes the wealth of a whole race of knaves.
That other, with a clustring train behind,
Owes his new honours to a sordid mind.
This next in court-fidelity excells,
The publick rifles, and his country sells.
May the proud chariot never be my fate,
If purchas'd at so mean, so dear a rate;

8

O rather give me sweet content on foot,
Wrapt in my virtue, and a good Surtout!

JOHN GAY (1685-1732)
Trivia; or the Art of Walking the Streets of London

A CITY SHOWER

Ah! where must needy poet seek for aid,
When dust and rain at once his coat invade?
Sole coat! where dust cemented by the rain
Erects the nap, and leaves a cloudy stain!
Now in contiguous drops the flood comes down,
Threatening with deluge this devoted town.
To shops in crowds the daggled females fly,
Pretend to cheapen goods, but nothing buy,
The Templar spruce, while every spout's abroach,
Stays till 'tis fair, yet seems to call a coach.
The tucked-up sempstress walks with hasty strides,
While streams run down her oiled umbrella's sides.
Here various kinds, by various fortunes led,
Commence acquaintance underneath a shed.
Triumphant Tories and desponding Whigs
Forget their feuds, and join to save their wigs.
Boxed in a chair the beau impatient sits,
While spouts run clattering o'er the roof by fits,
And even and anon with frightful din
The leather sounds; he trembles from within.

JONATHAN SWIFT (1667-1745)
Description of a City Shower

STREET CRIES

The crying of wares in the street is now comparatively rare in London, perhaps because the traffic so insistently shouts down this kind of appeal. But the use of the megaphone can add to the vocal din when it appears. At election times the candidates and the supporters parade the suburban streets with machinery which horribly amplifies their appeals for support. Our railway stations are also made raucous with megaphonic information which justifies Addison's following remarks about "cries very often not only incommodious but altogether useless to the public." After attending to these utterances to the best of our ability we often have to ask a guard or porter to interpret the contents of the raucous communication.

There is nothing which more astonishes a foreigner and frights a country squire than the Cries of London. My good friend Sir Roger often declares, that he cannot get them out of his head, or go to sleep for them, the first week that he is in town. On the contrary, Will. Honeycomb calls them the *Ramage de la Ville*, and prefers them to the sounds of larks and nightingales, with all the music of the fields and woods. I have lately received a letter from some very odd fellow upon this subject, which I shall leave with my reader, without saying anything further of it.

" Sir,

I am a man out of all business, and would willingly turn my head to anything for an honest livelihood. I have invented several projects for raising many millions of money without burthening the subject, but I cannot get the parliament to listen to me, who look upon me, forsooth, as a crack and a projector; so that despairing to enrich either myself or my country by this public-spiritedness, I would make some proposals to you relating to a design which I have very much at heart, and which may procure me an handsome subsistence, if you will be pleased to recommend it to the cities of London and Westminster.

" The post I would aim at is to be Comptroller-general of the London Cries, which are at present under no manner of rules or discipline. I think I am pretty well qualified for this place, as being a man of very strong lungs, of great insight into all the branches of our British trades and manufactures, and of a competent skill in music.

" The cries of London may be divided into vocal and instrumental. As for the latter, they are at present under a very great disorder. A freeman of London has the privilege of disturbing a whole street, for an hour together, with the twanking of a brass-kettle or a frying-pan. The watchman's thump at midnight startles us in our beds as much as the breaking in of a thief. I would therefore propose, that no instrument of this nature should be made use of, which I have not tuned and licensed, after having carefully examined in what manner it may affect the ears of her Majesty's liege subjects.

" Vocal cries are of a much larger extent, and, indeed, so full of incongruities and barbarisms, that we appear a distracted city to foreigners, who do not comprehend the meaning of such enormous outcries. Milk is generally sold in a note above ela, and it sounds so exceeding shrill, that it often sets our teeth on edge. The chimney-sweeper is confined to no certain pitch; he sometimes utters himself in the deepest bass, and sometimes in the sharpest treble; sometimes in the highest, and sometimes in the lowest note of the gamut. The same observation might be made on the retailers of small coal, not to mention broken glasses or brick-dust. In these, therefore, and the like cases, it should be my care to sweeten and mellow the voices of these itinerant tradesmen, before they make their appearance in our streets, as also to accommodate their cries to their respective wares;

and to take care in particular that those may not make the most noise who have the least to sell, which is very observable in the venders of card-matches, to whom I cannot but apply that old proverb of " Much cry, but little wool."

" Some of these last-mentioned musicians are so very loud in the sale of these trifling manufactures that an honest splenetic gentleman of my acquaintance bargained with one of them never to come into the street where he lived: but what was the effect of this contract? Why, the whole tribe of card-match-makers which frequent the quarter, passed by his door the very next day, in hopes of being bought off after the same manner.

" I am always pleased with that particular time of the year which is proper for the pickling of dill and cucumbers; but, alas, this cry, like the song of the nightingale, is not heard above two months. It would, therefore, be worth while to consider whether the same air might not in some cases be adapted to other words.

" It might likewise deserve our most serious consideration, how far, in a well-regulated city, those humourists are to be tolerated, who, not contented with the traditional cries of their forefathers, have invented particular songs and tunes of their own: such as was, not many years since, the pastry-man, commonly known by the name of the colly-molly-puff; and such as is at this day the vender of powder and wash-balls, who, if I am rightly informed, goes under the name of Powder Watt.

" I must not here omit one particular absurdity which runs through this whole vociferous generation, and which renders their cries very often not only incommodious, but altogether useless to the public; I mean that idle accomplishment which they all of them aim at, of crying so as not to be understood. Whether or no they have learned this from several of our affected singers, I will not take upon me to say; but most certain it is, that people know the wares they deal in rather by their tunes than by their words; insomuch, that I have some-times seen a country boy run out to buy apples of a bellows-mender, and ginger-bread from a grinder of knives and scissors. Nay, so strangely infatuated are some very eminent artists of this particular grace in a cry, that none but their acquaintance are able to guess at their profession; for who else can know that, ' Work if I had it,' should be the signification of a corn-cutter.

" Forasmuch, therefore, as persons of this rank are seldom men of genius or capacity, I think It would be very proper, that some man of good sense, and sound judgment, should preside over these public cries, who should permit none to lift up their voices in our streets, that have not tuneable throats, and are not only able to overcome the noise of the crowd, and the rattling of coaches, but also to vend their respective merchandises in apt phrases, and in the most distinct and agreeable sounds. I do therefore humbly recommend myself as a person rightly qualified for this post: and if I meet with fitting encouragement, shall communicate some other projects which I have by me, that may no less conduce to the emolument of the public.

> " I am, sir, etc.,
> " Ralph Crotchet."

JOSEPH ADDISON (1672-1719)
Essays

LOCUSTS AND BALLOONS

The duke and duchess of M—— breakfasted here on Monday, and seemed much pleased, though it rained the whole time, with an Egyptian darkness. I should have thought there had been deluges enough to destroy all Egypt's other plagues; but the newspapers talk of locusts—I suppose relations of your beetles, though probably not so fond of green fruit; for the scene of their campaign is Queen-square, Westminster, where there certainly has not been an orchard since the reign of Canute.

I have, at last, seen an air-balloon—just as I once did see a tiny review, by passing one accidentally on Hounslow-heath. I was going last night to lady Onslow at Richmond, and over Mr. Cambridge's field I saw a bundle in the air not bigger than the moon, and she herself could not have descended with more composure, if she had expected to find Endymion fast asleep. It seemed to light on Richmond-hill; but Mrs. H——was going by, and her coiffeure prevented my seeing it alight. The papers say, that a balloon has been made at Paris, representing the castle of Stockholm, in compliment to the king of Sweden: but that they were afraid to let it off— so, I suppose, it will be served up to him in a dessert. No great progress, surely, is made in these airy navigations, if they are still afraid of risking the necks of two or three subjects for the entertainment of a visiting sovereign. There is seldom a *feu de joie* for the birth of a dauphin that does not cost more lives. I thought royalty and science never haggled about the value of blood, when experiments are in question.

HORACE WALPOLE (1717-1797)
Diary

DON JUAN COMES TO LONDON

Through coaches, drays, choked turnpikes, and a whirl
Of wheels, and roar of voices, and confusion;
Here taverns wooing to a pint of " purl,"
There mails fast flying off like a delusion;
There barbers' blocks with periwigs in curl
In windows; here the lamplighter's infusion
Slowly distill'd into the glimmering glass
(For in those days we had not got to gas—);

Through this, and much, and more, is the approach
Of travellers to mighty Babylon:
Whether they come by horse, or chaise, or coach,
With slight exceptions, all the ways seem one.
I could say more, but do not choose to encroach
Upon the Guide-book's privilege. The sun
Had set some time, and night was on the ridge
Of twilight, as the party cross'd the bridge.

That's rather fine, the gentle sounds of Thamis—
Who vindicates a moment, too, his stream—
Though hardly heard through multifarious " damme's."
The lamps of Westminster's more regular gleam,
The breadth of pavement, and yon shrine where fame is
A spectral resident—whose pallid beam
In shape of moonshine hovers o'er the pile—
Make this a sacred part of Albion's isle.

The Druid's groves are gone—so much the better:
Stone-Henge is not—but what the devil is it?—
But Bedlam still exists with its sage fetter,
That madmen may not bite you on a visit;
The Bench too seats or suits full many a debtor;
The Mansion-House, too (though some people quiz it),
To me appears a stiff yet grand erection;
But then the Abbey's worth the whole collection.

The line of lights, too, up to Charing Cross,
Pall Mall, and so forth, have a coruscation
Like gold as in comparison to dross,
Match'd with the Continent's illumination,
Whose cities Night by no means deigns to gloss.
The French were not yet a lamp-lighting nation,
And when they grew so—on their new-found lantern,
Instead of wicks, they made a wicked man turn.

REGENT STREET IN CHRISTMAS TRIM

The store-keepers of Regent Street have their own organisation as well as their own pride. Before Christmas they combine to welcome the shopping crowds with a unified scheme of decoration and illumination and clever artistry is shown in carrying it out.

CUT FROM THE JOINT

Londoners lived on such scanty meat rations during and for some time after the war that the return of the roast was much appreciated. Here at Simpson's in the Strand, famous for its meat, the customer sees what he is getting as the carver brings round his trolley.

CHELSEA: A RIVERSIDE NIGHT

Whistler's painting caught the exquisite blues and greys of the twilit river
at Chelsea: the camera can also achieve notable nocturnes of the Thames
with the sentinel power-stations and the moorings for barges and the
craft owned by members of the Chelsea Yacht and Boat Club.

A row of gentlemen along the streets
Suspended, may illuminate mankind,
As also bonfires made of country-seats;
But the old way is best for the purblind:
The other looks like phosphorous on sheets,
A sort of *ignis fatuus* to the mind,
Which, though 'tis certain to perplex and frighten,
Must burn more mildly ere it can enlighten.

But London's so well lit, that if Diogenes
Could recommence to hunt his honest man,
And found him not amidst the various progenies
Of this enormous city's spreading spawn,
'T were not for want of lamps to aid his dodging his
Yet undiscover'd treasure. What I can,
I've done to find the same throughout life's journey,
But see the world is only one attorney.

Over the stones still rattling, up Pall Mall,
Through crowds and carriages, but waxing thinner
As thunder'd knockers broke the long-seal'd spell
Of doors 'gainst duns, and to an early dinner
Admitted a small party as night fell,—
Don Juan, our young diplomatic sinner,
Pursued his path, and drove past some hotels,
St. James's Palace and St. James's " Hells."

They reach'd the hotel: forth stream'd from the front
    door
A tide of well-clad waiters, and around
The mob stood, and as usual several score
Of those pedestrian Paphians who abound
In decent London when the daylight's o'er;
Commodious but immortal, they are found
Useful, like Malthus, in promoting marriage—
But Juan now is stepping from his carriage.

Into one of the sweetest of hotels,
Especially for foreigners—and mostly
For those whom favour or whom fortune swells,
And cannot find a bill's small items costly.
There many an envoy either dwelt or dwells
(The den of many a diplomatic lost lie),
Until to some conspicuous square they pass,
And blazon o'er the door their names in brass.

*   *   *

His morns he pass'd in business—which dissected,
Was like all business, a laborious nothing
That leads to lassitude, the most infected
And Centaur Nessus garb of mortal clothing,
And on our sofas makes us lie dejected,
And talk in tender horrors of our loathing
All kinds of toil, save for our country's good—
Which grows no better, though 'tis time it should.

His afternoons he pass'd in visits, luncheons,
Lounging, and boxing; and the twilight hour
In riding round those vegetable puncheons
Call'd " Parks," where there is neither fruit nor flower
Enough to gratify a bee's slight munchings;
But after all it is the only " bower "
(In Moore's phrase) where the fashionable fair
Can form a slight acquaintance with fresh air.

Then dress, then dinner, then awakes the world!
Then glare the lamps, then whirl the wheels, then roar
Through street and square fast flashing chariots hurl'd
Like harness'd meteors; then along the floor
Chalk mimics painting; then festoons are twirl'd;
Then roll the brazen thunders of the door,
Which opens to the thousand happy few
An earthly Paradise of " Or Molu."

There stands the noble hostess, nor shall sink
With the three-thousandth curtsy; there the waltz,
The only dance which teaches girls to think,
Makes one in love even with its very faults.
Saloon, room, hall, o'erflow beyond their brink,
And long the latest of arrivals halts,
'Midst royal dukes and dames condemn'd to climb,
And gain an inch of staircase at a time.

Thrice happy he who, after a survey
Of the good company, can win a corner,
A door that's in or boudoir out of the way,
Where he may fix himself like small " Jack Horner,"
And let the Babel round run as it may,
And look on as a mourner, or a scorner,
Or an approver, or a mere spectator,
Yawning a little as the night grows later.

But this won't do, save by and by; and he
Who, like Don Juan, takes an active share,
Must steer with care through all that glittering sea
Of gems and plumes and pearls and silks, to where
He deems it is his proper place to be;
Dissolving in the waltz to some soft air,
Or proudlier prancing with mercurial skill,
Where Science marshals forth her own quadrille.

LORD BYRON (1788-1824)
Don Juan

STREET SCENE, 1775

A series of pictures representing the streets of London in
the night, even at the comparatively recent date of this
tale, would present to the eye something so very different
in character from the reality which is witnessed in these
times, that it would be difficult for the beholder to

recognise his most familiar walks in the altered aspect of little more than half a century ago.

They were, one and all, from the broadest and best to the narrowest and least frequented, very dark. The oil and cotton lamps, though regularly trimmed twice or thrice in the long winter nights, burnt feebly at the best; and at a late hour, when they were unassisted by the lamps and candles in the shops, cast but a narrow track of doubtful light upon the footway, leaving the projecting doors and house-fronts in the deepest gloom. Many of the courts and lanes were left in total darkness; those of the meaner sort, where one glimmering light twinkled for a score of houses, being favoured in no slight degree. Even in these places, the inhabitants had often good reason for extinguishing their lamp as soon as it was lighted; and the watch being utterly inefficient and powerless to prevent them, they did so at their pleasure. Thus, in the lightest thoroughfares, there was at every turn some obscure and dangerous spot whither a thief might fly for shelter, and few would care to follow; and the city being belted round by fields, green lanes, waste grounds, and lonely roads, dividing it at that time from the suburbs that have joined it since, escape, even where the pursuit was not, was rendered easy.

It is no wonder that with these favouring circumstances in full and constant operation, street robberies, often accompanied by cruel wounds, and not unfrequently by loss of life, should have been of nightly occurrence in the very heart of London, or that quiet folks should have had great dread of traversing its streets after the shops were closed. It was not unusual for those who wandered home alone at midnight, to keep the middle of the road, the better to guard against surprise from lurking footpads; few would venture to repair at a late hour to Kentish Town or Hampstead, or even to Kensington or Chelsea, unarmed and unattended;

while he who had been loudest and most valiant at the supper-table or the tavern, and had but a mile or so to go, was glad to fee a link-boy to escort him home.

There were many other characteristics—not quite so disagreeable—about the thoroughfares of London then, with which they had been long familiar. Some of the shops, especially those to the eastward of Temple Bar, still adhered to the old practice of hanging out a sign; and the creaking and swinging of these boards in their iron frames on windy nights, formed a strange and mournful concert for the ears of those who lay awake in bed or hurried through the streets. Long stands of hackney-chairs and groups of chairmen, compared with whom the coachmen of our day are gentle and polite, obstructed the way and filled the air with clamour; night-cellars, indicated by a little stream of light crossing the pavement, and stretching out half-way into the road, and by the stifled roar of voices from below, yawned for the reception and entertainment of the most abandoned of both sexes; under every shed and bulk small groups of link-boys gamed away the earnings of the day; or one more weary than the rest gave way to sleep, and let the fragments of his torch fall hissing on the puddled ground.

Then there was the watch with staff and lantern crying the hour, and the kind of weather; and those who woke up at his voice and turned them round in bed, were glad to hear it rained, or snowed, or blew, or froze, for very comfort's sake. The solitary passenger was startled by the chairmen's cry of " By your leave there! " as two came trotting past him with their empty vehicle— carried backwards to show its being disengaged—and hurried to the nearest stand. Many a private chair, too, inclosing some fine lady, monstrously hooped and fur-belowed, and preceded by running-footmen bearing flambeaux—for which extinguishers are yet suspended before the doors of a few houses of the better sort—

made the way gay and light as it danced along, and
darker and more dismal when it had passed. It was not
unusual for these running gentry, who carried it with a
very high hand, to quarrel in the servant's hall while
waiting for their masters and mistresses; and, falling
to blows either there or in the street without, to strew
the place of skirmish with hair-powder, fragments of
bag-wigs, and scattered nosegays. Gaming, the vice
which ran so high among all classes (the fashion being
of course set by the upper), was generally the cause of
these disputes; for cards and dice were as openly used,
and worked as much mischief, and yielded as much
excitement below stairs, as above.

While incidents like these, arising out of drums and
masquerades and parties at quadrille, were passing at
the west end of the town, heavy stage-coaches and scarce
heavier waggons were lumbering slowly towards the
city, the coachmen, guard, and passengers, armed to the
teeth, and the coach—a day or so perhaps behind its time,
but that was nothing—despoiled by highwaymen; who
made no scruple to attack, alone and single-handed, a
whole caravan of goods and men, and sometimes shot a
passenger or two, and were sometimes shot themselves,
as the case might be. On the morrow, rumours of this
new act of daring on the road yielded matter for a few
hours' conversation through the town, and a Public
Progress of some fine gentleman (half drunk) to Tyburn,
dressed in the newest fashion, and damning the ordinary
with unspeakable gallantry and grace, furnished to the
populace at once a pleasant excitement and a wholesome
and profound example.

CHARLES DICKENS (1812-1870)
Barnaby Rudge

WAITING

" O come, O come," the mother pray'd
 And hush'd her babe: " let me behold
Once more thy stately form array'd
 Like autumn woods in green and gold!

" I see thy brethren come and go;
 Thy peers in stature, and in hue
Thy rivals. Some like monarchs glow
 With richest purple: some are blue

" As skies that tempt the swallow back;
 Or red as, seen o'er wintry seas,
The star of storm; or barr'd with black
 And yellow, like the April bees.

" Come they and go! I heed not, I.
 Yet others hail their advent, cling
All trustful to their side, and fly
 Safe in their gentle piloting

" To happy homes on heath or hill,
 By park or river. Still I wait
And peer into the darkness: still
 Thou com'st not—I am desolate.

" Hush! hark! I see a towering form!
 From the dim distance slowly roll'd
It rocks like lilies in a storm,
 And O, its hues are green and gold:

" It comes, it comes! Ah rest is sweet,
   And there is rest, my babe, for us! "
She ceased, as at her very feet
   Stopp'd the St. John's Wood omnibus.

C. S. CALVERLEY (1831-1884)
Fly Leaves

The London omnibus long ago changed its colour along with its
motive power, but this poem by Calverley has a delightful flavour for
myself since in my early boyhood I waited for the Green Atlas (horse-
drawn) bus to carry me from Hampstead to St. John's Wood and so
to the heaven that was Lord's cricket-ground. The fare was a penny
each way, entrance sixpence, score-card a penny: with a shilling in
pocket and some sandwiches I had threepence for the extras and threepence (carefully watched) could buy quite a lot then. So I respond
with a warmth of memory to the "stately form arrayed like autumn
woods in green and gold " as it clip-clopped down the Finchley Road.

LONDON SNOW

When men were all asleep the snow came flying,
In large white flakes falling on the city brown,
Stealthily and perpetually settling and loosely lying,
   Hushing the latest traffic of the drowsy town;
Deadening, muffling, stifling its murmurs failing;
Lazily and incessantly floating down and down:
   Silently sifting and veiling road, roof and railing;
Hiding difference, making unevenness even,
Into angles and crevices softly drifting and sailing.
   All night it fell, and when full inches seven
It lay in the depth of its uncompacted lightness,
The clouds blew off from a high and frosty heaven;
   And all woke earlier for the unaccustomed brightness
Of the winter dawning, the strange unheavenly glare:
The eye marvelled—marvelled at the dazzling whiteness;
   The ear hearkened to the stillness of the solemn air;
No sound of wheel rumbling nor of foot falling,
And the busy morning cries came thin and spare.
   Then boys I heard, as they went to school, calling,

They gathered up the crystal manna to freeze
Their tongues with tasting, their hands with snow-
    balling;
    Or rioted in a drift, plunging up to the knees;
Or peering up from under the white-mossed wonder,
" O look at the trees! " they cried, " O look at the trees! "
    With lessened load a few carts creak and blunder,
Following along the white deserted way,
A country company long dispersed asunder:
    When now already the sun, in pale display
Standing by Paul's high dome, spread forth below
His sparkling beams, and awoke the stir of the day.
    For now doors open, and war is waged with the snow;
And trains of sombre men, past tale of number,
Tread long brown paths, as toward their toil they go:
    But even for them awhile no cares encumber
Their minds diverted; the daily word is unspoken,
The daily thoughts of labour and sorrow slumber
At the sight of the beauty that greets them, for the charm
    they have broken.

ROBERT BRIDGES (1844-1930)
Shorter Poems

TYBURNIA

Tyburnia, or the northern wing, is that vast city which
has sprung up within the last twelve years from the sod,
known as the Paddington district. Having been built at
one time, it assumes in consequence a regularity of
appearance contrasting strangely with the older portions
of the Metropolis. Fine squares, connected by spacious
streets, the houses being of great altitude, give a certain
air of nobility to the district. The sameness, however,
caused by endless repetition of " Compo " decorations,
and the prevailing white colour of the houses, distresses
the eye, especially after the red brick of Grosvenor, and

the older and still great fashionable squares. Tyburnia
is principally inhabited by the gentry, professional men,
the great City merchants, and by those who are under-
going the transitional state between commerce and
fashion. Its boundaries may be said to be the Edgware-
road on the E., Bayswater on the W., Maida-hill on the
N., and Hyde Park and Kensington Gardens on the S.
The point of junction with the great centre of fashionable London being the Marble Arch at Cumberland
Gate, Hyde Park.

Murray's Guide to Modern London, 1851

The name of Tyburn Tree, scene of executions, had such ugly associations that it is surprising to find that the name Tyburnia was still
given in early Victorian times to a district then increasingly favoured
by the prosperous genteel. John Galsworthy's Forsytes were clustered
on this side of Hyde Park and would not have cared to be called
Tyburnians. Bayswater, mentioned as the western limit of the old
Tyburnia, is now the title usually given to all this area.

THE GARDEN SUBURB

I had often heard of the Hampstead Garden Suburb, of
the attempt of its inhabitants to create an atmosphere
of the Higher Culture, to recreate, as it were, the Golden
Age in that region. But I must now confess that it was
in a spirit of profane curiosity that I walked up towards
its courts and closes. And when I saw the notices of the
Societies for Mothercraft and Handicraft and Child
Study, the lectures on Reincarnation, the Holy Grail,
and the Teaching of the Holy Zoroaster, I'm afraid I
laughed. But how thin this laughter sounded amid the
quiet amenity, the beautiful distinction of this Utopia!
It was an afternoon of daydreams; the autumnal light
under the low clouds was propitious to inner recollec-
tion; and as I walked the street of this transcendenta
city, soothed by the sense of order and beautiful archi

tecture all around me, I began to feel that I too was an Idealist, that here was my spiritual home, and that it would be a seemly thing to give up the cinemas and come and make my abode on this hill-top. Pictures floated before my eyes of tranquil days, days of gardening and handicrafts and lectures, evenings spent in perusing the world's masterpieces.

Although I still frequent the cinemas, and spend too much time gazing in at the windows of expensive shops, and the reverie of that afternoon has come to no fruition, yet I feel myself a better person for it: I feel that it marks me off from the merely cynical and worldly. For I at last have had a Pisgah sight of the Promised City; I have made its ideal my own, if but for an afternoon, and only in a daydream.

LOGAN PEARSALL SMITH (1865-1946)
More Trivia

A COCKNEY'S EVENING SONG

Fades into twilight the last golden gleam
Thrown by the sunset on upland and stream;
Glints o'er the Serpentine—tips Notting Hill—
Dies on the Summit of proud Pentonville.

Day brought us trouble, but Night brings us peace;
Morning brought sorrow, but Eve bids it cease.
Gaslight and Gaiety, beam for a while;
Pleasure and Paraffin, lend us a smile.

Temples of Mammon are voiceless again—
Lonely policemen inherit Mark Lane
Silent is Lothbury—quiet Cornhill—
Babel of Commerce, thine echoes are still.

Far to the South—where the wanderer strays
Lost among graveyards and riverward ways,

Hardly a footfall and hardly a breath
Comes to dispute Laurence Poutney with Death.

Westward the stream of Humanity glides;—
'Busses are proud of their dozen insides.
Put up thy shutters, grim Care, for today—
Mirth and the lamplighter hurry this way.

Out on the glimmer weak Hesperus yields!
Gas for the cities and stars for the fields.
Daisies and buttercups, do as ye list;
I and my friends are for music or whist.

HENRY S. LEIGH (1837-1883)
Carols of Cockayne, 1874

SPRING IN PICCADILLY

Spring winds that blow
As over leagues of myrtle-blooms and may;
Bevies of spring clouds trooping slow,
Like matrons heavy bosomed and aglow
With the mild and placid pride of increase! Nay,
What makes this insolent and comely stream
Of appetence, this freshet of desire
(Milk from the wild breasts of the wilful Day!),
Down Piccadilly dance and murmer and gleam
In genial wave on wave and gyre on gyre?
Why does that nymph unparalleled splash and churn
The wealth of her enchanted urn
Till, over-billowing all between
Her cheerful margents, grey and living green,
It floats and wanders, glittering and fleeing,
An estuary of the joy of being?
Why should the lovely leafage of the Park
Touch to an ecstasy the act of seeing?

Praise God for giving
Through this His messenger among the days
His word the life He gave is thrice-worth living!
For Pan, the bountiful, imperious Pan—
Not dead, not dead, as impotent dreamers feigned,
But the gay genius of a million Mays
Renewing his beneficent endeavour!—
Still reigns and triumphs, as he hath triumphed and
    reigned
Since in the dim blue dawn time
The universal ebb-and-flow began,
To sound his ancient music, and prevails,
By the persuasion of his mighty rhyme,
Here in this radiant and immortal street
Lavishly and omnipotently as ever
In the open hills, the undissembling dales,
The laughing-places of the juvenile earth.
For lo! the wills of man and woman meet,
Meet and are moved, each unto each endeared,
As once in Eden's prodigal bowers befell,
To share his shameless, elemental mirth
In one great act of faith: while deep and strong,
Incomparably nerved and cheered,
The enormous heart of London joys to beat
To the measures of his rough, majestic song;
The lewd, perennial, overmastering spell
That keeps the rolling universe ensphered,
And life, and all for which life lives to long,
Wanton and wondrous and for ever well.

W. E. HENLEY (1849-1903)
London Voluntaries

OCTOBER SUNSET

For earth and sky and air
Are golden everywhere,
And golden with a gold so suave and fine
That looking on it lifts the heart like wine,
Trafalgar Square
(The fountains volleying golden glaze)
Shines like an angel-market. High aloft
Over his couchant Lions, in a haze
Shimmering and bland and soft,
A dust of chrysoprase,
Our Sailor takes the golden gaze
Of the saluting sun, and flames superb,
As once he flamed it on his ocean round . . .
The very blind man pottering on the kerb,
Among the posies and the ostrich feathers
And the rude voices touched with all the weathers
Of the long, varying year,
Shares in the universal alms of light.
The windows, with their fleeting, flickering fires,
The height and spread of frontage shining sheer,
The quiring signs, the rejoicing roofs and spires—
'Tis El Dorado—El Dorado plain,
The Golden City! And when a girl goes by,
Look! as she turns her glancing head,
A call of gold is floated from her ear!
Golden, all golden! In a golden glory,
Long-lapsing down a golden coasted sky,
The day not dies but seems
Dispersed in wafts and drifts of gold, and shed
Upon a past of golden song and story
And Memories of gold and golden dreams.

W. E. HENLEY (1849-1903)
Collected Poems

PARLIAMENT HILL FIELDS

Rumbling under blackened girders, Midland, bound for
     Cricklewood,
Puffed its sulphur to the sunset where that Land of
     Laundries stood.
Rumble under, thunder over, train and tram alternate
     go,
Shake the floor and smudge the ledger, Charrington,
     Sells, Dale and Co.,
Nuts and nuggets in the window, trucks along the lines
     below.

When the Bon Marché was shuttered, when the feet were
     hot and tired,
Outside Charrington's we waited, by the " STOP HERE
     IF REQUIRED,"
Launched aboard the shopping basket, sat precipitately
     down,
Rocked past Zwanziger the baker's, and the terrace
     blackish brown,
And the curious Anglo-Norman parish church of Kentish
     Town.

Till the tram went over thirty, sighting terminus
     again,
Past municipal lawn tennis and the bobble-hanging
     plane;
Soft the light suburban evening caught our ashlar-
     speckled spire,
Eighteen-sixty Early English, as the mighty elms
     retire
Either side of Brookfield Mansions flashing fine french-
     window fire.

Oh the after-tram-ride quiet, when we heard a mile
    beyond,
Silver music from the bandstand, barking dogs by High-
    gate Pond;
Up the hill where stucco houses in Virginia creeper
    drown—
And my childish wave of pity, seeing children carrying
    down
Sheaves of drooping dandelions to the courts of Kentish
    Town.

JOHN BETJEMAN (1906-   )
Collected Poems

TORRACORRA

This name is neither Mexican nor Antipodean. It may
suggest a snake-dance as described by D. H. Lawrence or
one of the back-blocks where Boldrewood's bushrangers
have now been peaceably transmuted into budding
Bradmans. But in fact the pentasyllabic-monster belongs
to London, West Central 1. It signifies the Tottenham
Court Road. But that must be explained.

When I was a boy, living in a tranquil crescent called
Hampstead Hill Gardens, I first travelled to and from
Oxford Street by way of Camden Town and this shopping
avenue called Tottenham Court Road; our vehicle was
a horse-bus. Going down hill from the Northern
Heights, as the house-agents love to call them—it will be
the North London Highlands before long—was easy
work. But coming up again was real coaching; we took
on an extra horse and became a three-in-hand at Chalk
Farm and then again at Rosslyn Hill in order to surmount these escarpments, to use the military writer's
term. The descent into London took us about forty
minutes and the reascent some fifty. There was a seat
beside the driver for which a small boy darted, braving

OUTSIDE THE PALACE

The sentries at Buckingham Palace were for many years posted outside the main gates, exposed to stares and questions they were not allowed to answer. In 1959 they were removed to the entry of the Palace itself. A policeman, who has freedom of speech, remains outside.

UPPER CHEYNE ROW, CHELSEA

Cheyne Row in Chelsea, near the grander parade of riverside Cheyne Walk, has some Queen Anne houses, including the home of Thomas and Jane Carlyle, No. 24, now a literary shrine on public view. Carlyle described the row as "all old-fashioned and tightly done up".

ST. PAUL'S AND ITS NEW SURROUNDINGS

The Cathedral, though damaged, survived the bombing of the Second World War. Many of the buildings around it were wrecked and have been replaced by new offices and warehouses yielding much greater accomodation.

REGENT STREET: DAMP BUT BLAZING

The cars are driving in from Regent Street to the hub of London's pleasure centre, Piccadilly Circus. Forty theatres and many large cinemas are within a small radius. Do the advertisements flash vulgarly? Perhaps, but there is gaiety in a town lit up, even with rain about.

the weather of the uncovered top-deck in order to profit
by the company, the general sense of equine acquaintance,
and the commanding position. So with a not outrageous
day and a good, genial, fruity conversational driver as
your guide and commentator on the London scene—
and such men there were—the journey could be total
bliss.

*   *   *

The horse-bus (and tram) were on their last, hard-
worked legs. We were soon to dive into the bowels of
Belsize Park and be taken for twopence—the horse-bus
fare had been threepence, I think—in the Tube to Oxford
Street in a quarter of the old time, speeding like magic-
ally accelerated moles under tunnelled Torracorra. It
was the custom, on the earliest Tube trains, to have a
guardian to every carriage. His job was to open and close
the doors and also to warn the passengers of the station
next ahead, so that they should be on tip-toe to alight.
Such admonitions were delivered with a grinding vocal
roar which telescoped all the details of the information
as an accident may telescope the railway carriages. Those
extraordinary, and surely to a foreigner quite incom-
prehensible, noises ended when the presence of guardians
in each coach was deemed superfluous.

But the relentless yelling survives in the curious
screams which are delivered by platform officials at the
central stations of the London Tubes when crowds are
largest at the rush-hour. We are commanded to hurry on,
with orders raucously bellowed into the ears of people
already being pushed and almost trampled down in the
scramble to get somehow wedged into the train. When
a person who is fighting desperately to insert himself
into a packed carriage has his ear-drums assaulted with
the kind of savage exhortation, he experiences the last,
infuriating horror of such travel. I cannot think why

the rulers of London Transport permit, or even encourage, this cacophonous discourtesy. The melancholy
wail of " Idor," which presumably means " Mind the
Doors," is harmless enough; it is the nagging stream of
"Hong, Hong," which presumably means "Hurry on "
when one is being hustled almost to extinction that
drives one to frenzy.

As we left Goodge Street going south in the old days
the voice of the guardian roared " Torracorranex," in-
forming us that our next stop would be the Tottenham
Court Road. So the street has remained Torracorra for
me; also it has retained a certain fascination, despite
all its drabness, because it was my first avenue to the
pleasures of the West End. Torracorranex! We were in
the heart of things.

The road was once a rural thoroughfare leading to
the Adam and Eve Pleasaunce, hard by Tottenham or
Tatnam Court which, the home of the Fitzroy family,
stood near our Fitzroy Square; this square is now
largely a hospital and office island with the Bohemian
waters lapping grubbily about it. The Adam and Eve is
still there at the corner of Warren Street and Hampstead
Road, and is now a very urban public-house. Gone are
the London gardens famous for their syllabubs, a dish
which sounds a trifle sickly nowadays since it had a milk
basis and was curdled with wine. It was popular with the
Restoration ladies who carried their virtue, rather pre-
cariously, for an airing in the famous pleasure-grounds
and tavern-gardens of the town.

* * *

Earlier, in the days of Shakespeare and Jonson, resort
to Tatnam had been common for the purpose of eating
cream and there was the sweet of the year when Torracorra smelled all April and May so that Gay could write
of a street car (named Desire?) making for amorous

thoughts in green shades, doubtless with syllabubs attending.

> Love flies the dusty town for shady woods,
> Then Tottenham Fields with roving beauty swarm.

There is still rusticity. Leaving Oxford Street you see the northern hills and woodlands on a summer evening surging gently up behind Camden Town: and on a clear day in winter you may have the same glimpse too. These slopes were long the cherished view of London's inhabitants; that is why what was left of the dwelling-houses in Euston Road had their gardens, later yards, in front of them. This was the verge of the town before the railways came and naturally the railways established their three great termini where the town began. The house-owners liked to sit and look outwards to the north-westerly heights whose agreeable curves moved skyward behind the villages of Somers Town, Kentish Town, and Camden Town; so they arranged their gardens for such sessions and, when you went from Warren Street to Euston, you could, until quite recently, see the houses on your right set back with what was once a gazebo or observation-post as well as a pleasaunce in front.

Lovers now, if they fly from the town for the shady copse, need not go very far. A journey of five miles will bring them to the great beeches of Kenwood. But they will discover small relief of that kind in Torracorra; the joys are urban and up to date, " jive " in London's Harlem or the racket of the Fun Fair. Cakes gluey with cream-substitute replace the syllabub. Hot-dogs and hamburgers abound. But still, with a clear sky, you may lift up your eyes unto the hills and feel some balm from that not far horizon.

It is an extraordinary place, this Torracorra, with its seigneurial past and its plebeian look. The imposing and historic shops on the East side are contrasted with some lamentable shabbiness on the West. It largely furnished Victorian London and a good deal of our own. Behind its plate-glass windows have gleamed a noble array of mahogany sideboards, of august four-posters, and of the shiniest bedroom suites in the modern style. Wandering down the street of a morning—I was a Bloomsburian once—I often thought what a pleasing surprise it would be for Maple's staff, if, when they clocked in, they discovered that a weary tramp, or even a couple, had somehow penetrated their vast mansion during the night and had gone happily to sleep in one of those great beds displayed in the vast windows. Some boozy Christopher Sly of St. Pancras, all fumes and rags, would well have become such an invasion. Indeed, the trick might have been played the Sly way, with a posse of rowdy students depositing a drunk and incapable member of their rout to sleep it off in such grandeur and then wake to find himself famous—or at least a " front-page top " in the early editions of the evening papers.

The great days of Torracorra were when Shoolbred stood shoulder to shoulder with Maple. In an age of shine and shoddy Shoolbred's was doomed by nature; it was a store as solemn as a kirk elder and reliable as oak. It retained the shop-walker, in solemn black, tail-coated I think, or even frock-coated, to the end. It retained leisure and a grave brand of courtesy. You could really shop in Shoolbred's instead of being caught in a wave of bargain-hunting, stunt-lured myriads. It sold everything and its catalogues were encyclopaedias. I miss my store-catalogue English in these times; " the same, japanned." Do we still japan? The particular glory of the house was its home equipment, beds, blankets, ironmongery and so on. It did not vulgarly bellow its bargains or beckon the young couple about to set up house in the suburbs; sagacious parents led them down Torracorra as the right, indeed the only, thing to do; here was the Mecca of the mattress-minded.

Up the East Side, from Charles Baker's where I bought my schoolboy suits, to Wolfe and Hollander and Bartholomew and Fletcher, it used to be solid worth all the way. Heal came in with the New Look, reminding the Road that it was the verge of Bloomsbury as well as the bed-maker for Baron's Court. Heal brought in style and Shearn gave it nuts. I never felt that the Torracorra was the right place for vegetarians. It was the natural sideboard for a large roast.

IVOR BROWN (1891-)
Winter in London

At Plays and Play

WINTER SPORTS

12th Century

During the holydays in summer the young men exercise themselves in the sports of leaping, archery, wrestling stone-throwing, slinging javelins beyond a mark, and also fighting with bucklers. Cytherea leads the dances of the maidens, who merrily trip along the ground beneath the uprisen moon. Almost on every holyday in winter, before dinner, foaming boars, and huge-tusked hogs, intended for bacon, fight for their lives, or fat bulls or immense boars are baited with dogs. When that great marsh which washes the walls of the city on the north side is frozen over, the young men go out in crowds to divert themselves upon the ice. Some, having increased their velocity by a run, placing their feet apart, and turning their bodies sideways, slide a great way: others make a seat of large pieces of ice like mill-stones, and a great number of them running before, and holding each other by the hand, draw one of their companions who is seated on the ice: if at any time they slip in moving so swiftly, all fall down headlong together.

Others are more expert in their sports upon the ice; for fitting to, and binding under their feet the shinbones of some animal, and taking in their hands poles shod with iron, which at times they strike against the ice, they are carried along with as great rapidity as a bird flying or a bolt discharged from a cross-bow. Sometimes two of the skaters having placed themselves a great distance apart by mutual agreement, come together from opposite

sides; they meet, raise their poles, and strike each other;
either one or both of them fall, not without some bodily
hurt: even after their fall they are carried along to a
great distance from each other by the velocity of the
motion; and whatever part of their heads comes in
contact with the ice is laid bare to the very skull. Very
frequently the leg or arm of the falling party, if he
chance to light upon either of them, is broken. But
youth is an age eager for glory and desirous of victory,
and so young men engage in counterfeit battles, that
they may conduct themselves more valiantly in real ones.

JOHN STOW (1525-1605)
Survey of London

In his *Survey*, John Stow made many quotations from William
Fitzstephen, a monk of Canterbury who wrote his *Descriptio Londiniae*
in the reign of Henry II and died in 1191. This passage is by Fitzstephen.

LONDON CRICKET

(1) BUMPERS

"July 16: Last week was played a match in White-
Conduit Fields by Islington; between 11 Londoners on
one side, and 11 men of Kent on the other side, for 5s. a
head; at which time, being in eager pursuit of the game,
the Kentish men having the wickets, two Londoners
striving with expedition to gain the ball, met each other
with that fierceness, that hitting their heads together
they both fell backwards without stirring hand or foot,
and lay deprived of sense for a considerable time, and
'tis not yet known (at that time) whether they will
recover. The Kentish men were beat."

from the *Weekly Journal or Saturday's Post, 1720*

(2) Getting Shirty

" On Monday, July 26, 1731, a great cricket match was play'd on Chelsea Common, between 11 of London, and the like number of Brompton, for £5 a-head, which was won by great odds by the former. As soon as the match was over a quarrel happened between a Londoner and a Brompton gentleman, occasioned by the latter's tearing the former's ruffles from off his shirt, swearing he had no property to them, when several engaged on both sides for nearly half an hour, and most of the Brompton gentlemen were forced to fly for quarters, and some retired home with black eyes, and broken heads, much to the satisfaction of the opposite side."

from the *Weekly Journal or Saturday's Post, 1731*

(3) London The Champion

Hail Cricket! glorious, manly, British Game!
First of all sports! be first alike in fame!
To my fir'd Soul thy busy transports bring,
That I may feel thy Raptures, while I sing!
O thou, sublime Inspirer of my Song!
What matchless trophies to thy worth belong!
Look round the earth, inclin'd to mirth, and see
What daring sport can claim the prize from thee!

Not puny Billiards, where, with sluggish pace,
The dull ball trails before the foolish face,
Where nothing can your languid spirits move,
Save when the Marker bellows out, Six love!
Nor yet that happier Game, where the smooth **Bowl**,
In circling mazes, wanders to the goal;

ST. BONIFACE: STEPNEY'S NEW LOOK

Churches as well as houses were obliterated by the German bombers which paid special attention to the docks and East End. A new Stepney arises and a better one. But lovers of tradition will be surprised at the spire of the new church of St. Boniface.

THE BOAT RACE: OXFORD LEAD

Although television now gives all viewers a complete picture of the University Boat Race, great crowds still flock to the banks to see only a portion of it. In this 1960 picture Oxford are leading Cambridge at Hammersmith Bridge on their way to victory.

CHELSEA FLOWER SHOW: ROCK GARDEN

The Chelsea Flower Show is an annual event which attracts crowds of garden-lovers and floral specialists in the month of May from all over the country. It is organised by the Royal Horticultural Society and is held in the grounds of the Royal Hospital founded by Charles II.

Not Tennis self, thy sister sport, can charm,
Or with thy fierce delights our bosoms warm.
For, to small space confined, ev'n she must yield
To nobler Cricket, the disputed field.

O parent Britain! minion of renown!
Whose far-extended fame all nations own;
Nurs'd on thy plains, first Cricket learnt to please,
And taught thy sons to slight inglorious ease;
And see where busy Counties strive for fame,
Each greatly potent at this mighty game!
Fierce Kent, ambitious of the first applause,
Against the world combin'd, asserts her cause;
Gay Sussex sometimes triumphs o'er the field,
And fruitful Surrey cannot brook to yield.
While London, Queen of Cities! proudly vies,
And often grasps the well-disputed prize.

JOHN LOVE
Cricket, An Heroic Poem
published in 1744

LONDON PLAYGOER, 1609

One of the more expensive seats in the London theatres for which
Shakespeare wrote was a stool at the side of the rush-strewn stage.
For the kind of young buck who wished to display himself this was
preferable to a place in the galleries or in "the lord's room."
Thomas Dekker, playright and satirical pamphleteer, published in
1609 "The Gull's Hornbook" i.e., the A.B.C. of a Lout About
Town. Gull did not mean to Dekker merely a person gulled or taken
in. His Gull was a boor pretending to smartness and wit.

It must be remembered that Dekker was writing to entertain and
was probably exaggerating the vulgar antics to be expected from
the stool-holders. When a play by an author of repute was being
given it is hardly credible that the better part of the audience
having come to see and hear a good play, would have tolerated such
oafish raggihg on the part of some noisy exhibitionists. None the
less, when all allowances have been made for the satirist's eagerness to amuse, Dekker's picture of his Gull at the theatre reminds

9

us that even Shakespeare's famous Globe could be a rough house in a rough age. The "Gatherers" mentioned were those who took the money at the doors. The "Sharers" were the established actors who had a share in the profits and controlled the business side of their ventures as well as the quality of the piece and its perform- ance. Shakespeare was a sharer as well as an actor and an author.

Sithence then the place is so free in entertainment, allowing a stool as well to the farmer's son as to your templar; that dour stinkard has the selfsame liberty to be there in his tobacco-fumes, which your sweet courtier hath; and that your carman and tinker claim as strong a voice in their suffrage, and sit to give judgement on the play's life and death, as well as the proudest Momus among the tribe of critic: it is fit that he, whom the most tailors' bills do make room for, when he comes, should not be basely, like a viol, cased up in a corner.

Whether therefore the gatherers of the public or private playhouse stand to receive the afternoon's rent; let our gallant, having paid it, presently advance him- self up to the throne of the stage; I mean not into the lords' room, which is now but the stage's suburbs; no, those boxes, by the iniquity of custom, conspiracy of waiting-women and gentlemen-ushers that there sweat together, and the covetousness of sharers, are con- temptibly thrust into the rear; and much new satin is there damned, by being smothered to death in darkness. But on the very rushes where the comedy is to dance, yea, and under the state of Cambyses himself, must our feathered estrich, like a piece of ordnance, be planted valiantly, because impudently, beating down the mews and hisses of the opposed rascality. . . .

Before the play begins, fall to cards; you may win or lose, as fencers do in a prize, and beat one another by confederacy, yet share the money when you meet at supper: notwithstanding, to gull the ragamuffins that stand aloof gaping at you, throw the cards, having first torn four or five of them, round about the stage, just upon the third sound, as though you had lost; it skills not if the four knaves lie on their backs, and out-face the audience; there's none such fools as dare take exceptions at them; because, ere the play go off, better knaves than they will fall into the company.

Now, sir; if the writer be a fellow that hath either epigrammed you, or hath had a flirt at your mistress, or hath brought either your feather or your red beard, or your little legs, etc. on the stage; you shall disgrace him worse than by tossing him in a blanket, or giving him the bastinado in a tavern, if, in the middle of his play, be it pastoral or comedy, moral or tragedy, you rise with a screwed and discontented face from your stool to be gone; no matter whether the scenes be good, or no; the better they are, the worse do you distaste them: and, being on your feet, sneak not away like a coward; but salute all your gentle acquaintance, that are spread either on the rushes, or on stools about you; and draw what troop you can from the stage after you; the mimics are beholden to you for allowing them elbow-room: their poet cries, perhaps, " a pox go with you "; but care not you for that; there's no music without frets.

Marry, if either the company or indisposition of the weather bind you to sit it out; my counsel is then that you turn plain ape: take up a rush, and tickle the earnest ears of your fellow gallants, to make other fools fall a laughing; mew at passionate speeches; blare at merry; find fault with the music; whew at the children's action; whistle at the songs; and, above all, curse the sharers, that whereas the same day you had bestowed forty shillings on an embroidered felt and feather, Scotch fashion, for your mistress in the court, or your punk in the city, within two hours after you encounter with the very same block on the stage, when the haberdasher swore to you the impression was extant but that morning. . . .

The next places that are filled, after the playhouses be emptied, are, or ought to be, taverns; into a tavern then let us next march, where the brains of one hogshead must be beaten out to make up another.

THOMAS DEKKER (1570?-1632)
The Gull's Hornbook

PULLING DOWN THEATRES

In our own time there has been much menace to and destruction of theatres because their sites could be more profitably employed for offices and flats. There is nothing new in this since the famous playhouses of the Elizabethan and Jacobean eras were broken up, for moral as well as economic reasons, to make tenements during the Civil War and the Cromwellian regime. The following catalogue of destruction, including the Globe made famous by Shakespeare, occurs in manuscript notes appended to an edition of Stow's Annals made by Edmund Howes. The dates may not all be correct since we know that the fatal fire at the Globe occurred in 1613. But that does not much affect the sad story of demolition. The spelling is as in the original manuscript.

The Globe play house on the Banks side in Southwarke, was burnt downe to the ground, in the yeare 1612. And now built up againe in the yeare 1613, at the great charge of King James, and many Noble men and others. And now pulled downe to the groun, by Sir Matthew Brand, On Munday the 15 of April 1644, to make tenements in the room of it.

The Black Friers players playhouse in Blacke Friers, London, which had stood many yeares, was pulled downe to the ground on Munday the 6 day of August 1655, and tennements built in the rome.

The play house in Salsbury Court, in Fleetstreete, was pulled downe by a company of souldiers, set on by the sectuaries of these sad times, On Saterday the 24 day of March 1649.

The Phenix in Druery Lane, was pulled downe also this day . . . by the same souldiers.

The Fortune Playhouse betweene White Crosse streete and Golding Lane was burnd downe to the ground in the yeare 1618. And built againe with brick worke on the outside in the yeare 1622. And now pulled downe on the inside by the souldiers this 1649.

The Hope, on the Banks side in Southwarke, commonly called the Beare Garden, a Play House for Stage Playes on Mundayes, Wednesdayes, Fridayes, and Saterdayes, and for the baiting of the Beares on Tuesdayes and Thursdayes, the stage being made to take up and down when they please. It was built in the year 1610, and now pulled downe to make tennementes, by Thomas Walker, a peticoate maker in Cannon Streete, on Tuesday the 25 day of March 1656. Seuen of Mr. Godfries beares, by the command of Thomas Pride, then the Sheriefe of Surry, were then shot to death, on Saterday the 9 day of February 1655, by a company of souldiers.

Manuscript notes (1656-8) appended to *Stow's Annals*

DICE AND DEVILRY

The day being shut in, you may properly compare this place to those Countries which lye far in the North, where it is as clear at midnight as at noonday: And though it is a house of Sin, yet you cannot call it a house of Darkness, for the Candles never go out till morning, unless the sudden fury of a losing Gamester make them extinct.

This is the time (when ravenous beasts usually seek their prey) wherein comes shoals of Huffs, Hectors, Setters, Gilts, Pads, Biters, Divers, Lifters, Filers, Budgies, Droppers, Crossbyters, etc., and these may all pass under the general and common appellation of Rooks. And in this particular, an Ordinary serves as a Nursery for

Tyburn; for if any one will put himself to the trouble of observation, he shall find that there is seldom a year wherein there are not some of this Gang hang as pretious Jewels in the ear of Tyburn: Look back and you will find a great many gone already, God knows how many are to follow.

These Rooks are in continual motion, walking from one Table to another, till they can discover some un-experienc'd young Gentleman, Casheer or Apprentice, that is come to this School of Virtue, being unskill'd in the quibbles and devices there practised; these they call Lambs, or Colls: Then do the Rooks (more properly called Wolves) strive who shall fasten on him first, follow-ing him close, and engaging him in some advantageous Bets, and at length worry him, that is, gets all his money, and then the Rooks (Rogues I should have said) laugh and grin, saying, the Lamb is bitten.

If you nick them, 'tis odds, if they wait not your coming out at night and beat you: I could produce you an hundred examples in this kind, but they will rarely adventure on the attempt unless they are backt with some Bully-Huffs, and Bully-Rooks, with others whose fortunes are as desperate as their own. We need no other testimony to confirm the danger of associating with these Anthropo-phagi or Man-Eaters, than Lincolns-Inn-Fields whilst Speerings Ordinary was kept in Bell-yard, and that you need not want a pair of Witnesses for the proof thereof, take in also Covent-Garden.

Neither is the House itself to be exempted, every night almost some one or other, who either heated with Wine, or made cholerick with the loss of his Money, raises a quarrel, swords are drawn, box and candlesticks thrown at one anothers head, Tables overthrown, and all the House in such a Garboyl, that it is the perfect Type of Hell.

CHARLES COTTON (1630-1687)
The Compleat Gamester

PEPYS PLEASED AND AFRAID

... So to my chamber, and there did some little business, and then abroad, and stopped at the Bear-garden-stairs, there to see a prize fought. But the house so full there was no getting in there, so forced to go through an alehouse into the pit, where the bears are baited; and upon a stool did see them fight, which they did very furiously, a butcher and a waterman. The former had the better all along, till by and by the latter dropped his sword out of his hand, and the butcher, whether not seeing his sword dropped I know not, but did give him a cut over the wrist, so as he was disabled to fight any longer. But, Lord! to see how in a minute the whole stage was full of watermen to revenge the foul play, and the butchers to defend their fellow, though most blamed him; and there they all fell to it knocking down and cutting many on each side. It was pleasant to see, but that I stood in the pit, and feared that in the tumult I might get some hurt. At last the rabble broke up, and so I away to White Hall and so to St. James's.

SAMUEL PEPYS (1633-1703)
Diary

MAKING A NIGHT OF IT

To the Duke of York's house, to see the new play, called "The Man is the Master," where the house was, it being not one o'clock, very full. But my wife and Deb. being there before, with Mrs. Pierce and Corbet and Betty Turner, whom my wife carried with her, they made me room; and there I sat, it costing me 8s. upon them in oranges, at 6d a-piece. By and by the King came; and we sat just under him, so that I durst not turn my back

all the play. The play is a translation out of French, and
the plot Spanish, but not anything extraordinary at all
in it, though translated by Sir W. Davenant, and so I
found the King and his company did think meanly of it,
though there was here and there something pretty: but
the most of the mirth was sorry, poor stuffe, or eating of
sack posset and slabbering themselves, and mirth fit for
clownes; the prologue but poor, and the epilogue little
in it but the extraordinariness of it, it being sung by
Harris and another in the form of a ballad.

Thence, by agreement, we all of us to the Blue Balls,
hard by, whither Mr. Pierce also goes with us, who met
us at the play, and anon comes Manuel, and his wife
and Knipp, and Harris, who brings with him Mr.
Banister, the great master of musick; and after much
difficulty in getting of musick, we to dancing, and then
to a supper of French dishes, which yet did not please me,
and then to dance and sing; and mighty great content
in all my company, and I did, as I love to do, enjoy myself. My wife extraordinary fine today, in her flower
tabby suit, bought a year and more ago, before my
mother's death put her into mourning, and so not worn
till this day: and everybody in love with it; and indeed
she is very fine and handsome in it. I having paid the
reckoning, which come to almost £4, we parted: my
company and William Batelier, who was also with us,
home in a coach, round by the Wall, where we met so
many stops by the Watches, that it cost us much time
and some trouble, and more money, to every Watch, to
them to drink; this being encreased by the trouble the
'prentices did lately give the City, so that the Militia and
Watches are very strict at this time; and we had like to
have met with a stop for all night at the Constable's
watch, at Mooregate, by a pragmatical Constable; but
we came well home at about two in the morning.

SAMUEL PEPYS (1633-1703)
Diary

TOWN PLEASURES DENIED

HIPPOLITA: To confine a woman just in her rambling Age! take away her liberty at the very time she should use it! O barbarous Aunt! O unnatural Father; to shut up a poor girl at fourteen, and hinder her budding; all things are ripen'd by the Sun: to shut up a poor girl at fourteen!

PRUE: 'Tis true, Miss, two poor young creatures as we are!

HIPPOLITA: Not suffer'd to see a play in a twelve month!

PRUE: Nor to go to Ponchinello nor Paradise!

HIP.: Not to take a Ramble to the Park nor Mulbery-garden!

PRUE: Nor to Tatnam-Court nor Islington!

HIP.: Nor to eat a sillybub in new Spring-garden with a Cousin!

PRUE: Nor to drink a Pint of Wine with a Friend at the Prince in the Sun!

HIP.: Nor to hear a Fiddle in good Company!

PRUE: Nor to hear the Organs and Tongs at the Gun in Moorfields!

HIP.: Nay, not suffer'd to go to Church, because the men are sometimes there! Little did I think I should ever have long'd to go to Church!

PRUE: Or I either, but between two maids!

HIP.: Nor see a man!

PRUE: Not come near a man!

HIP.: Nor hear of a man!

PRUE: No, Miss, but to be deny'd a man, and to have no use at all of a man!

WILLIAM WYCHERLEY (1640-1716)
The Gentleman Dancing-Master

LEGS AND THE MAN

Mr. Pope has passed a very just Censure on this Writer in
the two following Lines:

> " The Stage how loosely does Astraea tread,
>   Who fairly puts all Characters to Bed! "

In the Play before us there is a very remarkable Instance
of this putting to Bed. One of the Personages of the
Drama takes off his Breeches in the Sight of the Audience,
whose Diversion is of a complicated Nature on this
Occasion. The Ladies are first alarmed; then the Men
stare: The Women put up their Fans—" My Lady Betty,
what is the Man about?—Lady Mary, sure he is ' not in
earnest! ' " Then peep thro' their Fans—" Well, I vow,
the He-creature is taking off his odious Breeches—He—
he—Po!—is that all?—the Man has Drawers on."—
Then, like Mrs. Cadwallador in the new Farce,—" Well
to be sure, I never saw any Thing in the Shape of it."—
Mean time, the Delight of the Male Part of the Audience
is occasioned by the various Operations of this Phoeno-
menon on the Female Mind—" This is rare Fun, d-n me
—Jack, Tom, Bob, did you ever see any thing like this?—
Look at that Lady Yonder—See, in the Stage Box—how
she looks half-averted," etc., etc. It is Matter of Wonder
that the Upper Gallery don't call for an Hornpipe, or,
" Down with the Drawers," according to their Custom
of insisting upon as much as they can get for their
Money. But to be a little serious, it should be remembered by all Managers that this Play was written in the
dissolute Days of Charles the Second; and that Decency
at least is, or ought to be, demanded at present.

This passage occurs in an anonymous article appearing in *The London
Chronicle*, founded in 1757. The paper's critic made vigorous attacks
on the indecency of the plays produced. The reference here is to
" The Rover " by Mrs. Aphra Behn, which he later claimed to have
" driven from the boards."

CROWDED HOURS

At the theatre in Dorset Gardens, this day being Friday the 30th of April will be presented a Farce, call'd The Cheats of Scapin. And a Comedy of two acts only, call'd, The Comical Rivals, or the School Boy. With several Italian Sonatas by Signor Gasperini and others. And the Devonshire Girl, being now upon her Return to the City of Exeter, will perform three several Dances, particularly her last Entry in Imitation of Mademoiselle Subligni, and the Whip of Dunboyne by Mr. Claxton her Master, being the last time of their Performance till Winter. And at the desire of several Persons of Quality (hearing that Mr. Pinkethman hath hired the two famous French Girls lately arriv'd from the Emperor's Court). They will perform several Dances on the Rope upon the Stage being improv'd to that Degree far exceeding all others in that Art. And their Father presents you with the Newest Humours of Harlequin as perform'd by him before the Grand Signor at Constantinople. Also the Famous Mr. Evans lately arrived from Vienna will shew you wonders of another kind, Vaulting on the Manag'd Horse, being the greatest Master of that Kind in the World. To begin at Five so that all may be done by Nine a Clock.

Advertisement in the Daily Courant, 1703

PLEASURE OF GOSSIP

PAGE: Madam, Mr. Medley has sent to know whether a Visit will not be Troublesome this Afternoon?

LADY TOWNLEY: Send him word his visits never are so.

EMILIA: He's a very pleasant man.

LADY TOWN.: He's a very necessary man among us

Women; he's not scandalous i' the least, perpetually contriving to bring good Company together, and always ready to stop us a gap at Ombre[1]; then he knows all the little news o' the Town.

EMILIA: I love to hear him talk o' the Intrigues, let 'em be never so dull in themselves, he'll make 'em pleasant i' the relation.

LADY TOWN.: But he improves things so much one can take no measure of the Truth from him. Mr. Dorimant swears a Flea or a Maggot is not made more monstrous by a magnifying glass, than a story is by his telling it.

EMILIA: Hold, here he comes.

*　　*　　*

EMILIA: Leave your raillery, and tell us, is there any new Wit come forth, Songs or Novels?

MEDLEY: A very pretty piece of gallantry, by an eminent Author, call'd the diversions of Bruxells, . . . Then there is the Art of Affectations, written by a late beauty of Quality, teaching you how to draw up your Breasts, stretch up your neck, to thrust out your Breech, to play with your Head, to toss up your Nose, to bite your Lips, to turn up your Eyes, to speak in a silly soft tone of a Voice, and use all the Foolish French Words that will infallibly make your person and conversation charming, with a short apologie at the latter end in the behalf of young Ladies who notoriously wash and paint, though they have naturally good Complexions.

EMILIA: What a deal of stuff you tell us!

MED.: Such as the Town affords, Madam. The Russians, hearing the great respect we have for Foreign Dancing, have lately sent over some of their best Ballarins, who are now practicing a famous Ballat which will be suddenly danc'd at the Bear-Garden.

[1] A once very popular game of cards played by three persons

LADY TOWN.: Pray forbear your idle stories and give us an account of the state of Love, as it now stands.

MED.: Truly, there has been some revolutions in those Affairs, great chopping and changing among the old, and some new Lovers, whom malice, indiscretion, and misfortune, have luckily brought into play.

LADY TOWN.: What think you of walking into the next Room, and sitting down, before you engage in this business?

MED.: I wait upon you, and I hope, (though Women are commonly unreasonable) by the plenty of Scandal I shall discover, to give you very good Content, Ladies.

SIR GEORGE ETHEREGE (1635?-1692?)
The Man of Mode

WATCHING THE FIREWORKS

Dear George,—Whatever you hear of the Richmond fireworks, that is short of the prettiest entertainment in the world, don't believe it; I never really passed a more agreeable evening. Everything succeeded; all the wheels played in time; Frederick was fortunate, and all the world in good humour. Then for royalty—Mr. Anstis himself would have been glutted; there were all the Fitzes upon earth, the whole court of St. Germain's, the duke, the duke of Modena and two Anamaboes. The king and princess Emily bestowed themselves upon the mob on the river; and, as soon as they were gone, the duke had the music into the garden, and himself, with my lady Lincoln, Mrs. Pitt, Peggy Banks, and lord Holderness, entertained the good subjects with singing God save the King to them over the rails of the terrace. The duke of Modena supped there, and the duke was asked but he answered, it was impossible: in short, he could not adjust his dignity to a mortal banquet.

In the middle of all these principalities and powers,

was the duchess of Queensbury, in her forlorn trim, a
white apron, and white hood, and would make the duke
swallow all her undress. T'other day she drove post to
lady Sophia Thomas, at Parsons-green, and told her that
she was come to tell her something of importance.
" What is it? "—" Why, take a couple of beef-steaks,
clap them together, as if they were for a dumpling, and
eat them with pepper and salt; it is the best thing you
ever tasted: I could not help coming to tell you this: "
and away she drove back to town. Don't a course of folly
for forty years make one very sick?

HORACE WALPOLE (1717-1797)
Letter to George Montagu, May 18, 1749

LONDON PLAYGOER, VICTORIAN

Henry Mayhew is perhaps more remembered for his humanity than
for his humour. He made careful and compassionate studies of poverty
in " London Labour and the London Poor " (1851). But he was also one
of the founders of *Punch*, whose editorship he shared with Mark
Lemon. His volume called *London Characters* contains amusing
portraits of widely assorted types. In one chapter, writing as " The
Thumbnail Sketcher " he gave his opinions of the drama's patrons
who were to be met in the capital.

Their behaviour during the progress of the representation
of a new piece, on its first night, irritates him beyond
endurance. In the first place, there is almost always a
party who hiss, without any reference to the merits or
demerits of the piece. It is a somewhat curious fact that in
England hisses are seldom heard save on " first nights ";
and of the fifty or sixty new pieces that have been recently
produced at West-end London theatres, hardly a dozen
have altogether escaped hissing on the occasion of their
first performance. ' Caste ' was not hissed, neither was
the ' Doge of Venice ', nor the Haymarket ' Romeo and
Juliet', nor ' A Wife Well Won '; but these pieces form

the principal exceptions to the rule. But it is not so much of indiscriminate hissing, as of indiscriminate applause, that the Thumbnail Sketcher complains. A clap-trap sentiment, a burlesque 'break-down', a music-hall parody, a comic man coming down a chimney, an indelicate joke, a black eye, a red nose, a pair of trousers with a patch behind, a live baby, a real cab, a smash of crockery, a pun in a 'comedy', an illusion, however clumsy, to any topic of the day, a piece of costermonger's slang, or any strongly-marked tailoring eccentricity, is quite sure of a rapturous reception whenever it is presented to an audience. Then I take objection to people who crack nuts—to people who eat oranges and peppermint drops—to people who go out between all the acts, without reference to the inconvenience they occasion to their neighbours. I take objection to people who know the plot, and tell it, aloud, to their friends—to people who don't know the plot but guess at the dénouement—to people who borrow playbills and opera glasses—to donkeys who talk of actresses by their Christian names—and, above all, to those unmitigated nuisances who explain all the jokes to friends of slow understanding. The Thumbnail Sketcher, being about to treat of people he meets in theatres, thinks it is only fair to admit this prepossession against them, in order that it may be distinctly understood, that, as he cannot pledge himself to look at them in an unprejudiced light, everything that he may have to say of them may be taken *cum grano*. . . .

" The lady who follows is intended as a representative of that extensive element in most dress-circles which finds its way into theatres by the means of free admissions. It is a curious feature in theatrical management—and a feature which doesn't seem to exist in any other form of commercial enterprise—that if you can't get people to pay for admission, you must admit them for nothing. Nobody ever heard of a butcher scattering

steaks broadcast among the multitude because his
customers fall off, neither is there any instance on record
of a banker volunteering to oblige penniless strangers
with an agreeable balance. Railway companies do not
send free passes for general distribution to eel-pie shops,
nor does a baker place his friends on his free-list. But it is
a standing rule at most theatres that their managers
must get people to pay to come in, if possible, but at all
events they must get people to come in. A poorly-filled
house acts not only as a discouragement to the actors, but
it depresses the audience, and sends them away with evil
accounts of the unpopularity of the entertainment. The
people who find their way into a theatre under the
' admit two to dress-circle ' system, hail, usually, from
the suburbs, but not unfrequently from the lodging-
letting districts about Russell Square. They usually
walk to the theatres, and, consequently, represent an
important source of income to the stout shabby ladies
who preside over the bonnet and cloak departments.
They may often be recognised by the persistency with
which they devour acidulated drops during the performances.

Finally we meet the young gentlemen,

". . . one of those intolerable nuisances, who, having a
reputation for waggery within a select circle of admirers,
find, in the production of every piece in which pathetic
interest is an important feature, an opportunity for
displaying a knowledge of the hollowness of the whole
thing, and the general absurdity of allowing oneself to
be led away by mere stage clap-trap. He will remind
you, as Juliet is weeping over her dead Romeo, that a
petition for a divorce filed by the Romeo against Juliet,
and in which the comfortable Friar is included as co-
respondent, is high up in the Judge Ordinary's list. He
will sometimes affect to be bathed in tears, when there is

no excuse for any demonstration of the kind, and he will interrupt a scene of deep pathos with a ' Ha! ha! ' audible all over the house. He is very angry at anything in the shape of a vigorous denunciation, or a pathetic appeal of any kind; and he indulges in a musing exclamational commentary of ' Oh! I say, you know! ' ' Come, come.' ' So ho! gently there!' ' St-st-st ', and ' Really, I say— by Jove! ' which meets with much admiration from his believing friends, and general indignation from others in his immediate neighbourhood who have not the advantage of his acquaintance."

HENRY MAYHEW (1812-1887)
London Characters

EARLY DAYS OF SADLER'S WELLS

Soon after the Revolution, upon the Drama being emancipated from the shackles of the Puritans, a novel species of amusement first became general, under the name of Musick-houses. One of the earliest of these was Coleman's Musick-house near Lamb's Conduit, which soon became a place of much abandoned company. In fact, this was their general character, and, in the end, caused their putting down one after another. One of the most frequented, and one which long outlasted others, was that at Islington called Miles's Musick-house or Sadler's Wells. Epsom and Tunbridge Wells were in use before Sadler's Well acquired its modern reputation, and there was also another well at Islington near the same spot called Islington Wells or Islington Spa, to which we shall anon refer.

But as to Sadler's Well, in a tract referred to by Sir John Hawkins, Lysons, and Strutt, published by Thomas Malthus at the Sun in the Poultry, 1684, we are told that " the new well at Islington is a certain spring in the middle of a garden belonging to the musick-house built by Mr. Sadler on the north side of the great cistern that receives the New River water near Islington; the water whereof was, before the Reformation, much famed for several extraordinary cures performed thereby, and was thereupon accounted sacred, and called the Holy Well. The priests belonging to the Priory of Clerkenwell used to attend there, and made the people believe that the virtues of the water proceeded from the efficacy of their prayers. But upon the Reformation, the well was stopped up, on the supposition that the frequenting it was altogether superstitious; and so by degrees, it grew out of remembrance and was wholly lost. Mr. Sadler being made surveyor of the highways, and having good gravel in his garden, employed two men to dig there."

These men re-discovered the well, a large well of stone, arched over and curiously carved. Supposing that the fame of the well formerly had proceeded from some medicinal virtue, Mr. Sadler carried some of it to a doctor, who advised him to brew beer with it, and sell it in bottles, called roundlets. Dr. Merton and others recommended their patients to drink it. And they were told in a puff, that it was well to drink a glass of Rhenish or white wine with it, and for those who smoked, to take a pipe or two whilst the water worked. In fact, it was intended, as at all such places, to make it a resort for dissipation in the pretence of seeking health. The well appears to have been opened in June 1697, being recommended in the ' Post-boy ' and ' Flying-Post ' as a powerful chalybeate spring. Sadler would seem only to have held it till 1699, for in that year it was called Miles's Musick-house, though the well continued to hold the name of Sadler's Well.

A description of the people frequenting the well and music-house, which shows the rude, low, and disgusting character of the population resorting to such places at that period, is given in the ' Weekly Comedy ', a play ' then acted in the Coffee-houses of London.' Of this

' Weekly Comedy ' the first number was published about May 3, 1699, and it was issued periodically in half sheets, folio; apparently with remarks and anecdotes. It was by Edward Ward; and the same piece was afterwards inserted in his Miscellaneous Works, as the ' Humours of a Coffee-house.' These works of Ned Ward present a faithful, no doubt, but a most awful and disgusting picture of coarseness, obscenity, and vile debauchery of the common people of London at that date, in language which could not be read now in any decent family. In the third number of Ward's ' Comedy ', and in ' Dowke's Protestant Mercury ' of the same date, 1699, a story is related of a fellow at Sadler's Wells, who, after he had dined heartily on a buttock of beef, for the wager of five guineas ate a live cock—feathers, entrails, and all —with only a plate of oil and vinegar for sauce, and half a pint of brandy to wash it down; and offered, after an interval of two hours, to do the same thing again for five guineas more.

In the same paper of January 4, following, the same monster is stated to have eaten a live cat at a music-house in St. Katherine's. These horrible feats were attested by many credible people, who were eye-witnesses. According to Ward's account, not only butchers, bailiffs, prize-fighters, deer-stealers, and a world of " vermin trained up for the gallows," but fine ladies and gentlemen from the inns of court, from the wealthy circles, frequented the New Tunbridge and Sadler's Wells, at Islington, where they were regaled with cheese-cakes, custards, bottled ale and cyder, and with singing and dancing. In this motley crowd were conspicuous numerous women of the town, and the quality of the singing and dancing was of the lowest and most sensual kind. Mimicry and pantomime, and a sort of masquerading, made up the entertainment, which was witnessed by the more select, if any attending such places could merit the name, from galleries adjoining the organ-loft.

The celebrity of the springs at Sadler's Well and the Islington New Tunbridge, did not last long, but the music-halls and their attractions continued to draw crowds for several years. There is a rare tract called " God's Judgment against Murderers, or an account of a cruel and barbarous murther, committed on Thursday night, the 14th of August, at Sadler's Musick-house, near Islington, on the body of Mr. Waite, a lieutenant of a man-of-war, by one Mr. French, a lawyer of the Temple, showing how they quarrelled about women," etc., 1712. This tract, which calls the place Sadler's, otherwise Miles's Musick-house, gives it the character of a most abandoned resort " of unaccountable and disorderly people."

WILLIAM HOWITT (1792-1879)
The Northern Heights of London

THE HAPPY PLAYGOER

Is it a stale remark to say, that I have constantly found the interest excited at a play-house to bear an exact inverse proportion to the price paid for admission? Formerly, when my sight and hearing were more perfect, and my purse a little less so, I was a frequenter of the upper gallery in the old theatres. The eager attention, the breathless listening, the anxiety not to lose a word, the quick anticipation of the significance of the scene (every sense kept as it were upon a sharp lookout), which are exhibited by the occupiers of those higher and now almost out-of-sight regions (who, going seldom to a play, cannot afford to lose anything by inattention), suffer some little diminution, as you descend to the lower or two-shilling ranks; but still the joy is lively and un-allayed, save that by some little incursion of manners, the expression of it is expected to abate somewhat of its natural liveliness. The oaken plaudits of the trunk-maker would here be considered as going a little beyond the line.

In the Pit first begins that accursed critical faculty, which, making a man the judge of his own pleasures, too often constitutes him the executioner of his own and others! You may see the *jealousy of being unduly pleased, the suspicion of being taken in to admire*; in short, the vile critical spirit, creeping and diffusing itself, and spreading from the wrinkled brows and cloudy eyes of the front row sages and newspaper reporters (its proper residence), till it infects and clouds over the thoughtless, vacant countenance, of John Bull tradesmen, and clerks of counting-houses, who, but for that approximation, would have been contented to have grinned without rule, and to have been pleased without asking why.

The sitting next a critic is contagious. Still now and then, a *genuine spectator* is to be found among them, a shopkeeper and his family, whose honest titilations of mirth, and generous chucklings of applause, cannot wait or be at leisure to take the cue from the sour judging faces about them. Haply they never dreamed that there were such animals in nature as critics or reviewers; even the idea of an author may be a speculation they never entered into; but they take the mirth they find as a pure effusion of the actor-folks, set there on purpose to make them fun. I love the unenquiring gratitude of such spectators.

CHARLES LAMB (1775-1834)
Essays of Elia

ARMED GUARD FOR THE PLAYGOER

My friend Sir Roger de Coverley, when we last met together at the club, told me that he had a great mind to see the new tragedy with me, assuring me at the same time, that he had not been at a play these twenty years.

" The last I saw," said Sir Roger, " was *The Committee*, which I should not have gone to neither, had not I been told beforehand that it was a good Church of England Comedy." He then proceeded to inquire of me who this *Distressed Mother* was; and upon hearing that she was Hector's widow, he told me that her husband was a brave man, and that when he was a school-boy he had read his life at the end of the dictionary. My friend asked me, in the next place, if there would not be some danger in coming home late, in case the Mohocks should be abroad. " I assure you," says he, " I thought I had fallen into their hands last night; for I observed two or three lusty black men that followed me half way up Fleet Street, and mended their pace behind me in proportion as I put on to get away from them. You must know," continued the knight, with a smile, " I fancied they had a mind to hunt me; for I remember an honest gentleman in my neighbourhood, who was served such a trick in King Charles II's time, for which reason he has not ventured himself in town ever since. I might have shown them very good sport, had this been their design; for as I am an old fox-hunter, I should have turned and dodged, and have played them a thousand tricks they had never seen in their lives before." Sir Roger added that if these gentlemen had any such intention, they did not succeed very well in it; " for I threw them out," says he, " at the end of Norfolk Street, where I doubled the corner, and got shelter in my lodgings before they could imagine what was become of me. However," says the knight, " if Captain Sentry will make one with us tomorrow night, and if you will both of you call upon me about four o'clock, that we may be at the house before it is full, I will have my own coach in readiness to attend you, for John tells me he has got the fore-wheels mended."

The Captain, who did not fail to meet me there at the appointed hour, bade Sir Roger fear nothing, for that he had put on the same sword which he made use of at the battle of Steenkirk. Sir Roger's servants, and among the rest my old friend the butler, had, I found, provided themselves with good oaken plants, to attend their master upon this occasion. When we had placed him in his coach, with myself at his left hand, the Captain before him, and his butler at the head of his footmen in the rear, we convoyed him in safety to the play-house, where, after having marched up the entry in good order, the Captain and I went in with him, and seated him betwixt us in the pit, As soon as the house was full, and the candles lighted, my old friend stood up and looked about him with that pleasure, which a mind seasoned with humanity naturally feels in itself, at the sight of a multitude of people who seem pleased with one another, and partake of the same common entertainment. I could not but fancy myself, as the old man stood up in the middle of the pit, that he made a very proper centre to a tragic audience. Upon the entering of Pyrrhus, the knight told me that he did not believe the King of France himself had a better strut. I was indeed very attentive to my old friend's remarks, because I looked upon them as a piece of natural criticism; and was well pleased to hear him, at the conclusion of almost every scene, telling me that he could not imagine how the play would end.

* * *

Sir Roger went out fully satisfied with his entertainment, and we guarded him to his lodgings in the same manner that we brought him to the play-house; being highly pleased, for my own part, not only with the performance of the excellent piece which had been presented, but with the satisfaction which it had given to the good old man.

JOSEPH ADDISON (1672-1719)
Essays

GAY LADIES OF THE TOWN

A tavern near Newgate

MACHEATH, DRAWER

MACHEATH: What a fool is a fond wench! Polly is most confoundedly bit.—I love the sex. And a man who loves money, might as well be contented with one guinea, as I with one woman. The town perhaps hath been as much oblig'd to me, for recruiting it with free-hearted ladies, as to any recruiting Officer in the army. If it were not for us and the other gentlemen of the sword, Drury-lane would be uninhabited.

(AIR XXI *Would you have a young Virgin, etc.*)

If the heart of a man is deprest with cares,
The mist is dispell'd when a woman appears;
Like the notes of a fiddle, she sweetly, sweetly
Raises the spirits, and charms our ears.
    Roses and lillies her cheeks disclose,
    But her ripe lips are more sweet than those.
    Press her,
    Caress her,
    With blisses,
    Her kisses
Dissolve us in pleasure, and soft repose.

I must have women. There is nothing unbends the mind like them. Money is not so strong a cordial for the time. —Drawer.—(*Enter* DRAWER.) Is the Porter gone for all the ladies, according to my directions?

DRAWER: I expect him back every minute. But you know, Sir, you sent him as far as Hockley in the Hole, for three of the ladies, for one in Vinegar Yard, and for the rest of them somewhere about Lewkner's Lane, Sure some of them are below, for I hear the barr bell. As they come I will show them up.—Coming, coming.

MACHEATH, MRS. COAXER, DOLLY TRULL, MRS. VIXEN, BETTY DOXY, JENNY DIVER, MRS. SLAMMEKIN, SUKY TAWDRY, AND MOLLY BRAZEN.

MACHEATH: Dear Mrs. Coaxer, you are welcome. You look charmingly today. I hope you don't want the repairs of quality, and lay on paint.—Dolly Troll! kiss me, you slut; are you as amorous as ever, hussy? You are always so taken up with stealing hearts, that you don't allow your self time to steal any thing else.— Ah Dolly, thou wilt ever be a Coquette!—Mrs. Vixen, I'm yours, I always lov'd a woman of wit and spirit; they make charming mistresses, but plaguy wives.— Betty Doxy! come hither, hussy. Do you drink as hard as ever? You had better stick to good wholesome beer; for in troth, Betty, strong-waters will in time ruin your constitution. You should leave those to your betters.— What! and my pretty Jenny Diver too! As prim and demure as ever! There is not any Prude, though ever so high bred, hath a more sanctify'd look, with a more mischievous heart. Ah! thou art a dear artful hypocrite. —Mrs. Slammekin! as careless and genteel as ever! all you fine ladies, who know your own beauty, affect an undress.—But see, here's Suky Tawdry come to contradict what I was saying. Every thing she gets one way she lays out upon her back. Why, Suky, you must keep at least a dozen Tally-men. Molly Brazen! (She kisses him). That's well done. I love a free-hearted wench. Thou has a most agreeable assurance, girl, and art as willing as a Turtle.—But hark! I hear musick. The Harper is at the door. If musick be the food of

Love, play on. E'er you seat your selves, ladies,
what think you of a dance? Come in. (*Enter* HARPER).
Play the French Tune, that Mrs. Slammekin was so
fond of.

(*A Dance à la ronde in the French manner; near the end of it
this Song and Chorus.*)

(AIR XXII *Cotillon*)

Youth's the season made for joys,
   Love is then our duty;
She alone who that employs,
   Well deserves her beauty.
     Let's be gay,
     While we may,
Beauty's a flower despis'd in decay.

CHORUS. Youth's the season, etc.

Let us drink and sport today,
   Ours is not tomorrow.
Love with youth flies swift away,
   Age is nought but sorrow.
     Dance and sing,
     Time's on the wing,
Life never knows the return of spring.

CHORUS. Let us drink, etc.

MACHEATH: Now pray ladies, take your places. Here
Fellow. (*Pays the* HARPER). Bid the Drawer bring us
more wine. (*Ex.* HARPER). If any of the ladies chuse gin,
I hope they will be so free to call for it.

JENNY: You look as you meant me. Wine is strong
enough for me. Indeed, Sir, I never drink strong-waters,
but when I have a Cholic.

MACHEATH: Just the excuse of the fine ladies! Why, a lady of quality is never without the Cholic.

JOHN GAY (1685-1732)
The Beggar's Opera

SALUTE TO THE STAGE

The historic London theatre of Drury Lane had been passing through serious financial troubles when James Lacy, with David Garrick as actor-manager, came to its rescue and began some of the most illustrious seasons in English theatrical history. Dr. Johnson, once Garrick's tutor at Lichfield, not only recorded in brief the history of the London stage but made demands on players and audience for a new reign of manners, morality, and the actor's art.

When Learning's triumph o'er her barb'rous foes
First rear'd the stage, immortal Shakespeare rose;
Each change of many-coloured life he drew,
Exhausted worlds, and then imagin'd new:
Existence saw him spurn her bounded reign,
And panting Time toil'd after him in vain.
His pow'rful strokes presiding Truth impress'd,
And unresisted Passion storm'd the breast.
    Then Jonson came, instructed from the school,
To please in method, and invent by rule;
His studious patience and laborious art,
By regular approach assail'd the heart:
Cold approbation gave the ling'ring bays,
For those, who durst not censure, scarce could praise.
A mortal born, he met the general doom,
And left, like Egypt's kings, a lasting tomb.
    The wits of Charles found easier ways to fame,
Nor wish'd for Jonson's art, or Shakespeare's flame.
Themselves they studied, as they felt they writ;
Intrigue was plot, obscenity was wit.
Vice always found a sympathetic friend;
They pleased their age, and did not aim to mend.

Yet bards like these aspir'd to lasting praise,
And proudly hop'd to pimp in future days.
Their cause was gen'ral, their supports were strong,
Their slaves were willing, and their reign was long:
Till Shame regain'd the post that Sense betray'd
And Virtue call'd Oblivion to her aid.

Then crush'd by rules, and weaken'd as refin'd,
For years the pow'r of Tragedy declin'd;
From bard to bard the frigid caution crept,
Till Declamation roar'd whilst Passion slept;
Yet still did Virtue deign the stage to tread,
Philosophy remain'd, though Nature fled.
But forc'd, at length, her ancient reign to quit,
She saw great Faustus lay the ghost of Wit;
Exulting Folly hail'd the joyful day,
And Pantomime and Song confirm'd her sway.

But who the coming changes can presage,
And mark the future periods of the stage?
Perhaps, if skill could distant times explore,
New Behns, new Durfeys, yet remain in store;
Perhaps where Lear has rav'd, and Hamlet dy'd,
On flying cars new sorcerers may ride:
Perhaps (for who can guess th'effects of chance?)
Here Hunt may box, or Mahomet may dance.

Hard is his lot that, here by Fortune plac'd,
Must watch the wild vicissitudes of taste;
With ev'ry meteor of caprice must play,
And chase the new-born bubbles of the day.
Ah! let not Censure term our fate our choice.
The stage but echoes back the public voice;
The drama's laws, the drama's patrons give,
For we that live to please, must please to live.

Then prompt no more the follies you decry,
As tyrants doom their tools of guilt to die;
'Tis yours, this night, to bid the reign commence
Of rescued Nature and reviving Sense;

To chase the charms of sound, the pomp of show,
For useful mirth and salutary woe;
Bid scenic Virtue from the rising age,
And Truth diffuse her radiance from the stage.

DR. SAMUEL JOHNSON (1709-1784)
*Prologue spoken by Mr. Garrick at the opening
of the Theatre Royal, DruryLane, 1747.*

REMINISCENCES OF A DANCING MAN

Who now remembers Almack's balls—
    Willis's sometime named—
In those two smooth-floored upper halls
    For faded ones so framed?
Where as we trod to trilling sound
The fancied phantoms stood around,
    Or joined us in the maze,
Of the powdered Dears from Georgian years,
Whose dust lay in sightless sealed-up biers,
    The fairest of former days.

Who now remembers gay Cremorne,
    And all its jaunty jills,
And those wild whirling figures born
    Of Jullien's grand quadrilles?
With hats on head and morning coats
There footed to his prancing notes
    Our partner-girls and we;
And the gas-jets winked, and the lustres clinked,
And the platform throbbed as with arms enlinked
    We moved to the minstrelsy.

Who now recalls those crowded rooms
    Of old yclept " The Argyle,"
Where to the deep Drum-polka's booms
    We hopped in standard style?

Whither have danced those damsels now!
Is Death the partner who doth moue
   Their wormy chaps and bare?
Do their spectres spin like sparks within
The smoky halls of the Prince of Sin
   To a thunderous Jullien air?

THOMAS HARDY (1840-1928)
Time's Laughingstocks

PUNCH AND JUDY—THE SHOWMAN TALKS

The performer of Punch that I saw was a short, dark, pleasant-looking man, dressed in a very greasy and very shiny shooting-jacket. This was fastened together by one button in front, all the other button-holes having been burst through. Protruding from his bosom, a corner of the pandean pipes was just visible, and as he told me the story of his adventures, he kept playing with the band of his very limp and very rusty old beaver hat . . .

‘ Ah, it's a great annoyance being a public kerrackter, I can assure you, sir; go where you will, it's “ Punchy, Punchy! ” As for the boys, they'll never leave me alone till I die, I know; and I suppose in my old age I shall have to take to the parish broom. All our forefathers died in the workhouse. I don't know a Punch's showman that hasn't. One of my pardners was burried by the workhouse; and even old Pike, the most noted show-man as ever was, died in the workhouse—Pike and Porsini. Porsini was the first original street Punch, and Pike was his apprentice; their names is handed down to posterity among the noblemen and footmen of the land. They both died in the workhouse, and, in course, I shall do the same. Something else might turn up, to be sure. We can't say what the luck of this world is. I'm obliged to strive very hard—very hard indeed, sir, now, to get a living; and then not to get it after all—at times, compelled to go short, often.

'Punch, you know, sir, is a dramatic performance in two hacts. It's a play, you may say. I don't think it can be called a tragedy hexactly; a drama is what we names it. There is tragic parts, and comic and sentimental parts, too. Some families where I performs will have it most sentimental—in the original style; them families is generally sentimental theirselves. Others is all for the comic, and then I has to kick up all the games I can. To the sentimental folk I'm obliged to perform werry steady and werry slow, and leave out all comic words and business. They won't have no ghost, no coffin, and no devil; and that's what I call spiling the performance entirely. It's the march of hintellect wot's a doing all this—it is, sir . . .

'Our business is werry much like hackney-coach work; we do best in vet veather. It looks like rain this evening, and I'm uncommon glad on it, to be sure. You see, the vet keeps the children in-doors all day, and then they wants something to quiet 'em a bit; and the mothers and fathers, to pacify the dears, gives us a horder to perform. It mustn't rain cats and dogs— that's as bad as no rain at all. What we likes is a regular good, steady Scotch mist, for then we takes double what we takes on other days. In summer we does little or nothing; the children are out all day enjoying themselves in the parks . . .

'We in generally walks from twelve to twenty mile every day, and carries the show, which weighs a good half-hundred, at the least. Arter great exertion, our voice werry often fails us; for speaking all day through the " call " is werry trying, 'specially when we are chirupping up so as to bring the children to the vinders. The boys is the greatest nuisances we has to contend with. Wherever we goes we are sure of plenty of boys for a hindrance; but they've got no money, bother 'em! and they'll follow us for miles, so that we're often compelled to go miles to awoid 'em. Many parts is swarming with boys, such as Vitechapel. Spitalfield, that's the worst place for boys I ever come a-near; they're like flies in summer there, only much more thicker. I never shows my face within miles of them parts. Chelsea, again, has an uncommon lot of boys; and wherever we know the children swarm, there's the spots we makes a point of awoiding. Why, the boys is such a hobstruction to our performance, that often we are obliged to drop the curtain for 'em.' . . .

HENRY MAYHEW (1812-1887)
London Labour and the London Poor

CRYSTAL PALACE, SACRED MUSIC

All this past week the world has been occupied with the Handel Concerts at the Crystal Palace, which went off with the greatest success and éclat. I went to the first (" Messiah "), and the last (" Israel in Egypt "); they were amazingly grand, and the beauty of the locale, with the vast crowds assembled in it, made an imposing spectacle. The arrangements were perfect, and nothing could be easier than the access and egress, or more comfortable than the accommodation. But the wonderful assembly of 2,000 vocal and 500 instrumental performers did not produce musical effect so agreeable and so perfect as the smaller number in the smaller space of Exeter Hall. The volume of sound was dispersed and lost in the prodigious space, and fine as it undoubtedly was, I much prefer the concerts of the Harmonic Society.

CHARLES GREVILLE (1794-1865)
Diary

MUSICAL ROUNDABOUT IN BATTERSEA

Despite the mechanisation of the modern Fun Fair exemplified in Battersea Park, a quiet street in the same part of London can provide a simple pleasure for the smaller children with the horse-drawn roundabout. There is even music laid on and no risk of a crash.

NEW HOMES FOR OLD PEOPLE

Vigorous efforts have recently been made to provide comfort and amenity for those handicapped by age. Sarel House in the East End, built by the London County Council, offers a place in the sun as well as a roof over grey heads. It was opened in 1960.

LAMBETH PALACE: THE GARDEN FRONT

At Lambeth, on the south bank, there has been "the London Inn" of the Archbishop of Canterbury for seven centuries. Its most conspicuous feature is "Morton's Tower" seen on the right, which gives the Palace a fortress-look. More peaceful is this garden-view.

KENSINGTON PALACE: EAST FRONT

William III disliked the damp of Whitehall and had Sir Christopher Wren build him a new home in Kensington. Here Queen Victoria was born and spent her childhood. Princess Margaret moved into one of the small houses attached to the Palace after her wedding in 1960.

PICNIC AT THE PALACE

Picnics and fire-works at the Crystal Palace in Sydenham were for many decades a major London pleasure and spectacle.

They come, they come, with fife and drum,
  And gleaming pikes and glancing banners:
Though the eyes flash, the lips are dumb;
  To talk in rank would not be manners.
Onward they stride, as Britons can;
The ladies following in the Van.

Who, who be these that tramp in threes
  Through sumptuous Piccadilly, through
The roaring Strand, and stand at ease
  At last 'neath shadowy Waterloo?
Some gallant Guild, I ween, are they;
Taking their annual holiday.

To catch the destin'd train—to pay
  Their willing fares, and plunge within it—
Is, as in old Romaunt they say,
  With them the work of half-a-minute.
Then off they're whirl'd, with songs and shouting,
To cedared Sydenham for their outing.

I mark'd them light, with faces bright
  As pansies or a new coin'd florin,
And up the sunless stairs take flight,
  Close-pack'd as rabbits in a warren.
Honour the Brave, who in that stress
Still trod not upon Beauty's dress!

Kerchief in hand I saw them stand;
　In every kerchief lurk'd a lunch;
When they unfurl'd them, it was grand
　To watch bronzed men and maidens crunch
The sounding celery-stick, or ram
The knife into the blushing ham.

Dash'd the bold fork through pies of pork;
　O'er hard-boil'd eggs the saltspoon shook;
Leapt from its lair the playful cork:
　Yet some there were, to whom the brook
Seem'd sweetest beverage, and for meat
They chose the red root of the beet.

Then many a song, some rather long,
　Came quivering up from girlish throats;
And one young man he came out strong,
　And gave " The Wolf " without his notes.
While they who knew not song or ballad
Still munch'd, approvingly, their salad.

But ah! what bard could sing how hard,
　The artless banquet o'er, they ran
Down the soft slope with daisies starr'd
　And kingcups! onward, maid with man,
They flew, to scale the breezy swing,
Or court frank kisses in the ring.

Such are the sylvan scenes that thrill
　This heart! The lawns, the happy shade,
Where matrons, whom the sunbeams grill,
　Stir with slow spoon their lemonade;
And maidens flirt (no extra charge)
In comfort at the fountain's marge!

Others may praise the " grand displays "
　Where " fiery arch," " cascade," and " comet,"
Set the whole garden in a " blaze "!
　Far, at such times, may I be from it;

Though then the public may be " lost
In wonder " at a trifling cost.

Fann'd by the breeze, to puff at ease
 My faithful pipe is all I crave:
And if folks rave about the " trees
 Lit up by fireworks," let them rave.
Your monster fêtes, I like not these;
Though they bring grist to the lessees.

C. S. CALVERLEY (1831-1884)
Fly Leaves

ASPIRING ACTOR

One of the curious features of the London Theatres in the early part
of last century were those Private Stages on which the aspiring actor
could buy himself a part. Peregrine Proteus, the hero of a book by
Pierce Egan, made this approach to his later successful career " on the
boards."

Peregrine soon made the tour of all the private theatres
in the metropolis; and in several of them he had performed trifling parts, by way of practice; but he now
boldly resolved on making his appearance in Hamlet.
His success, or rather the gross flattery of his friends,
completely removed all idea of business from his head.
In the phraseology of the stage, Proteus had now rubbed
against the flats; smelt the lamp; and become quite *au
fait* with O.P. and P.S. Richard, Macbeth, Octavian, etc.,
were performed in succession, till he became tired of the
limits of a private theatre, and sighed to obtain public
approbation.

His wishes were soon gratified, by an opportunity
offering to him of his making an appearance at the
Haymarket Theatre; and our hero was determined to
embrace it at all events. The principal difficulty to be
overcome was the cash account. The benefit was

announced (under the usual gag) for the Widow of an Officer. The play was Othello; and the characters, generally, were sold. The Moor produced £20, and the gentle Desdemona was put up and bargained for at nearly the same price. Iago was performed by an experienced country actor, in order to keep the amateurs together in something like the scene. In fact, it was for the benefit of the latter stroller: no uncommon thing for distressed country actors. Proteus purchased the part of Cassio for £5, with the liberty of selling tickets to relieve his expenses. Othello was personified by a young man in a public office, who had plenty of money, but no talents for the stage; and Desdemona, equally deficient, might be termed as the worst of heroines: loud hisses greeted them through every scene; and the house was one continued scene of tumult and riot till the conclusion of the piece. Peregrine, in Cassio, made a complete hit: and his performance was marked by well-merited applause.

PIERCE EGAN (1772-1849)
Life of an Actor

Charles Dickens also took a look at (and a poor view of) these performances.

" Richard the Third—Duke of Glo'ster, 2*l.*; Earl of Richmond, 1*l.*; Duke of Buckingham, 15*s.*; Catesby, 12*s.*; Tressel, 10*s.* 6*d.*; Lord Stanley, 5*s.*; Lord Mayor of London, 2*s.* 6*d.*"

Such are the written placards wafered up in the gentleman's dressing-room, or the green-room (where there is any), at a private theatre; and such are the sums extracted from the shop-till, or overcharged in the office expenditure, by the donkeys who are prevailed upon to pay for permission to exhibit their lamentable ignorance and boobyism on the stage of a private theatre. This they do, in proportion to the scope afforded by the character for the display of their imbecility. For instance, the Duke of Glo'ster is well worth two pounds, because he has it all to himself; he must wear a real sword, and what is better still, he must draw it several times in the course of the piece. The soliloquies alone are well worth fifteen shillings; then there is the stabbing King Henry—decidedly cheap at three-and-sixpence, that's eighteen-and sixpence; bullying the coffin-bearers—say eighteen-pence, though it's worth much more—that's a pound. Then the love scene with Lady Ann, and the bustle of the fourth act can't be dear at ten shillings more—that's only one pound ten, including the " off with his head! "— which is sure to bring down the applause, and it very easy to do—" Orf with his ed " (very quick and loud;—then slow and sneeringly)—" So much for Bu-u-u-uckingham! "

The lady performers pay nothing for their characters, and it is needless to add, are usually selected from one class of society; the audiences are necessarily of much the same character as the performers, who receive, in return for their contributions to the management, tickets to the amount of the money they pay.

All the minor theatres in London, especially the lowest, constitute the centre of a little stage-struck neighbourhood. Each of them has an audience exclusively its own; and at any you will see dropping into the pit at half-price, or swaggering into the back of a box, if the price of admission be a reduced one, divers boys of from fifteen to twenty-one years of age, who throw back their coat and turn up their wristbands, after the portraits of Count D'Orsay, hum tunes and whistle when the curtain is down, by way of persuading the people near them, that they are not at all anxious to have it up again, and speak familiarly of the inferior performers as Bill Such-a-one, and Ned So-and-so or tell each other how a new piece called *The Unknown Bandit of the Invisible Cavern*, is in rehearsal; how Mister Palmer is to play *The Unknown*

Bandit; how Charley Scarton is to take the part of an English sailor, and fight a broadsword combat with six unknown bandits, at one and the same time (one theatrical sailor is always equal to half a dozen men at least); how Mister Palmer and Charley Scarton are to go through a double hornpipe in fetters in the second act; how the interior of the invisible cavern is to occupy the whole extent of the stage; and other town-surprising theatrical announcements. These gentlemen are the amateurs —the Richards, Shylocks, Beverleys, and Othellos—the Young Dorntons, Rovers, Captain Absolutes, and Charles Surfaces—of a private theatre.

A quarter before eight—there will be a full house tonight—six parties in the boxes, already; four little boys and a woman in the pit; and two fiddles and a flute in the orchestra, who have got through five overtures since seven o'clock (the hour fixed for the commencement of the performances), and have just begun the sixth. There will be plenty of it, though, when it does begin, for there is enough in the bill to last six hours at least.

The characters in the tragedy are all dressed, and their own clothes are scattered in hurried confusion over the wooden dresser which surrounds the room. That snuff-shop-looking figure, in front of the glass, is Banquo: and the young lady with the liberal display of legs, who is kindly painting his face with a hare's foot, is dressed for Fleance. The large woman, who is consulting the stage directions in Cumberland's edition of Macbeth, is the Lady Macbeth of the night; she is always selected to play the part, because she is tall and stout, and looks a little like Mrs. Siddons—at a considerable distance. That stupid-looking milksop, with light hair and bow legs—a kind of man whom you can warrant town-made—is fresh caught; he plays Malcolm tonight, just to accustom himself to an audience. He will get on better by degrees; he will play Othello in a month, and in a month more, will very probably be apprehended on a charge of embezzlement. The black-eyed female, with whom he is talking so earnestly, is dressed for the " gentlewoman." It is her first appearance, too—in that character. The boy of fourteen who is having his eyebrows smeared with soap and whitening, is Duncan, King of Scotland; and the two dirty men with the corked countenances, in very old green tunics, and dirty boots, are the " army."

" Look sharp below there, gents," exclaims the dresser, a red-headed and red-whiskered Jew, calling through the trap, " they're a-going to ring up. The flute says he'll be blowed if he plays any more, and they're getting precious noisy in front." A general rush immediately takes place to the half-dozen little steep steps leading to the stage, and the heterogeneous group are soon assembled at the side scenes, in breathless anxiety and motley confusion.

CHARLES DICKENS (1812-1870)
Sketches by Boz

DICKENS ACTS, TENNYSON NODS

To T. Carlyle, Esq.   *Sept. 23, 1845.*

" Nothink " for you today in the shape of inclosure, unless I inclose a letter from Mrs. Paulet to myself, which you will find as " entertaining " to the full as any of mine. And nothink to be told either, except all about the play; and upon my honour, I do not feel as if I had a penny-a-liner genius enough, this cold morning, to make much entertainment out of that. Enough to clasp one's hands, and exclaim, like Helen before the Virgin and Child, " Oh, how expensive! " But " how did the creatures get through it? " Too well; and not well enough! The public theatre, scenes painted by Stansfield, costumes " rather exquisite," together with the certain amount of proficiency in the amateurs, overlaid all idea of private theatricals; and, considering it as public theatrical, the acting was "most insipid," not one performer among them that could be called good, and none that could be called absolutely bad. Douglas Jerrold seemed to me the best, the oddity of his appearance greatly helping him; he played Stephen the Cull; Forster as Kitely, and Dickens as Captain Bobadil, were much on a par; but Forster preserved his identity, even through his loftiest flights of Macreadyism; while poor little Dickens, all painted in black and red, and affecting the voice of a man of six feet, would have been un-recognisable to the mother that bore him! On the whole, to get up the smallest interest in the thing, one needed to be always reminding oneself: "all these actors were once men!" and will be men again to-morrow morning. The greatest wonder for me was how they had con-trived to get together some six or seven hundred ladies and gentlemen (judging from the clothes) at this season of the year: and all utterly unknown to me, except some half-dozen.

So long as I kept my seat in the dress circle I recognised only Mrs. Macready (in one of the four private boxes), and in my nearer neighbourhood Sir Alexander and Lady Gordon. But in the interval betwixt the play and the farce I took a notion to make my way to Mrs. Mac-ready. John, of course, declared the thing "clearly impossible, no use trying it;" but a servant of the theatre, over-hearing our debate, politely offered to escort me where I wished; and then John, having no longer any difficulties to surmount, followed, to have his share in what advantages might accrue from the change.

Passing through a long dim passage, I came on a tall man leant to the wall, with his head touching the ceiling like a caryatid, to all appearance asleep, or resolutely trying it under the most unfavourable circumstances.

ROYAL WEDDING

London loves a royal occasion and crowds will wait all night for a good stance. The procession to Westminster Abbey is conducted with medieval pomp. Horse-power is once more the power of horses and only then can a London street-scene contain not a single motor-car.

PARLIAMENT SQUARE

Parliament Square was laid out by Barry, the architect of the Houses of Parliament. This oasis in a whirl of traffic was replanned during the nineteen-fifties with some shuffling of the statues of eminent statesmen. The Epstein statue of General Smuts has been a recent addition.

REMEMBRANCE DAY

Remembrance Day is observed on the second Sunday in November. The simple and dignified Cenotaph in Whitehall was designed by Sir Edwin Lutyens in 1919 and now is a memorial "To the Glorious Dead" who fell in both the World Wars of 1914-1918 and 1939-1945.

" Alfred Tennyson! " I exclaimed in joyful surprise.
" Well! " said he, taking the hand I held out to him, and
forgetting to let it go again. " I did not know you were
in town," said I. " I should like to know who you are,"
said he; " I know that I know you, but I cannot tell your
name." And I had actually to name myself to him. Then
he woke up in good earnest, and said he had been meaning to come to Chelsea. " But Carlyle is in Scotland,"
I told him with humility. " So I heard from Spedding
already, but I asked Spedding, would he go with me to
see Mrs. Carlyle? and he said he would." I told him if he
really meant to come, he had better not wait for backing,
under the present circumstances; and then pursued my
way back to the Macreadys' box; where I was received
by William (whom I had not divined) with a " Gracious
heavens! " and spontaneous dramatic start, which made
me all but answer, " Gracious heavens! " and start
dramatically in my turn. And then I was kissed all
round by his women; and poor Nell Gwyn, Mrs. M——
G—— seemed almost pushed by the general enthusiasm
on the distracted idea of kissing me also!

They would not let me return to my stupid place, but
put in a third chair for me in front of their box; " and
the latter end of that woman was better than the beginning." Macready was in perfect ecstasies over the
" Life of Schiller," spoke of it with tears in his eyes. As
" a sign of the times," I may mention that in the box
opposite sat the Duke of Devonshire, with Payne Collier!
Next to us were D'Orsay and " Milady! "

Between eleven and twelve it was all over—and the
practical result? Eight-and-sixpence for a fly, and a
headache for twenty-four hours! I went to bed as wearied
as a little woman could be, and dreamt that I was plunging through a quagmire seeking some herbs which were
to save the life of Mrs. Maurice; and that Maurice was
waiting at home for them in an agony of impatience,
while I could not get out of the mud-water!

Craik arrived next evening (Sunday), to make his compliments. I was lying on the sofa, headachy, leaving Craik to put himself to the chief expenditure of wind, when a cab drove up. Mr. Strachey? No. Alfred Tennyson alone! Actually, by a superhuman effort of volition he had put himself into a cab, nay, brought himself away from a dinner party, and was there to smoke and talk with me!—by myself—me! But no such blessedness was in store for him. Craik prosed, and John babbled for his entertainment; and I, whom he had come to see, got scarcely any speech with him. The exertion, however, of having to provide him with tea, through my own unassisted ingenuity (Helen being gone for the evening) drove away my headache; also perhaps a little feminine vanity at having inspired such a man with the energy to take a cab on his own responsibility, and to throw himself on providence for getting away again! He stayed till eleven, Craik sitting him out, as he sat out Lady H——, and would sit out the Virgin Mary should he find her here.

JANE WELSH CARLYLE (1801-1866)
Letter to her husband, Thomas Carlyle

IRVING AND THE PUBLIC

However, let us leave what is really a very sordid side of the subject, and return to the question of popular control in the matter of Art, by which I mean Public Opinion dictating to the artist the form which he is to use, the mode in which he is to use it, and the materials with which he is to work. I have pointed out that the arts which have escaped best in England are the arts in which the public have not been interested. They are, however, interested in the drama, and as a certain advance has been made in the drama within the last ten or fifteen years, it is important to point out that this

advance is entirely due to a few individual artists refusing to accept the popular want of taste as their standard,
and refusing to regard Art as a mere matter of demand
and supply.

With his marvellous and vivid personality, with a
style that has really a true colour-element in it, with his
extraordinary power, not over mere mimicry but over
imaginative and intellectual creation, Mr. Irving, had
his sole object been to give the public what they wanted,
could have produced the commonest plays in the commonest manner, and made as much success and money as
a man could possibly desire. But his object was not that.
His object was to realise his own perfection as an artist,
under certain conditions and in certain forms of Art. At
first he appealed to the few: now he has educated the
many. He has created in the public both taste and
temperament. The public appreciate his artistic success
immensely. I often wonder, however, whether the
public understand that that success is entirely due to the
fact that he did not accept their standard, but realised
his own. With their standard the Lyceum would have
been a sort of second-rate booth, as some of the popular
theatres in London are at present. Whether they understood it or not, the fact however remains, that taste and
temperament have, to a certain extent, been created in
the public, and that the public is capable of developing
these qualities. The problem then is, why do not the
public become more civilised? They have the capacity.
What stops them?

The thing that stops them, it must be said again, is
their desire to exercise authority over the artists and over
works of art. To certain theatres, such as the Lyceum
and the Haymarket, the public seem to come in a proper
mood. In both of these theatres there have been individual artists, who have succeeded in creating in their
audiences—and every theatre in London has its own
audience—the temperament to which Art appeals. And

what is that temperament? It is the temperament of receptivity. That is all.

If a man approaches a work of art with any desire to exercise authority over it and the artist, he approaches it in such a spirit that he cannot receive any artistic impression from it at all. The work of art is to dominate the spectator: the spectator is not to dominate the work of art. The spectator is to be receptive. He is to be the violin on which the master is to play. And the more completely he can suppress his own silly views, his own foolish prejudices, his own absurd ideas of what Art should be, or should not be, the more likely he is to understand and appreciate the work of art in question.

OSCAR WILDE (1856-1900)
The Soul of Man Under Socialism

The Lyceum Theatre is now a dance hall; but the "Old Vic" has become the nucleus of a National Theatre and has recently included Wilde among its classic dramatists. Mr. Irving became Sir Henry in 1895: he was the first British actor to be knighted.

THE BALLET, 1910

The address of ballet has moved from "The Orient" to Covent Garden and Sadler's Wells. The Palaces of Varieties have dwindled, but this picture of the Piccadilly and Leicester Square London is a fascinating "period" piece.

The Orient Palace of Varieties rose like a cliff from the drapery shops of Piccadilly. On fine summer dusks, in a mist of golden light, it possessed a certain magic of gaiety; seemed to capture something of the torch-lit merriment of a country fair. As one loitered on the island, lonely and meditative, the Orient was alluring, blazed upon the vision like an enchanted cave, or offered to the London wanderer a fancy of the scents and glossy fruits and warblers of the garden where Camaralzaman lost Badoura; and in autumn stained by rosy sunsets, the theatre expressed the delicate melancholy of the season. But when the rain dripped monotonously, when fogs transformed the town, when London was London vast and grey, the Orient became unreal like the bedraggled palaces of an exhibition built to endure for a little while. After all, it was an exotic piece of architecture, and evoked an atmosphere of falseness, the falseness of an Indian gong in a Streatham hall. Yet it had stood fifty years without being rebuilt. In addition to having seen two generations pass away, something in the character of its entertainment, in the lavishness of it decoration lent it the sacred permanence of a mausoleum, the mausoleum of mid-Victorian amusement.

The Orient did not march with the times, rising from insignificance. It never owned a chairman who announced the willingness of each successive comedian to oblige with a song. Old men never said they remembered the Orient in the jolly old days, for they could not have forgotten it. In essentials it remained the same as ever. Dancers had gone; beauties had shrivelled; but their ghosts haunted the shadowy interior. The silver-footed coryphées now kept lodging-houses; the swan-like ballerinas wore elastic stockings; but their absence was filled by others: they were as little missed as the wave that has broken. The lean old vanities quizzed and ogled the frail ladies of the Promenade and sniffed the smoke-wreathed air with a thought of pleasures once worth enjoyment. They spent now an evening of merely sentimental dissipation, but, because it was spent at the Orient, not entirely wasted; for the unchanged theatre testified to the reality of their youth. It may not have been able to rejuvenate them, but, as by a handkerchief that survives the departure of its owner, their senses were faintly stimulated.

*   *   *

Dressing-room number forty-five was a long low room with walls of whitewashed brick. There was one window, seldom opened. There was no electric light and the gas-jets gave a very feeble illumination, so feeble that everybody always put on too much grease paint in their fear of losing an effect. The girls dressed on each side of the room at a wide deal board with forms to sit upon. There was a large wardrobe in one corner, and next to Jenny's place an open sink. The room was always dark and always hot. There were about eighty stone stairs leading up to it from the stage, and at least half a dozen ascents in the course of the evening. The dresser was a blowsy old Irishwoman more obviously dirty than the room, and there were two ventilators which gave a perpetual draught of unpleasant air. The inspectors of the London County Council presumably never penetrated as far as Room 45, a fact that seems to show that the extent of municipal interference has been much exaggerated.

The dressing-rooms were half on one side of the stage, half on the other. Those on the side nearer to the stage-door were less unpleasant. The architect evidently believed in the value of first impressions. Anybody venturing into either warren without previous acquaintanceship would have been bewildered by the innumerable rooms and passages tucked away in every corner and branching off in every direction. Some of the former seemed to have been uninhabited for years. One in particular contained an ancient piano, two daguerrotypes and a heap of mouldering stuffs. It might have been the cell where years ago a Ballerina was immured for a wrong step. It existed like a monument to the despair of ambition.

The Orient stifled young life. The Corps de Ballet had the engulfing character of conventual vows. When a girl joined it, she cut herself off from the world. She went there fresh, her face a mist of roses, hope burning in her heart, fame flickering before her eyes. In a few years she would inevitably be pale with the atmosphere, with grinding work and late hours. She would find it easy to buy spirits cheaply in the canteen underneath the stage. She would stay in one line, it seemed for ever. She would not dance for joy again.

When Jenny went to the Orient first, she did not intend to stay long. She told the girls this, and they laughed at her. She did not know how soon the heavy theatre would become a habit; she did not realize what comfort exists in the knowledge of being permanently employed. But not even the Orient could throttle Jenny. She was not the daughter and granddaughter of a ballet girl. She had inherited no traditions of obedience. She never became a marionette to be dressed and undressed and jigged, horribly and impersonally. She yielded up her ambition, but she never lost her personality.

*   *   *

It is not to be supposed that the eighty or ninety ladies of the ballet were unhappy. On the contrary, they were very happy and, so far as it accorded with the selfishness of a limited company, they were well looked after. The managing director called them " Children," and was firmly convinced that he treated them as children. Actually, he treated them as dolls, and, in the case of girls well into the thirties, with some of the sentimental indulgence lavished on old broken dolls. Perhaps it was the crowd of men who waited every night at the end of the long narrow court that led from Jermyn Street down to the Orient stage-door, which has helped to preserve the vulgar and baseless tradition of frailty still sedulously propagated. Every night, about half-past eleven, the strange mixture of men waited for the gradual exodus of the ladies of the ballet. A group of men, inherently the same, had stood thus on six nights of the week for more than fifty years.

They had stood there with Dundreary whiskers, in rakish full capes and strapped overalls. They had waited there with the mutton-chop whiskers and ample trousers of the 'seventies. Down the court years ago had come the beauties, with their striped stockings and swaying crinolines and velvety chignons. Down the court they had tripped in close-fitting pleated skirts a little later, and later still with the protruding bustles and skin-tight sleeves of the 'eighties. They had taken the London starlight with the balloon sleeves of the mid-'nineties. They took the starlight now, as sweet and tender as the fairs of long ago. They came out in couples, in laughing companies, and sometimes singly with eager searching glances. They came out throwing their wraps around them in the sudden coolness of the air. They lingered at the end of the court in groups delicate as porcelain, enjoying the freedom and reunion with life. Their talk was hushed and melodious as the conversation of people moving slowly across dusky lawns. They were dear to the imaginative observer. He watched them with pride and affection as he would have watched fishing-boats steal home to their haven about sunset. Every night they danced and smiled and decked themselves for the pleasure of the world. They rehearsed so hard that sometimes they would fall down after a dance, crying on the stage where they had fallen from sheer exhaustion. They were not rich. Most of them were married, with children and little houses in teeming suburbs. Many, of course, were free to accept the escort of loiterers by the stage-door. The latter often regarded the ladies of the ballet as easy prey, but the ladies were shy as antelopes aware of the hunter crawling through the grasses. They were independent of masculine patronage; laughed at the fools with their easy manners and genial condescension. They might desire applause

over the footlights, but under the moon they were free
from the necessity for favour. They had, with all its
incidental humiliations, the self-respect which a great
art confers. They were children of Apollo.

SIR COMPTON MACKENZIE (1883-   )
Carnival

THEATRE OF VARIETIES

This kind of star-clustered programme of most various varieties has
largely vanished, but I myself vividly remember the loquacious
conjuror described as " Van Hogen Mogen," the secondary turns and
the " hanging gardens " of the packed auditorium.

Circle on circle the hanging gardens descend,
Sloping from upper darkness, each flower face
Open, turned to the light and laughter and life
Of the sun-like stage. And all the space between,
Like the hot fringes of a summer sky,
Is quick with trumpets, beats with the pulse of drums,
Athwart whose sultry thunders rise and fall
Flute fountains and the swallow flight of strings,
Music, the revelation and marvellous lie!
On the bright trestles tumblers, tamers of beasts,
Dancers and clowns affirm their fury of life.
  " The World-Renowned Van Hogen Mogen in
    The Master Mystery of Modern Times."
He talks, he talks; more powerfully than even
Music his quick words hammer on men's minds.
  " Observe this hat, ladies and gentlemen;
Empty, observe, empty as the universe
Before the Head for which this Hat is made
Was or could think. Empty, observe, observe."
The rabbit kicks; a bunch of paper flowers
Blooms in the limelight; paper tape unrolls,
Endless, a clue. " Ladies and gentlemen . . ."

Sharp, sharp on malleable minds his words
Hammer. The little Indian boy
Enters the basket. Bright, an Ethiop's sword
Transfixes it and bleeding is withdrawn.
Death draws and petrifies the watching faces.
" Ladies and gentlemen ": the great Van Hogen Mogen
Smiles and is kind. A puddle of dark blood
Slowly expands. " The irremediable
Has been and is no more."
Empty of all but blood, the basket gapes.
" Arise! " he calls, and blows his horn. " Arise! "
And bird-like from the highest gallery
The little Indian answers.
Shout upon shout, the hanging gardens reverberate.
Happy because the irremediable is healed,
Happy because they have seen the impossible,
Because they are freed from the dull daily law,
They shout, they shout. And great Van Hogen Mogen
Modestly bows, graciously smiles. The band
Confirms the lie with cymbals and bassoons,
The curtain falls. How quickly the walls recede,
How soon the petrified gargoyles re-become
Women and men! who fill the warm thick air
With rumours of their loves and discontents,
Not suffering even great Hogen Mogen—
Only begetter out of empty hats
Of rose and rabbit, raiser from the dead—
To invade the sanctity of private life.
The Six Aerial Sisters Polpetini
Dive dangerously from trapeze to far
Trapeze, like stars, and know not how to fall.
For if they did and if, of his silver balls,
Sclopis, the juggler, dropped but one—but one
Of all the flying atoms which he builds
With his quick throwing into a solid arch—
What panic then would shake the pale flower faces
Blooming so tranquilly in their hanging beds!

What a cold blast of fear! But patrons must not,
And since they must not, cannot be alarmed.
Hence Sclopis, hence (the proof is manifest)
The Six Aerial Ones infallibly
Function, and have done, and for ever will.

God save the King. Music's last practical joke
Still bugling in their ears of war and glory,
The folk emerge into the night.
Already next week's bills are being posted:—
Urim and Thummim, cross-talk comedians;
Ringpok, the Magian of Tibet;
The Two Bedelias; Ruby and Truby Dix;
Sam Foy and Troupe of Serio-Comic Cyclists . . .
Theatre of immemorial varieties,
Old mummery, but mummers never the same!
Twice nightly every night from now till doomsday
The hanging gardens, bedded with pale flower faces,
Young flowers in the old old gardens, will echo
With ever new, with ever new delight.

ALDOUS HUXLEY (1894-1963)
Poems

Inns and Lodgings

AT THE MERMAID

What things have we seen
Done at the Mermaid! Heard words that have been
So nimble and so full of subtle flame
As if that every one from whence they came
Had meant to put his whole wit in a jest,
And had resolved to live a fool the rest
Of his dull life. Then when there hath been thrown
Wit able enough to justify the town
For three days past, wit that might warrant be
For the whole city to talk foolishly
Till that were cancelled, and when that was gone
We left an air behind us which alone
Was able to make the two next companies
Right witty, though but downright fools mere wise.

FRANCIS BEAUMONT (1584-1616)
Letter to Ben Jonson

ANOTHER GLIMPSE

Souls of poets dead and gone,
What Elysium have ye known,
Happy field or mossy cavern,
Choicer than the Mermaid Tavern?
Have ye tippled drink more fine
Than mine host's Canary wine?
Or are fruits of Paradise
Sweeter than those dainty pies

Of venison? O generous food!
Drest as though bold Robin Hood
Would, with his maid Marian,
Sup and bowse from horn and can.

JOHN KEATS (1795-1821)
Lines on the Mermaid Tavern

THE HAPPY HOSTESS

Hot weather and thunder, and want of company are the hostess's grief, for then her ale sours. Your drink usually is very young, two days old: her chiefest wealth is seen, if she can have one brewing under another: if either the hostess, or her daughter, or maid will kiss handsomely at parting, it is a good shoeing-horn or birdlime to draw the company thither again the sooner. She must be courteous to all, though not by nature, yet by her profession; for she must entertain all, good and bad, tag and rag, cut and long-tail. She suspects tinkers and poor soldiers most, not that they will not drink soundly, but that they will not pay lustily.

She must keep touch with three sorts of men; that is, the malt-man, the baker, and the justice's clerks. She is merry, and half mad, upon Shrove Tuesday, May days, feast days, and morris-dances: a good ring of bells in the parish helps her to many a tester[1]; she prays the parson may not be a puritan: a bagpiper, and a puppet-play brings her in birds that are flush, she defies a wine tavern as an upstart outlandish fellow and suspects the wine to be poisoned. Her ale, if new, looks like a misty morning, all thick; well, if her ale be strong, her reckoning right, her house clean, her fire good, her face fair, and the town great or rich, she shall seldom or never sit without chirping birds to bear her company.

D. LUPTON
London and the Countrey Carbonadoed,[2] *1632*

[1] Sixpence   [2] Carbonadoed means hacked about or minced

THE HOSTESS TROUBLED

The setting of this episode is the street, but the events discussed took place in the Boar's Head Tavern in Eastcheap of which Mistress Quickly was Hostess.

Enter the LORD CHIEF JUSTICE, *and his men.*

LORD CHIEF JUSTICE: What is the matter? keep the peace here, ho!

HOSTESS: Good my lord, be good to me! I beseech you, stand to me!

LORD CHIEF JUSTICE: How now, Sir John! what are you brawling here? Doth this become your place, your time, and business? You should have been well on your way to York—Stand from him, fellow: wherefore hang'st upon him?

HOSTESS: O my most worshipful lord, an't please your Grace, I am a poor widow of Eastcheap, and he is arrested at my suit.

LORD CHIEF JUSTICE: For what sum?

HOSTESS: It is more than for some, my lord; it is for all,—all I have. He hath eaten me out of house and home; he hath put all my substance into that fat belly of his:— but I will have some of it out again, or I will ride thee o'nights like the mare.

FALSTAFF: I think I am as like to ride the mare, if I have any vantage of ground to get up.

LORD CHIEF JUSTICE: How comes this, Sir John? Fie! what man of good temper would endure this tempest of exclamation? Are you not ashamed to enforce a poor widow to so rough a course to come by her own?

FALSTAFF: What is the gross sum that I owe thee?

HOSTESS: Marry, if thou wert an honest man, thyself and the money too. Thou didst swear to me upon a par-cel-gilt goblet, sitting in my Dolphin-chamber, at the round table, by a sea-coal fire, upon Wednesday in Wheeson-week, when the prince broke thy head for liking his father to a singing-man of Windsor,—thou didst swear to me then, as I was washing thy wound, to marry me, and make me my lady thy wife. Canst thou deny it? Did not goodwife Keech, the butcher's wife, come in then, and call me gossip Quickly? coming in to borrow a mess of vinegar; telling us she had a good dish of prawns; whereby thou didst desire to eat some; whereby I told thee they were ill for a green wound? And didst thou not, when she was gone down stairs, desire me to be no more so familiarity with such poor people; saying that ere long they should call me madam? And didst thou not kiss me, and bid me fetch thee thirty shillings? I put thee now to thy book-oath: deny it, if thou canst.

FALSTAFF: My lord, this is a poor mad soul; and she says, up and down the town, that her eldest son is like you: she hath been in good case, and the truth is, poverty hath distracted her. But for these foolish officers, I beseech you I may have redress against them.

LORD CHIEF JUSTICE: Sir John, Sir John, I am well acquainted with your manner of wrenching the true cause the false way. It is not a confident brow, nor the throng of words that come with such more than impudent sauciness from you, can thrust me from a level consideration: you have, as it appears to me, practised upon the easy-yielding spirit of this woman, and made her serve your uses both in purse and in person.

HOSTESS: Yea, in truth, my lord.

LORD CHIEF JUSTICE: Pray thee, peace.—Pay her the debt you owe her, and unpay the villainy you have done her: the one you may do with sterling money, and the other with current repentance.

FALSTAFF: My lord, I will not undergo this sneap without reply. You call honourable boldness impudent sauciness: if a man will make court'sy, and say nothing, he is virtuous:—no, my lord, my humble duty remember'd, I will not be your suitor. I say to you, I do desire deliverance from these officers, being upon hasty employment in the king's affairs.

LORD CHIEF JUSTICE: You speak as having power to do wrong: but answer in the effect of your reputation, and satisfy the poor woman.

FALSTAFF: Come hither, hostess. (*Takes her aside.*)

Enter GOWER.

LORD CHIEF JUSTICE: Now, Master Gower, what news?

GOWER: The king, my lord, and Harry Prince of Wales are near at hand: the rest the paper tells.

(*Gives a letter.*)

FALSTAFF: As I am a gentleman,—

HOSTESS: Faith, you said so before.

FALSTAFF: As I am a gentleman:—come, no more words of it.

HOSTESS: By this heavenly ground I tread on, I must be fain to pawn both my plate and the tapestry of my dining-chambers.

FALSTAFF: Glasses, glasses, is the only drinking: and for thy walls,—a pretty slight drollery, or the story of the Prodigal, or the German Hunting in water-work, is worth a thousand of these bed-hangings and these fly-bitten tapestries. Let it be ten pound, if thou can'st. Come, an 'twere not for thy humours, there's not a better wench in England. Go, wash thy face, and draw the action. Come, thou must not be in this humour with me; dost not know me? come, come, I know thou wast set on to this.

HOSTESS: Pray thee, Sir John, let it be but twenty nobles: i' faith, I am loth to pawn my plate, so God save me, la.

FALSTAFF: Let it alone; I'll make other shift: you'll be a fool still.

CLOUDS OVER HAMPSTEAD HEATH

The view is westward from the highest point of Hampstead Heath (440 ft.) and shows the new suburbs that stretch for miles beyond this fortunate break in the world of brick. The Heath was saved for the public in 1872 at a cost of £45,000.

RICHMOND PARK: LONDON'S DEER FOREST

Richmond Park was enclosed for hunting by Charles I in 1637; public rights were established in 1758. A wooded area of 2,258 acres is thus open to the public only twelve miles from the centre of London. It contains a bird sanctuary and large herds of red and fallow deer.

ST. MARTIN'S-IN-THE-(FLOODLIT)-FIELDS

James Gibbs's beautiful spire of St. Martin's-in-the-Fields is seen from between the columns of the National Gallery in Trafalgar Square. The church was built in the years 1722-26 and is now floodlit at Christmas. It is the scene of many memorial services after the death of famous men and women.

HOSTESS: Well, you shall have it, though I pawn my gown. I hope you'll come to supper. You'll pay me all together?

FALSTAFF: Will I live?—(*To* BARDOLPH) Go, with her, with her; hook on, hook on.

HOSTESS: Will you have Doll Tearsheet meet you at supper?

FALSTAFF: No more words; let's have her.

WILLIAM SHAKESPEARE (1564-1616)
Henry IV, Part II

TAVERN ATTRACTIONS

" At Mr. Croome's, at the sign of the Shoe and Slap[1], near the Hospital Gate, in West Smithfield, is to be seen

THE WONDER OF NATURE

A Girl above Sixteen years of Age, born in Cheshire, and not above Eighteen inches long, having shed her Teeth several Times, and not a perfect Bone in any Part of her, only the Head, yet she hath all her senses to Admiration, and Discourses, Reads very well, Sings, Whistles, and all very pleasant to hear."

A Bill of 1667

Another notice (in 1718) is typical of the tavern's function as a dubious drug-store.

" The Anodyne Necklace for children's teeth, women in labour, and distempers of the head; price 5s. Recommended by Dr. Chamberlain. Sold up one pair of stairs at the sign of the Anodyne Necklace, without Temple Bar; at the Spanish Lady at the Royal Exchange, next Threadneedle Street; at the Indian Handkerchief, facing the New Stairs in Wapping, etc."

[1] The slap was a form of slipper

WAITER, PORT, AND POET

The Cock Tavern in Fleet Street, just east of Temple Bar, was long popular with lawyers and journalists working near-by. Its pint of port also gratified Lord Tennyson and was the medium of this libation to his Muse.

O plump head-waiter at The Cock,
    To which I most resort,
How goes the time? 'Tis five o'clock.
    Go fetch a pint of port:
But let it not be such as that
    You set before chance-comers,
But such whose father-grape grew fat
    On Lusitanian summers.

No vain libation to the Muse,
    But may she still be kind,
And whisper lovely words, and use
    Her influence on the mind,
To make me write my random rhymes,
    Ere they be half-forgotten;
Nor add and alter, many times,
    Till all be ripe and rotten.

I pledge her, and she comes and dips
    Her laurel in the wine,
And lays it thrice upon my lips,
    These favour'd lips of mine;
Until the charm have power to make
    New lifeblood warm the bosom,
And barren commonplaces break
    In full and kindly blossom.

I pledge her silent at the board;
  Her gradual fingers steal
And touch upon the master-chord
  Of all I felt and feel.
Old wishes, ghosts of broken plans,
  And phantom hopes assemble;
And that child's heart within the man's
  Begins to move and tremble.

Thro' many an hour of summer suns,
  By many pleasant ways,
Against its fountain upwards runs
  The current of my days:
I kiss the lips I once have kiss'd;
  The gas-light wavers dimmer;
And softly, thro' a vinous mist,
  My college friendships glimmer.

I grow in worth, and wit, and sense,
  Unboding critic-pen,
Or that eternal want of pence,
  Which vexes public men,
Who hold their hands to all, and cry
  For that which all deny them—
Who sweep the crossings, wet or dry,
  And all the world go by them.

Ah yet, tho' all the world forsake,
  Tho' fortune clip my wings,
I will not cramp my heart, nor take
  Half-views of men and things.
Let Whig and Tory stir their blood;
  There must be stormy weather;
But for some true result of good
  All parties work together.

Let there be thistles, there are grapes;
    If old things, there are new;
Ten thousand broken lights and shapes,
    Yet glimpses of the true.
Let raffs be rife in prose and rhyme,
    We lack not rhymes and reasons,
As on this whirligig of Time
    We circle with the seasons.

This earth is rich in man and maid;
    With fair horizons bound:
This whole wide earth of light and shade
    Comes out a perfect round.
High over roaring Temple-bar,
    And set in Heaven's third story,
I look at all things as they are,
    But thro' a kind of glory.

*   *   *

Head-waiter, honour'd by the guest
    Half-mused, or reeling ripe,
The pint, you brought me, was the best
    That ever came from pipe.
But tho' the port surpasses praise,
    My nerves have dealt with stiffer.
Is there some magic in the place?
    Or do my peptics differ?

The Muse, the jolly Muse, it is!
    She answer'd to my call,
She changes with that mood or this,
    Is all-in-all to all:
She lit the spark within my throat,
    To make my blood run quicker,
Used all her fiery will, and smote
    Her life into the liquor.

And hence this halo lives about
   The waiter's hands, that reach
To each his perfect pint of stout,
   His proper chop to each.
He looks not like the common breed
   That with the napkin dally;
I think he came like Ganymede,
   From some delightful valley.

ALFRED, LORD TENNYSON (1809-1892)
Will Waterproof's Lyrical Monologue

DR. JOHNSON'S LODGERS

When I first cheapened my lodgings, the Landlady told me, that she hoped I was not an Author, for the Lodgers on the first Floor had stipulated that the upper Rooms should not be occupied by a noisy Trade. I very readily, promised to give no Disturbance to her Family, and soon dispatched a Bargain on the usual Terms.

I had not slept many Nights in my new Apartment before I began to inquire after my Predecessors, and found my Landlady whose Imagination is filled only with her own Affairs, very ready to give me Information.

Curiosity, like all other Desires, produces Pain, as well as Pleasure. Before she began her Narrative, I had heated my Head with Expectations of Adventures and Discoveries, of Elegance in Disguise and Learning in Distress and was therefore somewhat mortified when I heard, that the first Tenant was a Taylor, of whom nothing was remembered but that he complained of his Room for want of Light, and, after having lodged in it a Month, in which he paid only a Week's Rent, pawned a Piece of Cloth which he was trusted to cut out, and was forced to make a precipitate Retreat from this Quarter of the Town.

The next was a young Woman newly arrived from the Country, who lived for five Weeks with great Regularity, and became by frequent Treats very much the Favourite of the Family, but at last received Visits so frequently from a Cousin in Cheapside, that she brought the Reputation of the House into Danger, and was therefore dismissed with good Advice.

The Room then stood empty for a Fortnight, so that my Landlady began to think that she had judged hardly, and often wished for such another Lodger. At last an elderly Man of a very grave Aspect, read the Bill, and bargained for the Room at the very first Price that was asked. He lived in very close Retirement, seldom went out till Evening, and then returned early, sometimes chearful, and at other Times dejected. It was remarkable, that whatever he purchased, he never had small Money in his Pocket, and though cool and temperate on other Occasions, was always vehement and stormy till he received his Change; He paid his Rent with great Exactness, and seldom failed once a week to requite my Landlady's Civility with a Supper. At last, such is the Fate of human Felicity! the House was alarmed at Midnight by the Constable, who demanded to search the Garrets. My Landlady assuring him that he had mistaken the Door, conducted him up Stairs, where he found the Tools of a Coiner; but the Tenant had crawled along the Roof to an empty House, and escaped; very much to the Joy of my Landlady, who declares him a very honest Man, and wonders why any Body should be hanged for making Money when such Numbers are in Want of it. She however confesses that she shall for the future always question the Character of those who take her Garret without beating down the Price.

The Bill was then placed again in the Window, and the poor Woman was teazed for seven Weeks by innumerable Passengers, who obliged her to climb with them every Hour up five Stories, and then disliked the Prospect, hated the Noise of a publick Street, thought the Stairs narrow, objected to a low Ceiling, required the Walls to be hung with fresher Paper, and asked Questions about the Neighbourhood, could not think of living so far from their Acquaintance, wished the Window had looked to the South rather than the West, told how the Door and the Chimney might have been better disposed, bid her half the Price that she asked, or promised to give her Earnest the next Day, and came no more.

At last, a short meagre Man, in a tarnished Waistcoat, desired to see the Garret, and when he had stipulated for two long Shelves and a larger Table, hired it at a low price. When the Affair was completed, he looked round him with great satisfaction, and repeated some Words which the Woman did not understand. In two Days he brought a great Box of Books, took Possession of his Room, and lived very inoffensively, except that he frequently disturbed the Inhabitants of the next Floor by unseasonable Noises. He was generally in Bed at Noon, but from Evening to Midnight he sometimes talked aloud with great Vehemence, sometimes stamped as in Rage, sometimes threw down his Poker, then clattered his Chairs, then sat down in deep Thought, and again burst out into loud Vociferations; sometimes he would sigh as oppressed with Misery, and sometimes shake with convulsive Laughter. When he encountered any of the Family he gave way or bowed, but rarely spoke, except that as he went up Stairs he often repeated,

This habitant, th' aerial regions boast,

hard Words, to which his Neighbours listened so often, that they learned them without understanding them. What was his Employment she did not venture to ask him, but at last heard a Printer's Boy enquire for the Author.

My Landlady was very often advised to beware of this strange Man, who, though he was quiet for the present, might perhaps become outrageous in the hot Months, but as she was punctually paid, she could not find any sufficient Reason for dismissing him, till one Night he convinced her by setting Fire to his Curtains, that it was not safe to have an Author for her Inmate.

She had then for six Weeks a Succession of Tenants, who left the House on Saturday, and instead of paying their Rent, rated their Landlady: At last she took in two Sisters, one of whom had spent her little Fortune in procuring Remedies for a lingering Disease, and was now supported and attended by the other; she climbed with Difficulty to the Apartment, where she languished for eight Weeks without Impatience or Lamentation, except for the Expense and Fatigue which her Sister suffered, and then calmly and contentedly expired. The Sister followed her to the Grave, paid the few Debts which they had contracted, wiped away the Tears of useless Sorrow, and returning to the Business of common Life, resigned to me the vacant Habitation.

Such, Mr. Rambler, are the Changes which have happened in the narrow Space where my present Fortune has fixed my Residence; so true is it that Amusement and Instruction are always at Hand to those who have Skill and Willingness to find them, and so just is the observation of Juvenal, that a single House will shew whatever is done or suffered in the World.

DR. SAMUEL JOHNSON (1709-1784)
The Rambler

A SPUNGING-HOUSE

The fate of debtors in England was for a long time a strange one, as readers of Dickens must be well aware. They were sent to prisons until their defaults were met—and how were they to earn money there to buy their way to freedom? Some of them seemed to have sufficient small cash to keep themselves in beer and victuals, for which they could send out. They could appeal to their friends to lend them more in order to pay off what they had already borrowed. Or they could languish, like Mr. Dorrit, for years.

Another form of incarceration, strangely, if shabbily, luxurious, was the spunging-house. To one of these Colonel Crawley, Becky Sharp's very reckless and somewhat illiterate husband, was removed by Mr. Moss, the bailiff. Here is Thackeray's description of the curious establishment kept by Mr. Moss and of the Colonel's appeal to his wife to sell up something to buy him out.

Friend Rawdon drove on then to Mr. Moss's mansion in Cursitor Street, and was duly inducted into that dismal place of hospitality. Morning was breaking over the cheerful house-tops of Chancery Lane as the rattling cab woke up the echoes there. A little, pink-eyed Jew-boy, with a head as ruddy as the rising morn, let the party into the house, and Rawdon was welcomed to the ground-floor apartments by Mr. Moss, his travelling companion and host, who cheerfully asked him if he would like a glass of something warm after his drive.

The Colonel was not so depressed as some mortals would be, who, quitting a palace and a *placens uxor*, find themselves barred into a spunging-house; for, if the truth must be told, he had been a lodger at Mr. Moss's establishment once or twice before. We have not thought it necessary in the previous course of this narrative to mention these trivial little domestic incidents; but the reader may be assured that they can't unfrequently occur in the life of a man who lives on nothing a year.

Upon his first visit to Mr. Moss, the Colonel, then a bachelor, had been liberated by the generosity of his aunt. On the second mishap, little Becky, with the greatest spirit and kindness, had borrowed a sum of money from Lord Southdown, and had coaxed her husband's creditor (who was her shawl, velvet-gown, lace pocket-handkerchief, trinket, and gimcrack purveyor, indeed) to take a portion of the sum claimed, and Rawdon's promissory note for the remainder. So on both these occasions the capture and release had been conducted with the utmost gallantry on all sides, and

Moss and the Colonel were therefore on the very best of
terms.

"You'll find your old bed, Colonel, and everything
comfortable," that gentleman said, "as I may honestly
say. You may be pretty sure it's kep' aired, and by the
best of company, too. It was slep' in the night afore last
by the Honourable Capting Famish, of the Fiftieth
Dragoons, whose mar took him out, after a fortnight,
jest to punish him, she said. But, Law bless you, I
promise you he punished my champagne, an had a party
'ere every night—reg'lar tip-top swells, down from the
clubs and the West End—Captain Ragg, the Honourable
Deuceace, who lives in the Temple, and some fellers as
knows a good glass of wine, I warrant you. I've got a
Doctor of Diwinity upstairs, five gents in the coffee-
room, and Mrs. Moss has a tably-dy-hoty at half-past
five, and a little cards or music afterwards, when we
shall be most happy to see you."

"I'll ring when I want anything," said Rawdon, and
went quietly to his bedroom. He was an old soldier, we
have said, and not to be disturbed by any little shocks of
fate. A weaker man would have sent off a letter to his
wife on the instant of his capture. "But what is the use
of disturbing her night's rest?" though Rawdon. "She
won't know whether I am in my room or not. It will be
time enough to write to her when she has had her sleep
out, and I have had mine. It's only a hundred-and-
seventy, and the deuce is in it if we can't raise that."
And so, thinking about little Rawdon (whom he would
not have know that he was in such a queer place), the
Colonel turned into the bed lately occupied by Captain
Famish, and fell asleep. It was ten o'clock when he woke
up, and the ruddy-headed youth brought him, with
conscious pride, a fine silver dressing-case, wherewith he
might perform the operation of shaving. Indeed, Mr
Moss's house, though somewhat dirty, was splendid
throughout. There were dirty trays, and wine-coolers

en permanence on the sideboard, huge dirty gilt cornices, with dingy yellow satin hangings to the barred windows which looked into Cursitor Street—vast and dirty gilt picture-frames surrounding pieces sporting and sacred, all of which works were by the greatest masters; and fetched the greatest prices, too, in the bill transactions, in the course of which they were sold and bought over and over again. The Colonel's breakfast was served to him in the same dingy and gorgeous plated ware. Miss Moss, a dark-eyed maid in curl-papers, appeared with the teapot, and, smiling, asked the Colonel how he had slep'? and she brought him in The Morning Post, with the names of all the great people who had figured at Lord Steyne's entertainment the night before. It contained a brilliant account of the festivities, and of the beautiful and accomplished Mrs. Rawdon Crawley's admirable personifications.

After a lively chat with this lady (who sat on the edge of the breakfast table in an easy attitude, displaying the drapery of her stockings and an ex-white satin shoe which was down at heel), Colonel Crawley called for pens and ink, and paper; and being asked how many sheets, chose one which was brought to him between Miss Moss's own finger and thumb. Many a sheet had that dark-eyed damsel brought in; many a poor fellow had scrawled and blotted hurried lines of entreaty, and paced up and down that awful room until his messenger brought back the reply. Poor men always use messengers instead of the post. Who has not had their letters, with the wafers wet, and the announcement that a person is waiting in the hall?

Now on the score of his application, Rawdon had not many misgivings.

" Dear Becky (Rawdon wrote),—I hope you slept well. Don't be frightened if I don't bring you in your coffy. Last night as I was coming home smoking, I met with an accadent. I was nabbed by Moss of Cursitor Street—

from whose gilt and splendid parler I write this—the same that had me this time two years. Miss Moss brought in my tea—she is grown very fat, and, as usual, had her stockens down at heal.

" It's Nathan's business—a hundred-and-fifty—with costs, hundred-and-seventy. Please send me my desk and some cloths—I'm in pumps and a white tye (something like Miss M.'s stockings)—I've seventy in it. And as soon as you get this, Drive to Nathan's—and offer him seventy-five down, and ask him to renew—say I'll take wine—we may as well have some dinner sherry; but not picturs, they're too dear.

" If he won't stand it. Take my ticker and such of your things as you can spare, and send them to Balls—we must of course, have the sum tonight. It won't do to let it stand over, as tomorrow's Sunday; the beds here are not very clean, and there may be other things out against me—I'm glad it an't Rawdon's Saturday for coming home. God bless you.

"   " Yours in haste,
"   "R. C.
" P.S.—Make haste and come."

This letter, sealed with a wafer, was dispatched by one of the messengers who are always hanging about Mr. Moss's establishment; and Rawdon, having seen him depart went out in the courtyard, and smoked his cigar with a tolerably easy mind—in spite of the bars over-head; for Mr. Moss's courtyard is railed in like a cage, lest the gentlemen who are boarding with him should take a fancy to escape from his hospitality.

Three hours, he calculated, would be the utmost time required, before Becky should arrive and open his prison doors; and he passed these pretty cheerfully in smoking, in reading the paper, and in the coffee-room with an acquaintance, Captain Walker, who happened to be there, and with whom he cut for sixpences for some hours, with pretty equal luck on either side.

But the day passed away and no messenger returned—
no Becky. Mr. Moss's tably-dy-hoty was served at the
appointed hour of half-past five, when such of the
gentlemen lodging in the house as could afford to pay
for the banquet came and partook of it in the splendid
front parlour before described, and with which Mr.
Crawley's temporary lodging communicated, when
Miss M. (Miss Hem, as her papa called her) appeared
without the curl-papers of the morning, and Mrs. Hem
did the honours of a prime boiled leg of mutton and
turnips, of which the Colonel ate with a very faint
appetite. Asked whether he would " stand " a bottle of
champagne for the company, he consented, and the
ladies drank to his 'ealth, and Mr. Moss, in the most
polite manner, " looked towards him."

W. M. THACKERAY (1811-1863)
Vanity Fair

PURL AND MISS POTTERSON

The Six Jolly Fellowship-Porters, already mentioned as a
tavern of a dropsical appearance, had long settled down
into a state of hale infirmity. In its whole constitution it
had not a straight floor, and hardly a straight line; but
it had outlasted, and clearly would yet outlast, many a
better-trimmed building, many a sprucer public-house.
Externally, it was a narrow lopsided wooden jumble of
corpulent windows heaped one upon another as you
might heap as many toppling oranges, with a crazy
wooden verandah impending over the water; indeed the
whole house, inclusive of the complaining flag-staff on
the roof, impended over the water, but seemed to have
got into the condition of a faint-hearted diver who has
paused so long on the brink that he will never go in at
all.

This description applies to the river-frontage of the

Six Jolly Fellowship-Porters. The back of the establishment, though the chief entrance was there, so contracted, that it merely represented in its connexion with the front, the handle of a flat-iron set upright on its broadest end. This handle stood at the bottom of a wilderness of court and alley: which wilderness pressed so hard and close upon the Six Jolly Fellowship-Porters as to leave the hostelry not an inch of ground beyond its door. For this reason, in combination with the fact that the house was all but afloat at high water, when the Porters had a family wash the linen subjected to that operation might usually be seen drying on lines stretched across the reception-rooms and bedchambers.

The bar of the Six Jolly Fellowship-Porters was a bar to soften the human breast. The available space in it was not much larger than a hackney-coach; but no one could have wished the bar bigger, that space was so girt in by corpulent little casks, and by cordial-bottles radiant with fictitious grapes in bunches, and by lemons in nets, and by biscuits in baskets, and by the polite beer-pulls that made low bows when customers were served with beer, and by the cheese in a snug corner near the fire, with the cloth everlastingly laid. This haven was divided from the rough world by a glass partition and a half door with a leaden sill upon it for the convenience of resting your liquor; but, over this half-door the bar's snugness so gushed forth, that, albeit customers drank there standing, in a dark and draughty passage where they were shouldered by other customers passing in and out, they always appeared to drink under an enchanting delusion that they were in the bar itself.

For the rest, both the tap and parlour of the Six Jolly Fellowship-Porters gave upon the river, and had red curtains matching the noses of the regular customers, and were provided with comfortable fireside tin utensils, like models of sugar-loaf hats, made in that shape that they might, with their pointed ends, seek out for themselves glowing nooks in the depths of the red coals, when they mulled your ale, or heated for you those delectable drinks, Purl, Flip, and Dog's Nose. The first of these humming compounds was a speciality of the Porters, which, through an inscription on its door-posts, gently appealed to your feelings as, "The Early Purl House." For, it would seem that Purl must always be taken early; though whether for any more distinctly stomachic reason than that, as the early bird catches the worm, so the early purl catches the customer, cannot here be resolved. It only remains to add that in the handle of the flat iron, and opposite the bar, was a very little room like a three-cornered hat, into which no direct ray of sun, moon, or star, ever penetrated, but which was superstitiously regarded as a sanctuary replete with comfort and retirement by gaslight, and on the door of which was therefore painted its alluring name: Cosy.

Miss Potterson, sole proprietor and manager of the Fellowship-Porters, reigned supreme on her throne, the Bar, and a man must have drunk himself mad drunk indeed if he thought he could contest a point with her. Being known on her own authority as Miss Abbey Potterson, some water-side heads, which (like the water) were none of the clearest, harboured muddled notions that, because of her dignity and firmness, she was named after, or in some sort related to, the Abbey at Westminster. But Abbey was only short for Abigail, by which name Miss Potterson had been christened at Limehouse Church, some sixty and odd years before.

CHARLES DICKENS (1812-1870)
Our Mutual Friend

A CURIOUS HOST

Thomas De Quincey, whose life, though sometimes desperately unhappy, proved that the taking of opium need be no bar to longevity, ran away from Manchester Grammar School and went to London at the age of seventeen. There he attempted a Bohemian life and found it hard going. He became the master of an ample, flowery, and sometimes extremely powerful prose style: we now are critical of the kind of writing which calls food "esculent material" but his faults of such elaboration were easily out-weighed by his virtues of vision and the fluent force to express it.

Soon after this, I contrived, by means which I must omit for want of room, to transfer myself to London. And now began the latter and fiercer stage of my long sufferings; without using a disproportionate expression, I might say, of my agony. For I now suffered, for upwards of sixteen weeks, the physical anguish of hunger in various degrees of intensity; but as bitter, perhaps, as ever any human being can have suffered who has survived it. I would not needlessly harass my reader's feelings by a detail of all that I endured; for extremities such as these, under any circumstances of heaviest misconduct or guilt, cannot be contemplated, even in description, without a rueful pity that is painful to the natural goodness of the human heart. Let it suffice, at least on this occasion, to say, that a few fragments of bread from the breakfast-table of one individual (who supposed me to be ill, but did not know of my being in utter want), and these at uncertain intervals, constituted my whole support.

During the former part of my sufferings (that is, generally in Wales, and always for the first two months in London), I was houseless, and very seldom slept under a roof. To this constant exposure to the open air I ascribe it mainly, that I did not sink under my torments. Latterly, however, when cold and more inclement weather came on, and when, from the length of my sufferings, I had begun to sink into a more languishing condition, it was, no doubt, fortunate for me, that the same person to whose breakfast-table I had access allowed me to sleep in a large, unoccupied house, of which he was tenant. Unoccupied, I call it, for there was no household or establishment in it; nor any furniture, indeed, except a table and a few chairs. But I found, on taking possession of my new quarters, that the house already contained one single inmate, a poor, friendless child, apparently ten years old; but she seemed hunger-bitten; and sufferings of that sort often make children look older than they are. From this forlorn child I learned, that she had slept and lived there alone, for some time before I came; and great joy the poor creature expressed, when she found that I was in future to be her companion through the hours of darkness.

The house was large; and, from the want of furniture, the noise of the rats made a prodigious echoing on the spacious staircase and hall; and, amidst the real fleshly ills of cold, and, I fear, hunger, the forsaken child had found leisure to suffer still more (it appeared) from the self-created one of ghosts. I promised her protection against all ghosts whatsoever; but, alas! I could offer her no other assistance. We lay upon the floor, with a bundle of cursed law papers for a pillow, but with no other covering than a sort of large horseman's cloak; afterwards, however, we discovered, in a garret, an old sofa-cover, a small piece of rug, and some fragments of other articles, which added a little to our warmth. The poor child crept close to me for warmth, and for security against her ghostly enemies. When I was not more than usually ill, I took her into my arms, so that, in general, she was tolerably warm, and often slept when I could not; for, during the last two months of my sufferings, I slept much in the daytime, and was apt to fall into transient dozings at all hours.

Meantime, the master of the house sometimes came in upon us suddenly, and very early; sometimes not till ten o'clock; sometimes not at all. He was in constant fear of bailiffs; improving on the plan of Cromwell, every night he slept in a different quarter of London; and I observed that he never failed to examine, through a private window, the appearance of those who knocked at the door, before he would allow it to be opened. He breakfasted alone; indeed, his tea equipage would hardly have admitted of his hazarding an invitation to a second person, any more than the quantity of esculent material, which, for the most part, was little more than a roll, or a few biscuits, which he had bought on his road from the place where he had slept.

During his breakfast, I generally contrived a reason for lounging in; and, with an air of as much indifference as I could assume, took up such fragments as he had left,— sometimes, indeed, there were none at all. In doing this, I committed no robbery, except upon the man himself, who was thus obliged (I believe), now and then, to send out at noon for an extra biscuit; for, as to the poor child, she was never admitted into his study (if I may give that name to his chief depository of parchments, law writings, etc.); that room was to her the Blue-beard room of the house, being regularly locked on his departure to dinner, about six o'clock, which usually was his final departure for the night.

But who, and what, meantime, was the master of the house, himself? Reader, he was one of those anomalous practitioners in lower departments of the law, who,— what shall I say?—who, on prudential reasons, or from necessity, deny themselves all the indulgence in the luxury of too delicate a conscience (a periphrasis which might be abridged considerably, but that I leave to the reader's taste); in many walks of life, a conscience is a more expensive incumbrance than a wife or a carriage; and just as people talk of " laying down" their carriages, so I suppose my friend, Mr. ——, had " laid down " his conscience for a time; meaning, doubtless, to resume it as soon as he could afford it. The inner economy of such a man's daily life would present a most strange picture, if I could allow myself to amuse the reader at his expense. Even with my limited opportunities for observing what went on, I saw many scenes of London intrigues, and complex chicanery, " cycle and epicycle, orb in orb," at which I sometimes smile to this day, and at which I smiled then, in spite of my misery. My situation, however, at that time, gave me little experience, in my own person, of any qualities in Mr. ——'s character but such as did him honour; and of his whole strange composition, I must forget everything but that towards me he was obliging, and, to the extent of his power, generous.

That power was not, indeed, very extensive. However, in common with the rats, I sate rent free; and as Dr. Johnson has recorded that he never but once in his life had as much wall-fruit as he could eat, so let me be grateful that, on that single occasion, I had as large a choice of apartments in a London mansion as I could possibly desire. Except the Blue-beard room, which the poor child believed to be haunted, all others, from the attics to the cellars, were at our service. " The world was before us," and we pitched our tent for the night in any spot we chose. This house I have already described as a large one. It stands in a conspicuous situation, and in a well-known part of London. Many of my readers will have passed it, I doubt not, within a few hours of reading this. For myself, I never fail to visit it when business draws me to London. About ten o'clock this very night, August 15, 1821, being my birthday, I turned aside from my evening walk, down Oxford Street, purposely to take a glance at it. It is now occupied by a respectable family, and, by the lights in the front drawing-room, I observed a domestic party, assembled, perhaps, at tea, and apparently cheerful and gay:—marvellous contrast, in my eyes, to the darkness, cold, silence, and desolation, of that same house eighteen years ago, when its nightly occupants were one famishing scholar and a neglected child.

THOMAS DE QUINCEY (1785-1859)
Confessions of an English Opium Eater

MR. PECKSNIFF'S CHOICE

M. Todgers's Commercial Boarding-House was a house of that sort which is likely to be dark at any time; but that morning it was especially dark. There was an odd smell in the passage, as if the concentrated essence of all the dinners that had been cooked in the kitchen since the house was built lingered at the top of the kitchen stairs to that hour, and, like the Black Friar in Don Juan, "wouldn't be driven away." In particular, there was a sensation of cabbage; as if all the greens that had ever been boiled there, were ever-greens, and flourished in immortal strength. The parlour was wainscoted, and communicated to strangers a magnetic and instinctive consciousness of rats and mice. The staircase was very gloomy and very broad, with balustrades so thick and heavy that they would have served for a bridge. In a sombre corner on the first landing, stood a gruff old giant of a clock, with a preposterous coronet of three brass balls on his head; whom few had ever seen—none ever looked in the face—and who seemed to continue his heavy tick for no other reason than to warn heedless people from running into him accidentally. It had not been papered or painted, hadn't Todgers's, within the memory of man. It was very black, begrimed, and mouldy. And, at the top of the staircase, was an old, disjointed, rickety, ill-favoured skylight, patched and mended in all kinds of ways, which looked distrustfully down at everything that passed below, and covered Todgers's up as if it were a sort of human cucumber-frame, and only people of a peculiar growth were reared there.

Mr. Pecksniff and his fair daughters had not stood warming themselves at the fire ten minutes, when the sound of feet was heard upon the stairs, and the presiding deity of the establishment came hurrying in.

M. Todgers was a lady, rather a bony and hard-featured lady, with a row of curls in front of her head, shaped like little barrels of beer; and on the top of it something made of net—you couldn't call it a cap exactly—which looked like a black cobweb. She had a little basket on her arm, and in it a bunch of keys that jingled as she came. In her other hand she bore a flaming tallow candle, which, after surveying Mr. Pecksniff for one instant by its light, she put down upon the table, to the end that she might receive him with the greater cordiality.

*   *   *

Surely there never was, in any other borough, city, or hamlet in the world, such a singular sort of a place as Todgers's. And surely London, to judge from that part of it which hemmed Todgers's round, and hustled it, and crushed it, and stuck its brick-and-mortar elbows into it, and kept the air from it, and stood perpetually between it and the light, was worthy of Todgers's, and qualified to be on terms of close relationship and alliance with hundreds and thousands of the odd family to which Todgers's belonged.

You couldn't walk about in Todgers's neighbourhood, as you could in any other neighbourhood. You groped your way for an hour through lanes and bye-ways, and court-yards, and passages; and you never once emerged upon anything that might be reasonably called a street. A kind of resigned distraction came over the stranger as he trod those devious mazes, and, giving himself up for lost, went in and out and round about and quietly turned back again when he came to a dead wall or was stopped by an iron railing, and felt that the means of escape might possibly present themselves in their own good time, but that to anticipate them was hopeless.

Instances were known of people who, being asked to dine at Todgers's, had travelled round and round for a weary time, with its very chimney-pots in view; and finding it, at last, impossible of attainment, had gone home again with a gentle melancholy on their spirits, tranquil and uncomplaining. Nobody had ever found Todgers's on a verbal direction, though given within a minute's walk of it. Cautious emigrants from Scotland or the North of England had been known to reach it safely, by impressing a charity-boy, town-bred, and bringing him along with them; or by clinging tenaciously to the postman; but these were rare exceptions, and only went to prove the rule that Todgers's was in a labyrinth, whereof the mystery was known but to a chosen few.

Several fruit-brokers had their marts near Todgers's; and one of the first impressions wrought upon the stranger's senses was of oranges—of damaged oranges, with blue and green bruises on them, festering in boxes, or mouldering away in cellars. All day long, a stream of porters from the wharves beside the river, each bearing on his back a bursting chest of oranges, poured slowly through the narrow passages; while underneath the archway by the public-house, the knots of those who rested and regaled within, were piled from morning until night. Strange solitary pumps were found near Todgers's hiding themselves for the most part in blind alleys, and keeping company with fire-ladders. There were churches also by dozens, with many a ghostly little churchyard, all overgrown with such straggling vegetation as springs up spontaneously from damp, and graves, and rubbish. In some of these dingy resting-places, which bore much the same analogy to green churchyards, as the pots of earth for mignonette and wall-flower in the windows overlooking them did to rustic gardens, there were trees; tall trees; still putting forth their leaves in each succeeding year, with such a languishing remembrance of their kind (so one might fancy, looking on their sickly boughs) as birds in cages have of theirs. Here, paralysed old watchmen guarded the bodies of the dead at night, year after year, until at last they joined that solemn brotherhood; and, saving that they slept below the ground a sounder sleep than even they had ever known above it, and were shut up in another kind of box, their condition can hardly be said to have undergone any material change when they in turn were watched themselves.

*   *   *

To tell of half the queer old taverns that had a drowsy and secret existence near Todgers's, would fill a goodly book; while a second volume no less capacious might be devoted to an account of the quaint old guests who frequented their dimly-lighted parlours. These were, in general, ancient inhabitants of that region; born, and bred there from boyhood; who had long since become wheezy and asthmatical, and short of breath, except in the article of story-telling: in which respect they were still marvellously long-winded. These gentry were much opposed to steam and all new-fangled ways, and held ballooning to be sinful, and deplored the degeneracy of the times; which that particular member of each little club who kept the keys of the nearest church professionally, always attributed to the prevalence of dissent and irreligion: though the major part of the company inclined to the belief that virtue went out with hair-powder, and that Old England's greatness had decayed amain with barbers.

CHARLES DICKENS (1812-1870)
Martin Chuzzlewit

THE BRONTËS' CHOICE

In 1848 the success of the novels by the Brontë sisters, appearing with the nom-de-plumes of Currer, Ellis, and Acton Bell, necessitated a declaration of the real authorship. It had been believed by some that there was only one author and he a man. The matter had to be cleared up with Mr. Smith and Mr. Williams of the publishing firm Smith, Elder & Co. Here follows Mrs. Gaskell's account of how it was done.

Though Messrs. Smith, Elder, & Co., distinctly stated in their letter that they did not share in such " belief ", the sisters were impatient till they had shown its utter groundlessness, and set themselves perfectly straight. With rapid decision, they resolved that Charlotte and Anne should start for London that very day, in order to prove their separate identity to Messrs. Smith, Elder, and Co., and demand from the credulous publisher his reasons for a " belief " so directly at variance with an assurance which had several times been given to him. Having arrived at this determination, they made their preparations with resolute promptness. There were many household duties to be performed that day; but they were all got through. The two sisters each packed up a change of dress in a small box, which they sent down to Keighley by an opportune cart; and after early tea, they set off to walk thither—no doubt in some excitement; for independently of the cause of their going to London, it was Anne's first visit there. A great thunder-storm overtook them on their way that summer evening to the station; but they had no time to seek shelter. They only just caught the train at Keighley, arrived at Leeds, and were whirled up by the night train to London.

About eight o'clock on the Saturday morning, they arrived at the Chapter Coffee-house, Paternoster Row—

a strange place, but they did not well know where else to go. They refreshed themselves by washing, and had some breakfast. Then they sat still for a few minutes, to consider what next should be done.

When they had been discussing their project in the quiet of Haworth Parsonage the day before, and planning the mode of setting about the business on which they were going to London, they had resolved to take a cab, if they should find it desirable, from their inn to Cornhill; but, amidst the bustle and " queer state of inward excitement " in which they found themselves, as they sat and considered their position on the Saturday morning, they quite forgot even the possibility of hiring a conveyance; and when they set forth, they became so dismayed by the crowded streets, and the impeded crossings, that they stood still repeatedly, in complete despair of making progress, and were nearly an hour in walking the half-mile they had to go. Neither Mr. Smith nor Mr. Williams knew that they were coming; they were entirely unknown to the publishers of *Jane Eyre*, who were not, in fact, aware whether the " Bells " were men or women, but had always written to them as to men.

On reaching Mr. Smith's, Charlotte put his own letter into his hands; the same letter which had excited so much disturbance at Haworth Parsonage only twenty-four hours before. " Where did you get this ? " said he, —as if he could not believe that the two young ladies dressed in black, of slight figures and diminutive stature, looking pleased yet agitated, could be the embodied Currer and Acton Bell, for whom curiosity had been hunting so eagerly in vain. An explanation ensued, and Mr. Smith at once began to form plans for their amusement and pleasure during their stay in London. He urged them to meet a few literary friends at his house; and this was a strong temptation to Charlotte, as amongst them were one or two of the writers whom she particu-

larly wished to see; but her resolution to remain unknown
induced her firmly to put it aside.

The sisters were equally persevering in declining Mr.
Smith's invitations to stay at his house. They refused to
leave their quarters, saying they were not prepared for a
long stay.

Not the least singular part of their proceedings was the
place at which the sisters had chosen to stay.

Paternoster Row was for many years sacred to publishers. It is a narrow flagged street, lying under the
shadow of St. Paul's. The dull warehouses on each side
are mostly occupied at present by wholesale booksellers;
if they be publishers' shops, they show no attractive front
to the dark and narrow street. Half-way up, on the left-
hand side, is the Chapter Coffee-house. I visited it last
June. It was then unoccupied. It had the appearance of a
dwelling-house, two hundred years old or so, such as one
sometimes sees in ancient country towns; the ceilings
of the small rooms were low, and had heavy beams
running across them; the walls were wainscotted
breast high; the staircase was shallow, broad, and dark,
taking up much space in the centre of the house. This
then was the Chapter Coffee-house, which, a century ago,
was the resort of all the booksellers and publishers; and
where the literary hacks, the critics, and even the wits,
used to go in search of ideas or employment. This was
the place about which Chatterton wrote, in those
delusive letters he sent to his mother at Bristol, while he
was starving in London. " I am quite familiar at the
Chapter Coffee-house, and know all the geniuses there."
Here he heard of chances of employment; here his
letters were to be left.

Years later, it became the tavern frequented by university men and country clergymen, who were up in
London for a few days, and, having no private friends or
access into society, were glad to learn what was going

on in the world of letters, from the conversation which they were sure to hear in the Coffee-room. In Mr. Brontë's few and brief visits to town, during his residence at Cambridge, and the period of his curacy in Essex, he had stayed at this house; hither he had brought his daughters, when he was convoying them to Brussels; and here they came now, from very ignorance where else to go. It was a place solely frequented by men; I believe there was but one female servant in the house. Few people slept there; some of the stated meetings of the Trade were held in it, as they had been for more than a century; and, occasionally, country booksellers, with now and then a clergyman, resorted to it; but it was a strange desolate place for the Miss Brontës to have gone to, from its purely business and masculine aspect. The old " grey-haired elderly man," who officiated as waiter, seems to have been touched from the very first with the quiet simplicity of the two ladies, and he tried to make them feel comfortable and at home in the long, low, dingy room upstairs, where the meetings of the Trade were held. The high narrow windows looked into the gloomy Row; the sisters, clinging together on the most remote window-seat (as Mr. Smith tells me he found them when he came, that Saturday evening, to take them to the Opera), could see nothing of motion, or of change, in the grim, dark houses opposite, so near and close, although the whole breadth of the Row was between. The mighty roar of London was round them, like the sound of an unseen ocean, yet every footfall on the pavement below might be heard distinctly in that unfrequented street. Such as it was, they preferred remaining at the Chapter Coffee-house, to accepting the invitation which Mr. Smith and his mother urged upon them; and, in after years, Charlotte says:—

" Since those days, I have seen the West End, the parks, the fine squares; but I love the City far better. The City seems so much more in earnest; its business, its rush, its roar, are such serious things, sights, sounds. The City is getting its living—the West End but enjoying its pleasure. At the West End you may be amused; but in the City you are deeply excited."

MRS. GASKELL (1810-1865)
The Life of Charlotte Brontë

CLUB-LIFE, PICKLES WELL EARNED

The STEAKS. A society of noblemen and gentlemen, 24 in number, who, in rooms of their own, behind the scenes of the Lyceum Theatre, partake of a five o'clock dinner of beef-steaks every Saturday, from November till the end of June. They abhor the notion of being thought a club, dedicate their hours to " Beef and Liberty", and enjoy a hearty English dinner with hearty English appetites. The room they dine in, a little Escurial in itself, is most appropriately fitted up—the doors, wainscoting, and roof, of good old English oak, ornamented with gridirons as thick as Henry VII's Chapel with the portcullis of the founder. Every thing assumes the shape or is distinguished by the representation of their favourite implement, the gridiron. The cook is seen at his office through the bars of a spacious gridiron, and the original gridiron of the society (the survivor of two terrific fires) holds a conspicuous position in the centre of the ceiling. Every member has the power of inviting a friend, and pickles are not allowed till after a third helping. The Steaks had its origin in the Beef-Steak Society, founded (1735) by John Rich, patentee of Covent-garden Theatre, and George Lambert, the scene-painter.

Murray's Guide to Modern London, 1851

LOVE AT THE BLUE BOAR

Mr. Weller having obtained leave of absence from Mr. Pickwick, who, in his then state of excitement and worry, was by no means displeased at being left alone, set forth, long before the appointed hour, and having plenty of time at his disposal, sauntered down as far as the Mansion House, where he paused and contemplated, with a face of great calmness and philosophy, the numerous cads and drivers of short stages who assemble near that famous place of resort, to the great terror and confusion of the old-lady population of these realms. Having loitered here, for half an hour or so, Mr. Weller turned, and began wending his way towards Leadenhall Market, through a variety of bye streets and courts. As he was sauntering away his spare time, and stopped to look at almost every object that met his gaze, it is by no means surprising that Mr. Weller should have paused before a small stationer's and print-seller's window; but without further explanation it does appear surprising that his eyes should have no sooner rested on certain pictures which were exposed for sale therein, than he gave a sudden start, smote his right leg with great vehemence, and exclaimed, with energy, " If it hadn't been for this, I should h' forgot all about it, till it was too late! "

The particular picture on which Sam Weller's eyes were fixed, as he said this, was a highly-coloured representation of a couple of human hearts skewered together with an arrow, cooking before a cheerful fire, while a male and female cannibal in modern attire, the gentleman being clad in a blue coat and white trousers, and the lady in a deep red pelisse with a parasol of the same, were approaching the meal with hungry eyes, up a serpentine gravel path leading thereunto. A decidedly indelicate young gentleman, in a pair of wings and nothing else, was depicted as superintending the cooking; a representation of the spire of the church in Langham Place, London, appeared in the distance; and the whole formed a " valentine," of which, as a written inscription in the window testified, there was a large assortment within, which the shopkeeper pledged himself to dispose of, to his countrymen generally, at the reduced rate of one-and-sixpence each.

" I should ha' forgot it; I should certainly ha' forgot it! " said Sam; so saying, he at once stepped into the stationer's shop, and requested to be served with a sheet of the best gilt-edged letter-paper, and a hard-nibbed pen which could be warranted not to splutter. These articles having been promptly supplied, he walked on direct towards Leadenhall Market at a good round pace, very different from his recent lingering one. Looking round him, he there beheld a sign-board on which the painter's art had delineated something remotely resembling a cerulean elephant with an aquiline nose in lieu of trunk. Rightly conjecturing that this was the Blue Boar himself, he stepped into the house, and inquired concerning his parent.

" He won't be here this three-quarters of an hour or more," said the young lady who superintended the domestic arrangements of the Blue Boar.

" Wery good, my dear," replied Sam. " Let me have nine-penn'oth o'brandy-and-water luke, and the ink-stand, will you, miss? "

The brandy-and-water luke, and the inkstand, having been carried into the little parlour, and the young lady having carefully flattened down the coals to prevent their blazing, and carried away the poker to preclude the possibility of the fire being stirred, without the full privity and concurrence of the Blue Boar being first had and obtained, Sam Weller sat himself down in a box near the stove, and pulled out the sheet of gilt-edged letter-paper, and the hard-nibbed pen. Then looking carefully at the pen to see that there were no hairs in it, and dusting down the table, so that there might be no crumbs of bread under the paper, Sam tucked up the cuffs of his coat, squared his elbows, and composed himself to write.

To ladies and gentlemen who are not in the habit of devoting themselves practically to the science of penmanship, writing a letter is no very easy task; it being always considered necessary in such cases for the writer to recline his head on his left arm, so as to place his eyes as nearly as possible on a level with the paper, and, while glancing sideways at the letters he is constructing, to form with his tongue imaginary characters to correspond. These motions, although unquestionably of the greatest asistance to original composition, retard in some degree the progress of the writer; and Sam had unconsciously been a full hour and a half writing words in small text, smearing out wrong letters with his little finger, and putting in new ones which required going over very often to render them visible through the old blots, when he was roused by the opening of the door and the entrance of his parent.

" Vell, Sammy," said the father.

" Vell, my Prooshan Blue," responded the son, laying down his pen. "What's the last bulletin about mother-in-law ? "

" Mrs. Veller passed a very good night, but is uncommon perwerse and unpleasant this mornin'. Signed upon oath, S. Veller, Esquire Senior. That's the last vun as was issued, Sammy," replied Mr. Weller, untying his shawl.

" No better yet ? " inquired Sam.

" All the symptoms aggerawated," replied Mr. Weller, shaking his head. " But wot's that you're a-doin' of ? Pursuit of knowledge under difficulties, Sammy ? "

" I've done now," said Sam, with slight embarrassment: " I've been a-writin'."

" So I see," replied Mr. Weller. " Not to any young 'ooman, I hope, Sammy ? "

" Why, it's no use a-sayin' it ain't," replied Sam; " it's a walentine."

" A what! " exclaimed Mr. Weller, apparently horror-stricken by the word.

" A walentine," replied Sam.

" Samivel, Samivel," said Mr. Weller, in reproachful accents, " I didn't think you'd ha' done it. Arter the warnin' you've had o' your father's wicious propen-sities; arter all I've said to you upon this here wery subject; arter activally seein' and bein' in the company o' your own mother-in-law, vich I should ha' thought wos a moral lesson as no man could never ha' forgotten to his dyin' day! I didn't think you'd ha' done it, Sammy, I didn't think you'd ha' done it! " These reflections were too much for the good old man. He raised Sam's tumbler to his lips and drank off its contents.

" Wot's the matter now ? " said Sam.

" Nev'r mind, Sammy," replied Mr. Weller, " it'll be a wery agonisin' trial to me at my time of life, but I'm pretty tough, that's vun consolation, as the wery old turkey remarked wen the farmer said he wos afeerd he should be obliged to kill him for the London market."

" Wot'll be a trial ? " inquired Sam.

" To see you married, Sammy—to see you a dilluded wictim, and thinkin' in your innocence that it's all wery capital," replied Mr. Weller. " It's a dreadful trial to a father's feelin's, that 'ere, Sammy."

" Nonsense," said Sam. " I ain't a-goin' to get married, don't you fret yourself about that; I know you're a judge of these things. Order in your pipe and I'll read you the letter. There! "

We cannot distinctly say whether it was the prospect of the pipe, or the consolatory reflection that a fatal dis-position to get married ran in the family, and couldn't be helped, which calmed Mr. Weller's feelings, and caused his grief to subside. We should be rather disposed to say that the result was attained by combining the two sources of consolation, for he repeated the second in a low tone, very frequently; ringing the bell meanwhile, to order in the first. He then divested himself of his upper coat; and lighting the pipe and placing himself in front of the fire with his back towards it, so that he could feel its full heat, and recline against the mantelpiece at the same time turned towards Sam, and, with a countenance greatly mollified by the softening influence of tobacco, requested him to " fire away."

Sam dipped his pen into the ink to be ready for any corrections, and began with a very theatrical air—

" ' Lovely—— ' "

" Stop," said Mr. Weller, ringing the bell. " A double glass o' the inwariable, my dear."

" Very well, sir," replied the girl; who with great quickness appeared, vanished, returned, and disappeared.

" They seem to know your ways here," observed Sam.

" Yes," replied his father, " I've been here before, in my time. Go on Sammy."

" ' Lovely creetur,' " repeated Sam.

" Tain't in poetry, is it? " interposed his father.

" No, no," replied Sam.

" Wery glad to hear it," said Mr. Weller. " Poetry's unnat'ral; no man ever talked poetry 'cept a beadle on boxin'-day, or Warren's blackin', or Rowland's oil, or some of them low fellows; never you let yourself down to talk poetry, my boy. Begin again, Sammy."

CHARLES DICKENS (1812-1870)
Pickwick Papers

EVENTS AND DATES
IN LONDON'S HISTORY

61 A.D. Londinium sacked by Boadicea.
 314 Diocese of London founded.
1009 Danes attacked London.
1049 Westminster Abbey begun.
1078 The White Tower built (oldest part of the Tower of London).
1079 City of London granted first charter.
1123 St. Bartholomew's Hospital founded.
1189 First Lord Mayor of London elected.
1209 First London Bridge in stone completed.
1215 King John's charter to London.
1295 Stone of Destiny removed from Scone to London.
1440 Eton College established.
1476 Caxton set up his printing press at Westminster.
1483 Murder of the Princes in the Tower.
1530 St. James's Palace built.
1561 Westminster School founded.
1576 First theatre built in London.
1599 Globe Theatre built.
1605 Gunpowder Plot to blow up Houses of Parliament.
1611 Charterhouse School founded (later moved to Godalming, Surrey).
1619 Dulwich College founded.
1661 First dock built at Blackwall.
1661 Covent Garden market opened.
1665 The *London Gazette* first issued.
1665 The Great Plague.
1666 The Great Fire.
1671 Original Drury Lane Theatre founded.
1671 Attempt to steal crown jewels from the Tower.
1676 Royal Observatory opened at Greenwich (removed in 1953 to Sussex).
1677 Street lamps first used.
1682 Chelsea Royal Hospital founded by Charles II.
1694 Bank of England founded.
1703 Buckingham Palace built.
1712 St. Paul's Cathedral rebuilt by Sir Christopher Wren.
1724 Guy's Hospital founded.
1809 Gas lighting introduced in Pall Mall.
1812 Theatre Royal, Drury Lane, opened.
1829 Sir Robert Peel introduced the Metropolitan Police Force.
1836 London University founded.
1846 The *Daily News* founded by Charles Dickens.

1847 British Museum opened.
1851 The Marble Arch moved from Buckingham Palace to its present site.
1851 The Great Exhibition in Hyde Park.
1860 Tramways introduced in London.
1871 Albert Hall completed.
1872 Burlington House completed.
1879 First London telephone exchange opened.
1883 Royal College of Music opened.
1886 Tilbury Dock constructed.
1888 London County Council formed.
1894 The Tower Bridge opened.
1895 London School of Economics founded.
1897 First motor omnibus ran from Victoria to Charing Cross.
1897 Blackwall Tunnel constructed.
1897 Queen Victoria's Diamond Jubilee.
1909 Port of London Authority constituted.
1909 Declaration of London.
1911 Coronation of King George V and Queen Mary.
1913 New front for Buckingham Palace designed by Sir Aston Webb.
1917 Imperial War Museum founded.
1920 The Cenotaph in Whitehall, designed by Lutyens, unveiled by King George V.
1921 George V Dock constructed.
1922 The County Hall opened.
1924-5 British Empire Exhibition.
1925 Madame Tussaud's burned down.
1931 Whipsnade Zoo opened.
1936 B.B.C.'s first regular television service from Alexandra Palace.
1936 Crystal Palace destroyed by fire.
1937 Coronation of King George VI and Queen Elizabeth.
1941 Westminster Abbey, Houses of Parliament and British Museum badly damaged by bombs.
1944 Over 2,300 flying bombs fell in London.
1946 London Airport at Heathrow opened.
1947 Marriage of Princess Elizabeth and Prince Philip in Westminster Abbey.
1950 Stone of Destiny stolen from Westminster Abbey (returned early 1951).
1951 Festival of Britain on the South Bank.
1953 Coronation of H.M. Queen Elizabeth II.
1954 Roman Temple of Mithras discovered during excavations.
1955 Inauguration of helicopter service between London Airport and the South Bank.
1959 The Mermaid Theatre opened at Puddle Dock.

INDEX OF AUTHORS, SOURCES, FIRST LINES